Rail/Road/Air Link

  Rail/Road/Air Link

  Rail/Road/Air Link

  Rail/Air Link

In certain cases it may be necessary to delete one
of the words from the title.

  Rail/Road/Air Link

  Rail/Road/Air Link

British Rail

A New History

CHRISTIAN WOLMAR

MICHAEL JOSEPH

PENGUIN MICHAEL JOSEPH

UK | USA | Canada | Ireland | Australia
India | New Zealand | South Africa

Penguin Michael Joseph is part of the Penguin Random House group of companies
whose addresses can be found at global.penguinrandomhouse.com

First published 2022
001

Copyright © Christian Wolmar, 2022

Picture credits can be found on page 375

The moral right of the author has been asserted

Set in 14/17pt Garamond MT Std
Typeset by Jouve (UK), Milton Keynes
Printed and bound in Great Britain by Clays Ltd, Elcograf S.p.A.

The authorized representative in the EEA is Penguin Random House Ireland,
Morrison Chambers, 32 Nassau Street, Dublin D02 YH68

A CIP catalogue record for this book is available from the British Library

ISBN: 978–0–241–45620–0

www.greenpenguin.co.uk

To my grandsons, Luka and Quinn, and my step-grandsons, Alfie and Louie, who hopefully will all love the railways as much as I do.

Contents

Introduction   ix

PART ONE

British Railways

1. The Sparks Effect   3
2. The Inheritance   17
3. New for Old   55
4. Beeching's Double Act   75

PART TWO

British Rail

5. Establishing an Identity   105
6. War on Rail   129
7. The Changing Shape of the Train   159
8. All Change   187
9. Beginning the Break-Up   225
10. The Task Ahead   243
11. BR   275

CONTENTS

12. The Pinnacle   309

13. Epilogue   331

Acknowledgements   349

Timeline of Major Events   351

A Note on the Ministry   353

References   355

A Selective Bibliography   371

Index   377

Introduction

The public image of British Railways is permeated by a series of clichés. Passengers were forced to eat 'curly-ended stale sandwiches' and their trains were delayed by the 'wrong kind of snow'.

Let's just dispose of these two famous tropes. While there may, in the early days of BR, have been some stale sandwiches which were made available on the counter of the various cafés, on display under a glass dome, they were disposed of at the end of the day, long before they could develop curly edges. For the most part, the staleness of British Railways sandwiches was just used as the butt of oft-repeated jokes from stand-up comedians and in sitcoms. In fact, British Railways brought in expert chefs and well-known foodies such as Clement Freud and Prue Leith, who actually became a British Railways Board director, and the organization pioneered the idea of shrink-wrapped sandwiches.

As for 'the wrong kind of snow', no BR executive ever uttered that much-repeated phrase. It originated in an interview by James Naughtie on BBC Radio 4's *Today* programme in February 1991 after a spell of very cold weather had delayed trains across the network. British

Rail's Director of Operations, Terry Worrall, was asked to comment on the adverse effects of the heavy snowfall and explained that 'we are having particular problems with the type of snow, which is rare in the UK', because it was powdery and far colder than usual. Naughtie then cheekily suggested, 'Oh, I see, it was the wrong kind of snow', which Worrall refuted, merely emphasizing 'it was a different kind of snow'. This exchange was then picked up by the London *Evening Standard*, which splashed across its front page that 'British Rail blames the wrong type of snow', and it swiftly became a media cliché.

These are only the two most notorious myths surrounding British Railways. I mention them here because they are still important in setting the tone of much coverage of BR and yet bear no relation to any measured assessment of the organization's achievements and failings. Even as I wrote this introduction in the summer of 2021, Grant Shapps, the Transport Secretary, revived one of these tropes when announcing the restructuring of the industry, saying 'we won't be going back to the days of British Rail and its terrible sandwiches'.[1] There are plenty more similar myths examined in this book: the trains were never on time; the stations were dirty; the staff unhelpful; and the management out of its depth. These portrayals of a state-run industry that provided a vital service were important in creating the climate of public opinion which led to its privatization in the 1990s, just as the tales of straight bananas and banning double-decker buses influenced the referendum on membership of the European Union in 2016.

Despite this constant undermining of its efforts to provide a good railway service, British Railways was the last significant privatization of the Conservative era which ran from 1979 to 1997, because of fears that the public's affection for the organization would make it an unpopular move. And so it proved. The public may well have been critical of British Railways as an organization, but they did not really want their trains messed about with by some buccaneering capitalists who might slash and burn, as Beeching had done a generation previously. Therefore, despite the oft-repeated criticisms, British Railways remained relatively popular with the public and politicians feared a backlash if it were privatized. As a result, contrary to many people's recollection, it was not Margaret Thatcher who sold off the railway, as she had been aware of the particularly strong feelings that the British have about trains.

It was, therefore, left to her successor, John Major, to do the deed. The Conservative manifesto for the 1992 general election, which they were not expected to win, contained a few scant lines on the privatization of the railway, but contained no details as to how this would be done. The rushed sell-off that ensued dismantled an organization which had, after half a century of existence, created a workable structure that had delivered a much improved service. The unified integrated structure was split into more than 100 sections, governed by a system which was far more expensive to operate and ultimately proved unworkable.

It was such an embarrassment to its creators that in

John Major's 900-page autobiography, published almost a decade after he left office, there is barely a mention of what was one of his most contentious and high profile policies. In researching a TV programme on which I appeared, the producer wrote to Major asking for an explanation of the reasoning behind rail privatization. Surprisingly, the programme received a fairly comprehensive answer, in which Major set out the reasons behind the break-up and sale in a letter dated 15 May 2008:

> Some critics have claimed that British Rail was privatised for ideological reasons. This is nonsense. The impetus for privatisation was my wish to improve public services.
>
> I thought British Rail was inefficient; had been inadequately funded for 50 years; was hidebound by tradition; and poorly managed. In the aftermath of privatisation, the appalling state of the nationalised service is often forgotten.
>
> I believed a transfer to the private sector would improve British Rail through the use of private sector skills, thereby making it possible to raise funds for investment from the market, in sums a publicly-funded railway could never have managed. This was, of course, essential to the improvement of every aspect of British Rail's services. In short: my purpose was to produce a better railway.

He goes on to make points about the structure of the industry:

This structure was determined after widespread consultation. Initially I was in favour of a vertically-integrated rail system, but persuasive arguments encouraged me to move away from that concept. I was influenced by the fact that the safest transport industry in the country was also the most fragmented: namely Civil Aviation. The Airlines lease their aircraft; Airports are in multiple ownership; Air traffic control is another separate entity. Overall, the airline industry is sub-divided into far more component parts than was the railway following privatisation.

I did not believe the British Rail monolith was the best model for the industry. These days, every part of industry is disaggregated with more specialisation, subcontracting and flexibility than ever before. It would have been odd if British Rail had not followed a similar structure.

Major goes on to blame the Labour government elected in 1997 for 'the very hostile environment that ultimately brought about the collapse of Railtrack', the organization which had taken over all the infrastructure of British Railways, such as stations, signalling and tracks, and concludes:

> The main argument against returning to a national railway is an obvious one: in the future – as in the past – no Government would ever provide the railways with adequate funding. This was, of course, one of the principal reasons for the calamitous state of the service pre-1993, and the one which encouraged me to privatise it.

There is a lot to dispute with that description of the network under British Railways, as I set out in this book. The suggestion that the railway was in a 'calamitous state' before privatization is simply wrong. Yes, it had suffered from a loss of passengers, as always happens in times of economic hardship, and investment levels were far below what was needed, but much of that was the result of decisions taken by Major's own government. However, as this book explains, the railway was, indeed, in a 'calamitous state' – but in 1948, when BR was created, not fifty years later, when it was dismantled.

In the final chapter, I set out the chaotic process of privatization and how it was, contrary to Major's argument, motivated purely by ideology. The ultimate structure came not of some well thought-out process but rather from a government that embarked on a policy without any idea where it would lead.

As to the explanation of why Major omitted to mention rail privatization in his autobiography: I bumped into him at a County Hall event in London in 2014, held to celebrate the twenty-first anniversary of the passing of the 1993 Railways Act that laid the groundwork for privatization. I asked him about the omission, and he merely responded that there had not been sufficient time or space to include it. This seemed an unconvincing answer, to say the least, given that he had had a long time to write his autobiography and that the controversy over the railway often featured on the front pages of the newspapers at the time.

In setting out what I see as this corrective to the

history of British Railways, I would like to emphasize that I am not motivated by nostalgia. For me, steam engines are rightly consigned to history, and rattling along branch lines at 30 mph is not something I miss. Indeed, in writing more than a dozen books about the railway I have never indulged in melancholic moans on the theme of 'it was so much better in the old days'. Rather, my deep affection for the railway stems from the sheer pleasure of what is undoubtedly the best form of travel – apart from the bicycle for shorter journeys – and in learning about the role it has played in its near two centuries of existence.

Therefore, this book about British Railways does not seek to suggest the organization was without fault. Rather, it explores how British Railways was a victim of its history and of the whim of politicians who had little understanding about its achievements and, indeed, its real failings. Many of Major's arguments will be assessed. As the privatization experiment is now a quarter of a century old – half the time of BR's existence – it has been given a good opportunity to prove its worth. In fact, as I write, and indeed since early March 2020 when the Covid-19 pandemic began to reduce numbers using the railway, the industry has been in a state of turmoil unprecedented in peacetime.

The railway is in a state of chaos, wrecked financially by the pandemic and by the subsequent government messaging, which turned a crisis into a long-term disaster by terrifying potential passengers about the risks of taking the train. The franchising arrangement, created a quarter of a century ago in order to stimulate competition, is now dead, and finding a replacement structure has proved difficult for a government motivated more by ideology than by a desire to do the best for the industry and its passengers.

The publication of this book is indeed timely. In May 2021, the government led by Boris Johnson finally set out its vision for the railway in a White Paper entitled *Great British Railways*. This was the result of a process set in motion by the previous administration, led by Theresa May, when a wide-ranging timetable change in May 2018 resulted in chaos and thousands of cancellations because the various parts of the railway had not been coordinated in the absence of any overall 'guiding mind'. As a result, the new timetable proved unworkable, as parts of the infrastructure were unable to support the extra trains which were scheduled to operate. The review was led by Keith Williams, a former British Airways chief executive and, later, chairman, but its publication was delayed first by internal wrangling and then the pandemic. Eventually, the document was published as the Williams–Shapps review, with the name of the Transport Secretary added, and with the status of a White Paper setting out a series of radical changes to the structure of the industry, notably the ending of the franchising system created at privatization. The franchises will be replaced with a series of management contracts whose scope is far more limited, giving the newly created Great British Railways direct control over the timetabling and operation of passenger trains. It is, therefore, a part renationalization to add to the taking back into state ownership of Network Rail, Railtrack's successor, in 2014. Great British Railways will incorporate Network Rail, as well as allocate the contracts to run services, devise the timetable, take a strategic view of the railway and coordinate investment plans.

However, there are many details of the change which will need primary legislation passed through Parliament, and decisions still need to be made over precisely how much autonomy the new organization will have, notably in relation to the Department for Transport. The new structure of the railway is by no means a re-creation of British Rail, but it is undoubtedly a partial retreat from the fully privatized model created when British Rail was broken up.

There is much ground to make up in terms of understanding the history of British Rail, as demonstrated by Grant Shapps's frequent references to sandwiches during media interviews at the launch of Great British Railways. If the discussion is defined by simplistic references to a myth about an aspect of BR services that has nothing to do with its core purpose of enabling people to travel round the country, then it is clear that the politicians pushing through the reform of the industry in the 2020s have not learnt the lesson of history. The debate over the future shape of the railway should be better informed than that. There is much to be gained from taking a deep and unbiased look at the achievements and failings of British Rail, which is what this book sets out to do. I hope it offers precisely that and contributes to the discussions about the future of this great and much-loved industry.

Christian Wolmar, summer 2021

PART ONE
British Railways

I

The Sparks Effect

It was a moment of awe tinged with nostalgia. On 18 April 1966, the first electric passenger train left Euston station bound for Manchester. The unseasonal snow, which had fallen just four days previously, had fortunately just melted and the crowds around the train were able to enjoy the sight of the rather ungainly electric locomotive hauling its long train of carriages up the Euston incline on which previous generations of steam locomotives had always struggled. It was the culmination of nearly a decade of work to electrify the route, which had been delayed a number of times by ministerial indecision as well as by doubts over whether the scheme was worthwhile. While the watching crowds were indeed excited, there was, too, a sense of loss because no longer would great powerful locomotives bearing names of long-dead duchesses and princesses stutter amid clouds of smoke and steam as they began their journey northwards. There was something soulless about the box-like electric locomotives whose greater power was exerted quietly, almost apologetically, in contrast to the loud excess of the steam engines they were replacing.

The switch from steam to electric heralded other significant changes. There had been sacrifice, too, notably the Victorian-era Euston station, which had just been demolished to accommodate the longer and more frequent trains. Out, too, went many named trains, the 'Expresses' and 'Mails', and instead all the fast services running between Britain's main centres of population were branded as Inter-City (later, in a grammatical lapse, renamed InterCity), which was to be the flagship of British Rail.

Among the crowd of watching railway managers, there was nervousness, too. This scheme had to prove its worth. It wasn't just the key West Coast route out of Euston to Birmingham, Manchester, Liverpool and Glasgow that depended on the success of this new modern form of traction; the entire newly developed Inter-City brand required electrification to be a triumph. BR was relying on the 'sparks effect' to be the railway's saviour. 'Modernization' was the watchword and electrification was seen as the key to creating a railway fit for the latter part of the twentieth century. The West Coast Main Line had been selected because it was so obviously in need of improvement. Not only was it the oldest and busiest main-line railway in the world, it was also responsible for more than 10 per cent of BR's passenger income.

The completion of the scheme and the grand opening marked a new era for British Railways as Chris Green, who joined BR's management trainee scheme after graduating from Oxford University, recalls: 'My parents did not understand why I wanted to join an industry with no future. But this showed that the railway did have one.'[1]

The electrification of the West Coast Main Line was the centrepiece of British Railways' Modernisation Plan, which had been announced in 1955. It had set out a fifteen-year programme of bringing the railway up to date and, crucially, making it financially self-supporting. The plan included a phased introduction of electric and diesel vehicles to replace coal-fired steam engines, which were seen as dirty, inefficient and old-fashioned. In fact, the Modernisation Plan had foreseen a much wider programme of electrification across the network but this was stymied somewhat by the reluctance of many senior BR managers, who were concerned about the temporary upheaval caused by putting up overhead wires, which was by then the established method of electrifying lines, rather than the third rail used mostly on the Southern Region. While reluctantly recognizing that steam was no longer viable, many of the old hands preferred the less disruptive adoption of diesel traction. Therefore the East Coast Main Line, from London King's Cross through Peterborough to Leeds, Newcastle and Edinburgh, was a few years later provided with the most powerful diesel locomotives ever used by British Railways – the Deltics – rather than having the wires put up. These Deltics, far more akin to the steam locomotives they replaced than the quiet, box-shaped electric locomotives, were a great favourite with rail enthusiasts, until the electrification of the line was belatedly completed in the early 1990s.

Diesel was undoubtedly better than coal, but it failed to deliver all the advantages of electricity. It was still a rather dirty and inefficient fuel, but allowed one person, rather than two, to drive the train. Although the capital cost of electrification is high, given the need to install wiring and other infrastructure, such as substations and connections to the National Grid, in the long term it offers greater savings than diesel because of the higher efficiency of electricity as a power source. Moreover, it is cleaner, allows for far faster acceleration and is environmentally more sustainable, especially when obtained from renewable sources. The Modernisation Plan was supposed to be the turning point for the railway, paving the way for this nineteenth-century invention to finally be updated to twentieth-century standards, but sadly the electrification of Britain's railway is a typical tale of dither, hesitation and lack of courage.

The electrification of the almost 500 miles of line on the West Coast route cost £175 million (about £4,100 million in 2021 money) and caused significant disruption, with weekend closures and speed restrictions being a regular feature during the four-year construction period. The British Transport Commission had decided in 1956 that, apart from the Southern Region, where the third-rail system had been introduced throughout the electrified sections, all future projects would use twenty-five kilovolt (kV) overhead wiring, which was deemed the most economic for long-distance routes. This was more powerful than the system used in previous schemes and had been widely adopted in Europe. Electrification was carried out in stages, starting in the North with a pilot scheme, the eight-mile Styal loop line between Manchester and Crewe, being opened first. This was quickly followed by the rest of the route between Manchester and Crewe, which was completed in 1960, and by Liverpool to Crewe two years later. This low-key start to the project, away from the prying eyes of Whitehall, was part of a deliberate and astute strategy by British Railways, designed to bounce ministers into agreeing to electrify the entire route.

Although these initial schemes were presented as trials, it would have been illogical to electrify such a large part of the network in the North-West unless the intention was always to continue southwards all the way to Euston. According to Michael Bonavia, a senior rail manager at the time, the British Railways Board had cleverly pulled the wool over the eyes of ministers in pushing forward the electrification scheme. The Ministry of Transport appeared not to notice until too late that a substantial part of the scheme was already being worked on before full permission for the whole project had been given. Bonavia notes: 'This number of bites at the cherry [the three early sections] annoyed the Ministry of Transport, which criticized the way in which extended commitments were being incurred without an overall scheme based on clear financial justification, and a comparison between the expected results from electrification and those from a changeover to diesel traction.'

There was a lengthy but, as Bonavia puts it, 'unsatisfactory' correspondence between the ministry, the London Midland Region of British Railways, which was responsible for the scheme, and the British Transport Commission, which oversaw the British Railways Board: 'The Ministry never quite shook off the feeling that it had been pushed into authorising a huge scheme before receiving satisfactory answers to all the questions it had raised.'[2] Indeed, the way the ministry had been well and truly bounced into the scheme by British Railways was demonstrated by the fact that it did not give its approval until January 1961, by which time electric trains were already running between Manchester and Crewe. The next section, Crewe to Liverpool, was completed in early 1962, and the line between Euston and Manchester was fully electrified for testing by 1965, with the route through Birmingham finished a couple of years later. This episode is a cameo of the way that British Railways interacted with government throughout its history. While it was quasi-independent and able to operate without constant oversight, its overall finances were subject to government whim, as we will see in subsequent chapters. The same trick was played by the section of the ministry dealing with roads, as civil servants would give permission for a series of bypasses on a particular route which then, logic dictated, might as well be connected by nice new sections of dual carriageway through the countryside in between.

The construction work was carried out by a private company, British Insulated Callender's Cables (BICC), which later became Balfour Beatty. BICC's widespread knowledge of electrification projects both at home and overseas, in places as diverse as Australia, Brazil and India, was an important factor, because Britain's tardiness at adopting rail electrification meant there was not enough experience within British Railways to carry out the work.

The long history of the project ensured that the opening

of the newly electrified route from Euston to Manchester and Liverpool was a big moment for both British Railways and Britain's railway, representing a historic change in a country which had been slow to modernize its network. This scheme, which was an attempt to boost revenue through investing to create a better service, was a significant move away from the long-standing attempt to get the nationalized rail company to balance its books solely by focusing on reducing costs and closing lines. Indeed, in the previous decade the industry had yo-yoed between two contrasting attempts at achieving commercial viability. The Modernisation Plan had been conceived as a one-off investment programme but, as we shall see, it had failed to meet its transformational goal. When Richard Beeching arrived in 1961 to run Britain's railway, he executed a sharp U-turn, as he envisaged making major cuts to the network as the only route to profitability.

Now, at last, technology was being harnessed to boost passenger numbers. 'Electrification', according to Bonavia, 'was beginning to be seen as the most important single element in a modernised railway system and one that might not merely help to retain existing traffic but attract new business by offering a faster, more reliable and cleaner service.'

It was, he added, the 'sparks effect', which may have been impossible to quantify but which, he said, 'never failed to appear once electrification had been carried out'.[3] Indeed, much of the Southern Railway network had been electrified between the two world wars – albeit using the third-rail system – and the newly transformed

9

routes had invariably thrived, with passenger numbers increasing significantly while the costs of operation fell sharply. This had been true more recently, too, of the Liverpool Street to Shenfield commuter line, which was electrified in the aftermath of the Second World War, resulting in passenger numbers increasing by almost 50 per cent in the first year after the wires went up.

The transformation of the West Coast Main Line was, therefore, much more than the adoption of new technology. Ivor Warburton, another management trainee of the period, who later was in charge of services on the West Coast, believes that 'the start of regular operations on the route on April 18th, 1966, was the only time that I can recall the BBC and all the rest of the media doing a positive story on British Railways. It was the first day of 100 mph operation on the West Coast, which gave a time between London and Manchester of just over two and a half hours.'[4]

The West Coast was the first line to be improved as part of a wider strategy to develop the Inter-City brand for Britain's long-distance rail journeys. In addition to electrification, several major stations, such as Birmingham New Street, Manchester Piccadilly and Coventry, were rebuilt, and in all eighty-nine stations were reconstructed or refurbished. It was, as mentioned above, in London that the most controversial change was made. Euston, the London terminus since the completion of the line in 1838, was demolished and replaced with a soulless, modernist passenger hall, which was widely said to be like an airport lounge – except far worse, because there were not even any seats for passengers waiting to board. The old station had contained two features of enormous architectural merit: the Great Hall, which was by far the most impressive railway waiting room in Britain, with a classic double staircase by which passengers reached their trains, and which John Betjeman described as 'one of London's finest rooms'; and above it, away from public view, a Baroque boardroom big enough to hold 400 people, which possessed a 'deeply-coffered ceiling embellished with massive curved consoles and plaster bas-reliefs in each corner, the whole beautifully lit by attic windows'.[5] Both these, along with the Doric arch or *propylaeum* that had stood outside the station as a mark of the grandeur of the Victorian railway, were swept away as a demonstration of British Railways' determination to modernize the network. There was, indeed, no place for sentiment, or for old buildings whatever their architectural merit, in BR's modernization programme.

Apart from the demolition of Euston station, there were numerous other, and much less controversial, improvements. Most notably, the new rolling stock, consisting of Mark 2 carriages (so named because they were the second generation of coaches developed by British Railways) proved enormously popular from the start. They boasted air conditioning, which was considered a luxury at the time and greatly boosted their appeal, even if it meant that opening the windows was no longer possible. The timetable was also transformed. While previously there had been three or four trains at most to each destination daily, now there was at least one every two hours, and soon on the London–Birmingham route a half-hourly service was introduced to meet demand. The process of turning trains around was radically altered as well. In the past, carriages at Euston were always taken out to the depot a few miles up the line and then brought back later in the day when needed. Trains might have half a dozen carriages or twice that number, depending on demand, but now they were in 'fixed formation', always the same length and no longer hauled off to the depot at the end of every journey. While this may seem like a technical detail, it was the sort of change that allowed trains to be run far more efficiently and frequently.

For the first time, British Railways set about seriously marketing its new product, even using TV advertising. The notion that traffic levels were static and people could not be attracted to the railway was abandoned. As one long-standing rail manager put it to me: 'In the past, marketing had been considered to be fluff around an elephant's arse. Now they started actively selling tickets.'[6] Pricing, which once had been fixed in stone, now became more flexible, with affordable return fares and special deals designed to attract people to visit London for the day.

There was, too, an unprecedented marketing campaign. As soon as the first section of the line was electrified, British Railways promoted the scheme with a poster showing a new electric train speeding past railworkers, and boasting of 'Forging Ahead' with what it called 'this vast scheme'. Then, to mark the improvement in train services between London and the North-West, British Railways produced a glossy booklet, *Your New Railway*, partly funded by various suppliers who took out advertisements, but still priced at the considerable sum of 2s. 6d. (12.5p). The regional general manager, H. C. Johnson, proudly proclaimed in the introduction that this was 'A fast, modern highway for passengers and freight, running through the industrial heart of the country, [which was] the result of eight years' hard work by railway civil, electrical and signal engineers.'[7] In a lengthy account of why electrification had been chosen over diesel (a far more detailed explanation than you would expect to see today), one of the authors, Colin Jones, said: 'It requires a greater capital outlay than dieselization to get going but incurs a smaller wage bill to run'; and there was even the justification for why this particular type of electric technology had been chosen, which was because 'experimental work by French Railways had revealed the considerable advantages to be gained by adopting a new system altogether – the 25-kilovolt alternating-current 50-cycles system with overhead collection'. There was also a little boast in the conclusion: 'The whole scheme, originally scheduled for completion in the early 1970s will now be in full operation by early 1967.'[8]

The pamphlet also stressed the importance for freight of the West Coast improvements:

The impact upon freight working will be even greater, for electric working forms part of a wider revolution now taking place on this side of the railways' business. Traffic is being concentrated in full train loads, rather than wagon loads, and moved at high uniform speeds along the nation's main trade arteries. In this way, the railways can exploit their inherent advantages over road transport and, by providing fast, reliable, bulk transport they can best serve the needs of the nation.[9]

This was a further indication of the way that British Railways was beginning to change.

While today it might seem obvious that such a scheme should be accompanied by a publicity campaign, this was new ground for British Railways, which hitherto had been 'production-led' – in other words, focused on providing train travel without much thought given to why and who for. Even something as simple as producing a publicity brochure extolling the virtues of the scheme marked a departure from the past. There was, though, no doubting that BR's management were right to stress that the West Coast electrification scheme, along with all the other improvements, marked the beginning of a new era for their industry. Chris Green, who later rose to become boss of InterCity, was a marketing assistant on the West Coast when it was electrified: 'It transformed people's view of the railway. It was no longer seen as only an industry in decline.' As for the demolition of Euston station, Green says that the new passenger hall was a deliberate attempt to make taking the train more like air travel:

> We wanted to be seen as an industry with a future. British Railways wanted to be associated with the same modern approach and thought it ought to provide the same sort of service as an airline. And it worked. Passenger

numbers doubled in three years when the Ministry of
Transport had said we would not see any growth.[10]

Indeed. And the public was won over too. O. S. Nock,
who was a prolific author of railway books at the time,
was commissioned to write the story of the electrification
and found himself surprisingly impressed:

> The new services are not merely fast in a relative sense,
> they are really fast. At one time a journey between Lon-
> don and Liverpool, or London and Manchester, would
> have been considered as 'long-distance' travel; but in
> this era, when cities such as Zurich and Rome are within
> two hours' flying time to London airport, the new rail-
> way services have been geared to the tempo of this
> modern age.[11]

This was important in ensuring that British Railways
would be able to invest in future schemes. The government may have been somewhat finessed into supporting
the West Coast electrification, but its success made it easier for the Board to push through other schemes that
required investment to boost patronage. But attitudes
both within and outside the railway did not change overnight. The West Coast electrification was a triumph, but
while it was clear that the conversion to electric power
provided numerous direct and indirect benefits, it was
still the subject of much argument within BR. It would
take another fifteen years before the big Deltic diesels
introduced a few years earlier on the East Coast would be
replaced with electrically powered trains, because of

struggles both within and outside BR about the future direction of the railway. The West Coast modernization demonstrated how railways could be improved, but it was some time before everyone was convinced that the railway did have a future and that this really was the 'Age of the Train'.

2

The Inheritance

By the time the Modernisation Plan which led to the electrification of the West Coast Main Line was launched in 1955, British Railways had been in existence for seven years, during what was a particularly fraught period in the history of the nation's railway network.

The manifesto of the Labour government elected in the immediate aftermath of the Second World War had promised nationalization of the railway and therefore it could be argued that the project was driven by politics. That would be a mistake since, in reality, nationalization was born of necessity. No one but the state would pay for the rebuilding of a system which was on its knees and which had been starved of investment during the conflict. The war had destroyed the railway, not as a direct result of the efforts of the Luftwaffe, but rather because the system was exhausted by the depredations and requirements of warfare, as well as suffering significant underinvestment at a time of overuse.

Interestingly, given the fierce debates about railway

ownership in subsequent years, the decision to national-
ize the network, taken by the Labour government elected
in 1945, was relatively uncontroversial. At the time, there
was far more cross-party consensus about the need for
strong government involvement in industry. This was the
era of big state-owned organizations, such as the BBC,
the Central Electricity Board and London Transport,
which had all been created by Tory-dominated governments in the interwar period. Another major transport
industry, aviation, was already in public hands, with the
creation just before the war of BOAC, the British Overseas Airways Corporation. As Terry Gourvish, the official
historian of British Railways, explains, 'An increasing
body of opinion in all parties certainly favoured a greater
measure of governmental control in the interests of both
industry and the consumer.'[1] The most fervent opposition, unsurprisingly, came from the private owners of the
various railway companies.

The system of the four private regional companies had
been created in the aftermath of the First World War by
consolidating more than 100 disparate railway companies,
but even this simplified structure was no longer relevant
in a war-ravaged country struggling to meet the demands
of post-war reconstruction. A unified national system
was widely accepted as the only viable solution. Even
before the war, the Big Four, as they were known, had
struggled financially, and of the four only the Great Western had paid a dividend in 1938. During the conflict, the
railway was run into the ground carrying 50 per cent more
freight and operating many additional passenger trains to

keep up with both civilian and military demands. The rolling stock was outdated and the locomotives time-expired, with no fewer than 40 per cent having been constructed before the First World War.

A unified and integrated system owned and controlled by the state, a model which had been widely adopted elsewhere in Europe, was clearly the way forward. The Big Four merged to form British Railways, an enormous organization with about 640,000 staff (in truth, no one was certain about the exact number); 20,000 steam locomotives (almost exactly one for every route mile); 56,000 coaches; and more than one million freight wagons. A further half million freight wagons had to be bought by the nascent British Railways from their private owners at a fixed price, even though many were outdated or in a poor condition and had to be scrapped immediately. These weren't the only assets that moved into public ownership. The Big Four had essentially been transport conglomerates with interests beyond running trains. Between them they owned fifty-four hotels, numerous manufacturing and repair workshops, ships, ports and harbours, several major bus companies and a huge fleet of road vehicles to collect and deliver goods at stations. There were, too, no fewer than 7,000 horses, some of which were still in harness fifteen years later.

Many of the hotels, along with much of the marine business, were hived off to other parts of the British Transport Commission, which had been created by the Labour government as a huge state-owned transport conglomerate. The Commission also embraced long-distance road haulage, canals and London Transport in an attempt to create an integrated, state-owned transport system for the whole country. Inevitably, however, the Commission struggled to establish an equilibrium between the different modes of transport, not least because of the fundamental conflict between road and rail. Moreover, from the outset, the nationalized railway was denied the resources it desperately needed to recover from the war because the Commission's primary focus was on roads.

While the railway was supposedly run by a Railway Executive that reported to the Transport Commission, this extra layer of bureaucracy resulted in a lack of clarity about who was in charge. Was it the Commission or the Executive? No one seemed sure. The Commission, led by Sir Cyril Hurcomb (later Baron Hurcomb) – a long-serving senior civil servant with extensive transport experience – clashed frequently with Sir Eustace Missenden, who had been given the chairmanship of the Railway Executive. Hurcomb not only had the upper hand in terms of the hierarchy but he was also a far more experienced and accomplished administrator. Missenden, who had headed the Southern Railway, the smallest of the Big Four, reluctantly became chairman of the Railway Executive, a job no one else wanted. He was stolid, competent, but completely out of his depth. Suspicious of civil servants and politicians, he accepted the role only on condition that he could retire at the first possible opportunity. As a result, Hurcomb, at the Commission, was able to direct most of the available resources to the other industries under his control.

The divide between the two organizations, whose offices were just three miles apart (the Commission was at 55 Broadway, the huge London Transport headquarters over St James's Park Tube station, while the Railway Executive was located at 222 Marylebone Road, opposite Marylebone station), led to dither and inaction in the early days of British Railways. BR was not an organization that hit the road running, and the structure was widely perceived as being worse than the pre-war arrangement, as Gourvish suggests: 'In contrast to the way in which the railways had been run during the war, British Railways appeared to most railwaymen to be an enormous formless body, with the chiefs miles away at 222 Marylebone Road and the Commission even further away in its ivory tower at 55 Broadway.' This bad start was to dog the initial years of British Railways and helps to explain why its early history was marked by mistakes and poor planning. There were also long-term implications, according to Gourvish: 'The nationalisation period got off on the wrong organisational foot, and the structure erected in 1947 was the first of several defective solutions offered in [BR's first] quarter century.'[2]

The ability of British Railways and the larger Transport Commission to attract the right staff was hampered by the Labour government's reluctance to allow them to pay salaries that matched those in the private sector. Hurcomb was on just £7,000 (£260,000 in 2021 money), reduced by £1,500 to take account of his civil service pension. Similar sums were paid to other state industry bosses, such as the men (they were all men) heading the National Coal

Board or British Electricity Authority, and meant that these jobs tended to be filled by retired businessmen and civil servants with generous pensions, rather than up-and-coming, ambitious young executives.

As ever in British politics, the new structure was not designed with careful consideration of how best to run a railway, or how to attract enough people of sufficient calibre. Rather, as Gourvish succinctly describes the nationalization proposals, 'What mattered was political and administrative expediency. Discussion of the implications of the legislation for the economic operation of road and rail transport was conspicuously absent.'[3] Despite the dilapidated condition of the network, the owners of the Big Four had fought hard to ensure they were generously compensated by the state for the loss of their assets, even though profitability was minimal, and achieved only by not investing sufficiently to bring the railway back to its pre-war condition. Both passenger and freight traffic had fallen dramatically in the immediate post-war period, which was hardly surprising as few people had much money to spend.

Even though little of the war damage had been repaired in the two and a half years between the election of the Labour government and nationalization on 1 January 1948, the vociferous lobbying by shareholders of the Big Four proved to be successful. The result was that the newly created British Railways was saddled with a historic debt of £900 million (£33,500 million in 2021), on which it was required to pay a fixed interest of 3 per cent annually to the owners of the private assets it had taken over, despite their poor condition. This would blight the early years of British Railways, as Gourvish concludes: 'The postponement of essential maintenance and renewals, coupled with the more intensive use of the network and the effects of war damage, proved to be a most unfortunate legacy for post-war managements. The results were felt well into the period of nationalised railways.'[4]

In fairness, the efforts of the Big Four to improve the railway in the post-war period had been hampered by a shortage of both materials and skilled people and by the lengthy big freeze of early 1947. Consequently, the railway was in a far worse state at the time of nationalization than it had been in the late 1930s. This, as Gourvish points out, had a damaging effect on services:

> Starved of investment and hampered by the enormous backlog of repairs and renewals, the industry could do no more than offer a product much inferior to that of pre-war days. Services were slower and more unreliable; and government restrictions, for example, that on passenger train-mileages in 1947, prevented the companies from responding fully to the market.

It was, Gourvish concluded, not an ideal situation 'in which to contemplate the difficult transition from regulated regional monopoly to the public ownership of an integrated system'.[5]

The situation was made worse by a fundamental contradiction in the government's attitude to the finances of the railway, a state of affairs that overshadowed BR during its first two decades until the passage of the 1968

Transport Act. A key part of BR's remit was the onerous obligation to transport any load – from circuses and house movers to sewage and bundles of wool – at rates that were determined by an external government-appointed body, the Railway Rates Tribunal, which did not always take into account the particular costs involved. At nationalization, with petrol still rationed and buying a car beyond the means of working-class and even many middle-class people, the railway was still the only available form of transport for vast swathes of the population. British Railways' fundamental ethos at its creation recognized this. This 'common carrier' obligation may have been imposed on it by government, but many BR managers saw it as their duty to provide the service that people expected.

British Railways, therefore, was permanently in a kind of limbo between the public and private sectors. On the one hand, it had the obligations of a state-owned body, which were to fulfil certain requirements which benefitted society but were not profitable; while on the other, it was required to act like a conventional commercial organization to meet the financial constraints placed upon it by ministers. No wonder, then, that British Railways struggled to establish its own identity during these difficult early years. It was not until the 1968 Act that a clear distinction was made between the commercial parts of the business and the social aspects, which were not financially viable and consequently would always be dependent on subsidy (see Chapter 6).

The Railway Executive didn't help matters, with

decision-making that was rooted in the past when it should have been creating a new structure fit for the second half of the twentieth century. The Executive was dominated by old-fashioned rail managers who were embedded in the culture of competition between the rail companies, which in the interwar period had resulted in strong and very different traditions developing in the Big Four. Indeed, some of these differences, covering vital aspects of railway operations such as signalling, locomotive design and passenger services, pre-dated the Big Four. The Great Western – 'God's Wonderful Railway', as it termed itself – which had originally been built to a different gauge, had been particularly keen to differentiate itself from the way that other parts of the network were run. However, instead of trying to break down this structure and impose a new set of rules for the overall unified business, the Executive ensured its continuation with the establishment of regions with boundaries that almost mirrored those of the Big Four. Six regions were created out of the four old railways by hiving off Scotland and by splitting the London & North Eastern Railway into two at Doncaster. This failure to break up the old regional fiefdoms delayed standardization across the network until halfway through BR's existence and consequently resulted in considerable waste of money.

Although services improved slightly in BR's first year, mainly because there was no repetition of the previous year's big freeze that had halted trains on many routes, the railway was ticking over rather than embarking on a programme of modernization, which many of its counterparts in Europe had started, boosted by money from the Marshall Plan, the huge US lending programme aimed at supporting the war-damaged economies of Western Europe.

One urgent issue for British Railways was the choice of power source. Again, the conservative nature of the Railway Executive was a barrier to progress. The old-timers who sat on the Executive were from the pre-war era, when most railway managers had focused on improving the efficiency and performance of steam locomotives instead of investing in the modern forms of traction that were being adopted widely in much of Europe. The Executive shunned both diesel and electric power and pushed ahead with a programme to design and build a new generation of standard steam engines for use across the railway network. While this decision partly reflected a lack of foresight, it was also influenced by the widespread availability of domestically mined coal, which contrasted with the shortage of oil, which had to be imported and paid for with scarce foreign currency.

There was another, more technical reason for the rejection of diesel power. British trains run on the same tracks as most of the rest of the world – 4 ft 8½ in standard gauge, dating back to George Stephenson's adoption of it on his two pioneering railways, the Stockton & Darlington and the Liverpool & Manchester. As an aside, there are various explanations for this choice, none particularly convincing, such as it is the width of two horses' rear ends when attached to a cart, or that it was the distance between the two ruts on which the wheels of various precursors to the railway travelled. However, while most European countries also adopted the 4 ft 8½ in gauge, there is a key difference. Their 'loading gauge', which is the space in a tunnel or other constrained area needed to allow free passage of the train, is wider and higher than that in the UK. Diesel engine technology in the 1940s was not sufficiently advanced for a powerful – and sizeable – vehicle, of the type used in mainland Europe, to comply with the tighter loading gauge here. Therefore, although many small shunters used in yards were often diesel powered, BR managers felt it was not technically possible to introduce diesel trains on the main lines.

Despite these caveats, the Railway Executive's enthusiastic support for a steam locomotive building programme can only be fully explained by the widespread romantic feeling for the raw power of steam. What railway manager – train lovers all – could not but rave at the sight of a steam locomotive thundering through the countryside, puffing out clouds of thick white steam at regular intervals? They overlooked the fact that electric- and diesel-powered trains were already, by then, far more efficient and cheaper to operate. David Henshaw, author of a study on the Beeching closures, pithily put the creation of new locomotive types in context: 'The British Transport Commission had inherited 400 odd [in fact, 448] classes of steam locomotives and dealt with the problem by producing another 12 standard classes.'[6] The need for standard types arose because managers in the various regions in the new BR structure – which, as we have seen, were essentially based on the Big Four – were reluctant to use types of locomotives that had been developed in a rival area. No self-respecting London Midland manager would, for example, accept a Great Western-designed locomotive on his patch, such was the rivalry and the lack of standardization in BR's early days. Worse still, the new regions continued building bespoke steam locomotives. The Western Region, following the traditions of the Great Western Railway, which uniquely had survived since its creation in 1833 through to nationalization, was particularly profligate in pressing ahead with constructing its own types of locomotives. Overall, between 1948 and 1960, when British Railways' last steam locomotive, *Evening Star*, was built, a total of 2,500 steam engines were produced, 999 of them in the new standard designs.*

The reluctance to switch to diesel had a particularly damaging impact on the finances of regional and branch lines. Steam locomotives were an inherently inefficient and unwieldy form of traction for these types of lines, not least because turning round at the end of the line required a shunting move to take the locomotive from one end of the train to the other. Much more efficient were the 'railbus' and the diesel multiple unit, which essentially were coaches with an engine underneath that powered the train. These had first been introduced in Ireland in the 1930s, and a few 'railcars' had made it on to the Great Western in the same decade. By the late 1940s,

---

* A few more were built for export, and there have also been a couple of new steam engines constructed since then by rail enthusiasts intent on recreating facsimile locomotives to use for rail tours and trips.

these trains, which had a driving cab at each end, were operating across the world, especially on branch lines, where they could be turned around simply by the driver walking to the other end of the train. They were faster, cleaner and more fuel efficient than steam-hauled trains; but despite this, the British Transport Commission was unwilling to adopt this technology, quite possibly because it was also responsible for bus services, which might have lost their competitive edge as a result. As Henshaw points out, 'even in 1951, the BTC was designing and building steam push-pull units that were slow, dirty and expensive to operate. And they were being delivered to the lightly loaded branch lines that were most in need of modernisation.'[7]

As for electrification, the high level of investment required to fit equipment on major routes was seen as a deterrent in Britain, although it hadn't proved a barrier in other parts of the world. The technology had existed since the late nineteenth century; indeed, London's first deep Tube line, the City & South London, was powered by electricity when it opened in 1890, and by then many tramlines had been modernized to use electric power rather than horses. Some suburban rail lines around London and Liverpool were converted in the first decade of the twentieth century, at the same time as the rapidly expanding London Underground became all-electric.

Electrification had, in fact, been supported by a government committee set up in the aftermath of the First World War, but there was little progress between the wars. Only the Southern Railway, which ran most rail services south of London, adopted the new technology with enthusiasm, thanks to its forward-looking general manager, Herbert Walker. The rolling programme of electrification undertaken by the Southern Railway in the interwar period was one of the great railway successes of the Big Four.

Of course, a conventional business would have raised prices to cover the cost of electrification. But following nationalization, fares were controlled by government, not British Railways, which meant this option was effectively closed off. The lessons from the success of the pre-war electrification of much of the Southern Railway and the more recent electrification of the Liverpool Street to Shenfield line, which had resulted in sharp increases in passenger numbers, had not been learnt. The only other electrification scheme progressed at this time was the line between Manchester and Sheffield through the three-mile-long Woodhead tunnel which was finally completed in 1954. Its subsequent failure – the tunnel was closed in 1981 – was partly due to the choice of a different type of electrification system to the one that was eventually deployed on the West Coast Main Line and elsewhere on the network.

These early mistakes proved costly for British Railways throughout the first half of its existence. Michael Bonavia, who worked at the British Transport Commission and later wrote a book on BR's early years, argued that the steam locomotive policy was 'doubly unfortunate' because it perpetuated the use of a technology that should have been phased out much earlier. The failure to introduce diesel and electric traction as part of a planned programme meant British Railways had a lack of experience with these modern technologies 'which was to cost the railways dearly'.

> Furthermore, being late off the mark led to undue haste in traction conversion . . . if only a steady progress into diesel and electric traction had been planned and started in 1948, coupled with limited building and rebuilding of the most successful company steam locomotive designs, a great deal of money would have been saved.[8]

Rather than push for alternative types of traction, the Executive embarked on a programme to determine which of the contrasting types of express, general purpose and freight locomotives used by the Big Four were the best and could be used as the basis for future models. But rather than conducting these tests systematically in controlled conditions on a special track, they were run on several main-line routes. Moreover, locomotive performance varied greatly according to driving style. Some drivers used up far more fuel than others, or approached signals more cautiously. Trainspotters were thrilled by the sight of locomotives operating away from their normal routes, but there was an element of fiddling while Rome burned, since across the world railways were already planning the phasing out of steam.

While the important question of traction was batted back and forth between the Railway Executive and the Transport Commission, members of the former were busy choosing a livery for the newly unified organization, and a series of 'beauty contests' were held across the country which attracted widespread interest among both the press and the public. The first took place at Kensington Olympia in west London with a parade of the best cleaned-up locomotives from the Big Four and the public being asked to choose between the contrasting greens of the Great Western, the London & North Eastern and the Southern Railways. In the summer of 1948, fourteen trains in experimental liveries were placed in service on main-line and cross-country routes as a public relations exercise, with members of the public being invited to send their comments to the Executive. Ultimately, much of this fuss over colours and designs was to no avail since, as Bonavia points out, 'the shortage of staff for cleaning locomotives and washing machines for coaching stock made the whole exercise pretty unrealistic'.[9]

A similarly protracted discussion took place over the choice of a heraldic insignia to adorn British Railways rolling stock. The Commission eventually chose a design by the sculptor Cecil Thomas which showed a lion astride a giant wheel that had a bar bearing the words 'BRITISH RAILWAYS' in capital letters. The author of a history of BR, Tanya Jackson, relates how the 'bicycling lion' insignia proved rather unpopular among staff and quickly gained the nickname of 'ferret and dartboard' because, as she put it, 'the fact that the lion was stretched out over the top of the wheel gave its body an exaggerated yet thin look and the fact it had its mouth open made it look like a vomiting anorexic'.[10] The lion would later cause trouble for British Railways. An updated version of the insignia was created to give the organization a coat of arms, but when it was simplified to use as a badge on the locomotives, one heraldic nerd noticed that the lion was facing left rather than right, as it had done originally. This fell foul of the rules of the College of Arms, which do not allow such alterations to be made to heraldic insignia. It was too late, though, and the left-looking lions survived, and could even be seen on caps worn by railway staff.

All these tangential issues took up much executive time and energy and were something of a diversion obscuring the poor state of the railway. Most seriously, the lack of investment and the poor state of both rolling stock and infrastructure not only caused delay and disruption to services but posed a danger to the travelling public. In the run-up to nationalization there was a spate of accidents, culminating in two crashes in the space of three days in October 1947, with a combined death toll of sixty: two commuter trains collided in fog at South Croydon, and at Goswick in Northumberland the prestigious *Flying Scotsman* derailed after it failed to slow down when diverted to a loop as a result of work being carried out on the track. Significantly, the Chief Inspecting Officer of the Railways, in his annual report that year, blamed the poor safety record on the backlog of track maintenance in the aftermath of the war and on the failure to replace the old semaphore signalling with the far safer system of colour lights. These modern signals were much more easily seen in the dense fogs that were a frequent occurrence in the years before the 1956 Clean Air Act that would mandate smokeless fuel for domestic purposes.

Worse was to follow. The failure of British Railways to

address safety concerns and to use technology to reduce the risk of accidents was highlighted by the two most deadly rail disasters ever in England, which both occurred in the 1950s. In October 1952, an express from Scotland ploughed into a commuter train at Harrow and Wealdstone station in west London, killing 112 people; and five years later, in Lewisham, south London, ninety people were killed when an express ran into a local service. Both disasters would have been prevented by the installation of the Automatic Warning System, a device which alerts drivers and leads to an automatic brake application if a signal is passed at danger. But despite these shocking accidents, AWS was not made mandatory and only a pilot scheme involving fifty-four locomotives was introduced. It would not be until after privatization, and two more disasters in the 1990s involving signals passed at danger at, respectively, Southall and Ladbroke Grove in west London, that a similar system was made mandatory. The death toll in each of the two terrible 1950s accidents in London has only been exceeded in the whole history of railways in the UK by the troop train disaster at Quintinshill, Dumfriesshire, during the First World War, in which 226 were killed in a collision involving three trains.

Inevitably, service standards had also deteriorated markedly; carriages and stations had a neglected air, as Phil Kelly, a lifelong Liverpudlian rail enthusiast, recalled: 'When we went to the seaside in the early 1950s, Wigan Wallgate and Southport Chapel Street stations appeared not to have been painted since the 1920s. There was soot everywhere and you never saw a clean station, though I can't remember seeing any litter – and even that may just be nostalgia.'[11]

Worse, journey times were significantly longer than in the days of the Big Four. A survey of main-line timetables in 1950 showed that all but one of the services were slower than they were before the war, the exception being the London to Brighton run, which had remained at sixty minutes. Nor was the difference just a matter of a few minutes. London to York, for instance, was seventy-five minutes longer, and the journey time from London to Glasgow had increased by 110 minutes compared with 1938. Progress was slow. It was not until 1953, eight years after the end of the conflict, that British Railways was able to boast that the track was back to its pre-war standard and that trains were running at 90 mph on some main lines. Several services on the London Midland Region averaged 60 mph, but overall performance remained below pre-war timings.

In an effort to make services appear better, British Railways restored many of the popular named trains that were supposed to be a cut above the rest. The Pullman service *Queen of Scots* started running between London and Glasgow via Leeds, a somewhat roundabout journey, while the *Capitals Limited*, later renamed *The Elizabethan* in honour of the young Queen, was a non-stop summer service from King's Cross to Edinburgh. Pullmans were the elite form of rail travel. Originating in the USA, the Pullman Company supplied restaurant cars, and at times even whole trains, on which passengers paid a premium for a better service and a higher standard of catering. The

UK subsidiary of Pullman remained a private company until 1954, when it was taken over by the British Transport Commission, which used it as a flagship for BR's passenger services. Within a few years, BR operated a dozen all-Pullman services and more than 200 carriages on other trains.

The combination of the common carrier obligation and commercial targets led British Railways into providing all kinds of additional services, some of which were highly profitable while others were of dubious value and rather dated. There was a focus on the luxury end of the market, as this was highly profitable and was seen as good for BR's image, since it attracted the movers and shakers of the age to the railway, guaranteeing that the industry had supporters in high places. In my book *Fire and Steam*, I quoted a lecturer in railway studies who came from a comfortable middle-class family and recalled his holiday journeys in the early 1950s on the Yorkshire Pullman from Hull Paragon station:

> We always took morning coffee and lunch. The bowler-hatted station master would appear just before departure which was a real event. I remember the 'schlump' rather than the clatter of the door being shut, the quietness of the Pullman car disturbed only by the chinking of crockery and cutlery as we got under way, the masses of people on stations watching the train go through, and the eyes of the senior conductor piercing anyone who had the temerity to say they were not taking lunch.[12]

However, maintaining standards in the face of constant

pressure from government to reduce costs was not easy. In response to the need for economies and to changing mores, British Railways embarked on a cull of restaurant cars, which had been provided on nearly all long-distance trains, given that journeys took significantly longer than today. Full restaurant services were dropped from more than 100 daily services, to be replaced on some trains by a cafeteria, a self-service canteen rather like those to which many people had become accustomed in the armed services during the war. On other trains, trolleys which included a tea urn were introduced. Hitherto, they had been confined to platforms, where they were wheeled alongside carriages waiting to depart in order to serve passengers on the train through the windows that in those pre-air-conditioned days could be opened. Neither of these new arrangements was entirely satisfactory: large queues built up at the cafeterias as people dallied over their choice of dish; trolleys were blocked on crowded trains, and unions pointed out that the hot urns were something of a safety risk.

Because journeys were so much slower than today, sleeper cars were commonplace on long-distance routes. Indeed, they were the routine form of travel for the eight-hour journey between London and Scotland in an era when there were no motorways and the small number of domestic flights were prohibitively expensive for most travellers. Many other routes from London to regional cities had sleeper services, and they also ran on a number of routes directly linking provincial cities, such as Manchester–Plymouth. British Railways improved the offering for third-class passengers in sleepers, reducing their compartments from four berths to two. Sleeper cars were seen as a good business for BR and a new fleet of carriages was soon built to replace the motley stock inherited from the Big Four. They were steel framed, unlike the much less safe wooden coaches which surprisingly were still common at the time of nationalization, and offered greatly improved facilities – notably, according to one regular traveller, David Meara, 'a wash basin with hot and cold running water, and underneath it, on a hinged door, a chamber pot', which had a kind of self-emptying device: 'When the pot was slotted into the door and pushed up, the contents were deposited directly onto the track. It was primitive and somewhat unhygienic, but it worked.'[13] Nevertheless, despite such indignities, travel in these new coaches was advertised in a publicity leaflet as 'a luxury experience', offering 'interior-sprung mattresses, fresh linen, carpeted comfort, plenty of hot water, an electric razor point, morning tea and biscuits in bed, and the attendant only a bell push away'. On the East Coast, there was even 'a limited supply of hot water bottles for those who like home comforts', and a later poster recommended people to 'travel in your pyjamas'.[14]

Another innovation of the time came from the recognition that, although travellers preferred to take the train to Scotland, they also wanted to drive when they arrived there. The solution offered by British Railways was to put the car on the train, thereby reviving a tradition from the early days of the railway when it was not uncommon for rich aristocrats to simply load their personal travelling coach on to a flat wagon, which was then hitched to the back of a train for a modest fee. Consequently, in 1955, the Anglo-Scottish Car Carrier service, later renamed Motorail, was born. The initial service ran from King's Cross and was so successful that soon it operated five days per week. The train, which carried twenty motor cars, left London at 7.45 p.m. with packed suppers provided for the motorists, and arrived in Perth, 415 miles away, at 5.30 a.m., just in time for an early breakfast while the vehicles were unloaded. Soon King's Cross and its later replacement in Holloway, a couple of miles north of the station, proved unsatisfactory for the volume of traffic and a purpose-built Motorail station was constructed in west London at Kensington Olympia (a thrill for local trainspotters like me, as I would pop along with my dad to watch the cars being loaded in the evening). Again, the publicity leaflet emphasized the ease of travelling this way and, cleverly, tried to show that the train had all the advantages of motoring: 'Like thousands of other carefree motorists, begin your holiday at a railway station. Make for the open road – by train. Climb into your sleeping berth and arrive fresh as a daisy to pick up your car at your destination the next morning.' In fact, there were three different types of service: either travelling on the same train as the car; or at the same time but on separate trains; or thirdly, the '*Car* tourist' service, which allowed motorists to send their vehicle up on the night train while they travelled by day.

Motorail was well patronized, particularly in the summer when the service suited the hunting and shooting crowd heading north of the border in August for the Glorious Twelfth, the start of the shooting season for red grouse. Gerald Moule, a Scottish man of the cloth, told Meara about how he once bumped into the Prime Minister on this train. Moule, travelling with his parents, noticed that a lot of guns and other hunting equipment were being loaded on to the train:

> on entering the restaurant car which served as a bar there in the midst was the Prime Minister, Harold Macmillan, holding court with several shooting friends. After our nightcap, my parents and I returned to our bunks. However the PM's party seemed to be set for going on well into the early hours while the car sleeper train thundered North to Scotland.[15]

Tanya Jackson reckons Motorail was one of BR's big success stories and, 'with the growing frustration of long-distance motoring coupled with the petrol price hikes of the 1970s, was to be very well patronised for more than a decade'.[16] The success ensured other routes were added, and though most were abandoned in the 1980s, the London–Scotland service survived until rail privatization in 1997. BR, rather mischievously, found another use for its car-carrying wagons. A gigantic car crusher, named 'the Proler' after the American company which owned it, was sited next to the railway line at Willesden. BR secured the contract to deliver the cars to the crusher and provided two daily trains loaded with wrecks.

For those not availing themselves of Motorail but still needing a car at their destination, British Railways entered into a partnership with Victor Britain Rent-a-Car (later to become Godfrey Davis) to provide hire cars. For the payment of an additional five shillings (25p) on their ticket, passengers could reserve a car, ranging from a Morris Minor to a Ford Zephyr, at their destination. Helpfully, the leaflet assured purchasers that 'in the unlikely event of no car being available, your 5/- will be refunded'. Very generous.

In order to improve what today's marketing people would call 'the journey experience', as well as, crucially, safety, British Railways soon developed a new type of standard coach, known as Mark 1. By then, many modern coaches across the world, including Pullmans running in the UK, were constructed in an integral way; in other words, the bogie – the underframe supported by the wheels – and the superstructure, which houses the passengers, were constructed as one unit. British Railways considered the idea but rejected it as this integral design required much more steel, which remained in short supply in the post-war period. Instead, British Railways opted to develop the frames and the superstructure separately, using a standard underframe which supported different designs of carriage, including the new sleeper cars mentioned above. This had the advantage of enabling the train operator to retain the expensive and longer-lasting underframes, while replacing the upper body which tended to wear out faster, especially as the early Mark 1s used much wood-veneer panelling that needed replacing regularly. Oddly, BR would attach little labels to these panels, indicating the provenance of the wood.

Mark 1 coaches were produced in a wide variety of internal designs, which still included non-corridor compartment trains for suburban services. Each compartment, which had doors on both sides of the train, consisted of two sets of facing seats (therefore tempting the unruly and the unwashed to put their feet on the opposite one in defiance of numerous signs telling them not to do so), with room for four people on each side. This type of carriage had the advantage of speeding up access and egress at busy times, but its crucial failing was the lack of access to toilets or catering facilities. As some 'suburban' journeys could take up to two hours, this oversight tested the bladders of all but the hardiest. One advantage for women was the 'ladies only' compartment, which survived on many suburban trains until the 1970s.

These BR-built compartment trains did serve an alternative purpose for the gay community, in what were then known as 'gentlemen's clandestine activities'. John Richards, one of the Windrush generation, the first wave of West Indian immigrants, who like many of his compatriots worked on the railway, described how light bulbs were removed in some of the compartments of carriages used on the late trains out of Victoria station. Removal of both light bulbs in a compartment would make it completely dark, and Richards was bemused by the activity on the platform as the last train to Orpington was about to leave:

I could never quite understand at first why, at that time of night, chaps used to wander up and down platform 2 at Victoria alongside the coach with most compartments darkened right up until the whistle blew. The scenario seemed even more bizarre when, at Brixton, many alighted and raced about and boarded another compartment.[17]

This was a time, of course, when homosexuality was still illegal.

Most carriages were built with corridors, but retained separate compartments for six people accessed by a gangway and a sliding door to reach the seats. More than 2,000 of these carriages were built by British Railways, as well as a few hundred with an open-plan layout. In all cases, care was taken to align the seating with the windows, a way of making journeys more pleasant that more modern carriage designers often ignore. One oddity was that the window of the central compartment was designed to open inwards so that a stretcher could be passed through it – admittedly with some difficulty. This was, in fact, the only concession made to the disabled traveller on the railway, and wheelchair users wishing to avoid this perilous process had no option but to travel in the unheated guard's van with little natural lighting. Shockingly, this situation remained unchanged well into the 1980s.

In several other respects, too, the new carriages were primitive. The single-glazed windows weren't exactly soundproof and, of more concern to passengers, failed to keep out the cold – a situation that wasn't helped by an inadequate heating system based on steam generated by the locomotive. Because the heat tended to dissipate as it travelled along the train, this resulted in what became known as the 'Goldilocks effect', since it was too hot near the engine, all right in the middle and cold at the back. Simon Bradley, in his history of Britain's railway, says 'a sortie to the buffet car of a train of corridor Mark 1s on a winter's evening was an adventure in microclimates' – especially in the connections between carriages, where swirling freezing cold winds were the norm in the winter. But on a bad day, even the corridors along the carriages could be:

> the territory of the draughts, which seemed somehow to come from all directions at once, but with a general impetus in line with the direction of travel. A steady roar of air currents forced an entry through the gaps around the upper windows along the corridor. The draughts . . . raged unhindered in the under-lit vestibules at the carriage ends.[18]

Using steam heating also highlighted a lack of foresight, since new methods of keeping the carriages warm had to be installed once diesel locomotives took over. Nor was there any way for the driver or guard to communicate with passengers. Remarkably, it took until 1970 to install public address systems on trains, and in the early days the technology was very primitive, since the announcements were pre-recorded and triggered at intervals by a device that measured the distance from the starting point. Staff had to preload cassettes on to the system, which had been developed over the space of six years by the wonderfully named Ripper Robots Ltd of Cranfield in Bedfordshire.

There were two toilets at one end of each carriage, which were somewhat difficult to find as they were hidden by the wooden veneer. But, as with the sleepers, there was only one place where the contents of the toilet bowl would go – straight on to the ballast. This was despite the fact that retention tanks had long been a feature on railways across the world and that the practice of dumping faeces on the tracks was clearly unhygienic, posing a significant health risk to the men who patrolled the lines. Yet the famous sign, 'Please do not flush the toilet while the train is standing in a station' – an injunction that was all too easily ignored – remained relevant even into the 2020s on a few services.

In terms of comfort, Mark 1 coaches were better than their predecessors but were still basic in terms of facilities, with only first class boasting a carpeted floor. The seats, as was traditional, were stuffed with horsehair and covered with moquette, which was mostly wool with a dense pile. This was, however, better than the railways in many other countries, where wooden seats remained the norm.

In one important respect, though, the Mark 1 carriages represented a great improvement – safety. The flimsiness of the largely wooden-framed previous generation of carriages was all too often exposed in accidents resulting in a large number of fatalities. The steel body frames of Mark 1s proved far more resilient. As late as the 1970s, the Chief Inspecting Officer of the Railways was noting that the Mark 1 carriages had been a major contribution to the fall in accident casualties since 1955 because of their reinforced ends and the use of a stronger type of coupling between the carriages, which together reduced the likelihood of 'telescoping', a phenomenon which inevitably contributed to high death tolls in accidents. On the other hand, one downside of the new carriages was that, due to poor design, they could only be used for 100 mph running if there was very regular and costly maintenance, which limited BR's ability to provide faster passenger services. For the most part, passengers had to be satisfied with 90 mph. Nevertheless, despite these faults, more Mark 1s were built than any other type of carriage in the history of Britain's railway, and many survived well into the twenty-first century.

Unfortunately, steel shortages slowed the replacement programme. At nationalization, British Railways had inherited 56,000 passenger carriages, a quarter of which had been built before the First World War. Much of this older stock was used for excursion trains, which remained an important part of the railway's business. Unlike today's railway, BR always had spare rolling stock it could use for 'specials' and rail excursions, which were either to specific destinations or, in some cases, a 'mystery tour', with day trippers not knowing where they would be going. These could be very lengthy. Chris Randall, a rail journalist, recalls a mystery tour that went from Brighton in Sussex to Morecambe in Lancashire, where inevitably 'it rained all day'. Chris Green, who was based at Nottingham in the early 1980s, points out that these were incredibly popular and profitable:

> We did mystery trains, putting 400 people on a train who did not know where they were going and in the peak of

the summer we did twenty or thirty of those per week –
we could take them to Skegness, Blackpool or wherever;
we had a lot of freedom from BR management to do
this.[19]

There had long been a tradition in the railway for 'specials', trains either run by railway companies to a specific
destination in order to meet demand for events such as
the Coronation, major sporting occasions or simply the
start of the holiday season. There were even specials for
trainspotters, a burgeoning activity in this period before
television and computer games. Rather sadly, one regular
feature was the 'last trip to . . .' type of special, a valedictory before a branch line was closed.

Race specials were still popular, notably to Ascot, when
well-heeled punters would take the train dressed in their
finery, and Doncaster, which attracted a less affluent crowd
but in the past had needed more than 1,000 special trains
over the course of its four-day meetings. The most common sports specials were for football matches, serving a
rather different and more difficult clientele than the race
trains. Some football grounds, such as Cardiff's Ninian
Park, even had their own stations to accommodate football specials. While lucrative, they were problematic,
creating a dilemma for both the football and railway
authorities. As football hooliganism, which at times
resulted in extreme violence, took hold, the pictures of
wrecked carriages with windows smashed started appear-
ing regularly in the national press. Simon Bradley recounts
how a train returning to Liverpool was 'set on fire by the

occupants, using as fuel the contents of mailbags they had stolen from Leicester station'.[20] This was after youths had trashed a train at the station with a hatchet from an emergency kit, with the result that '228 windows were destroyed, with 128 compartment mirrors and picture glasses, 86 blinds, 38 window straps, 180 light bulbs and 8 fire extinguishers'. In another incident, Tottenham Hotspur fans on their way back from a heavy defeat at Derby damaged a train so badly they had to be ejected at two small stations in Bedfordshire and promptly terrorized the local villagers by smashing windows and attacking cars. The authorities did not know how to respond. On the one hand, they feared that scrapping the specials would unleash thousands of unruly and drunken supporters on to regular services; but on the other, the widespread publicity given to the pictures of wrecked trains presented the railway in a very poor light.

Among the more unusual specials were those that took hordes of Londoners as hop pickers to the late summer harvest in Kent. This was a huge operation, centred on London Bridge station. As with football specials, part of the motivation of running these specials was to keep the hop pickers, who could be unruly, off scheduled services and away from other passengers. In 1944, the last full year of the Second World War, 164 special services carried nearly 80,000 hop pickers, many of them women with children in tow, to the fields. But this was already something of a dying trade due to mechanization, and in 1958 the last two hop picker specials ran.

Even cyclists were accommodated in special trains,

with extra guards' vans to carry their bicycles to their destination, from where they would start their ride back home, as shown in an evocative 1955 British Transport Film, *Cyclists Special*. Indeed, much use was made of these films to demonstrate not just the availability of services but to present the railway system in a positive light.

While British Railways organized many of these specials and excursion trains, people could also charter a train or carriage themselves. If they did not have enough takers to charter a whole train, British Railways regularly published a helpful brochure, *Party Outings*, with information on how to organize groups from special-interest clubs or societies. The fares were cheap, but the rolling stock tended to reflect the price. If there was no catering car, individual meal trays were provided.

The most profitable specials, though, were for the holiday market. Although some people were starting to travel by car to their holiday destination, British Railways, with much spare rolling stock, was eager to retain this business at a time when it was still customary for people to holiday in the UK. Most holiday specials ran on Saturdays and the West Country was an especially popular destination. Exeter St David's, the hub of the rail network in Devon and Cornwall, saw up to 120,000 people pass through the station on one Saturday in August 1953. And 'on a normal summer Saturday, no fewer than 130 long-distance expresses either stop or pass through the station'.[21] This was not easy to manage, particularly if there was a mishap, which was not unusual as old unreliable locomotives were often used as well as carriages that should have been long past their use-by date. The worst overcrowding on the tracks from this great addition of trains was on 27 July 1957, when, according to the authors of *Summer Saturdays in the West* – who wrote with the precision of experienced trainspotters – it was the most 'chaotic day ever in the West of England ... [since] between 8.24 a.m. and 9.37 p.m., eighty down [heading West] trains arrived at Newton Abbot and were an average of 122 minutes late. Every train arriving between 1.15 p.m. and 5.15 p.m. was more than two hours late.'[22] In those days, long before mobile phones, there must have been a lot of seaside B & B landladies fretting about whether their clients would ever arrive, and a lot of evening meals missed.

Such mayhem didn't stop British Railways from responding to the demand for ever more specials, despite not having sufficient capacity on the tracks to deal with the extra trains. Whereas normally around 190 daily services would operate on a routine day in British Railways' Western Region, by 1960, on a summer Saturday, the number had increased to 450. The problem for British Railways, and indeed for any rail system in the world, is that it is simply impossible to meet such high demand, which only occurs on a few weekends a year, without spending a disproportionate amount of money on expanding the infrastructure. It was only the availability of spare rolling stock which sat in sidings for the rest of the year that made such an increase in services possible.

One great innovation was to make use of retired rolling stock sitting on an unused siding next to a station.

These 'camping coaches' could be booked very cheaply through the railway, with the proviso that four adult return tickets from their home station were bought for a six-berth coach, or six for an eight-berth one. According to the brochure, camping coaches could be found in 'specially selected places in England, Scotland and Wales', where they offered 'a cheap and ideal holiday for the family'. The local railway staff, and particularly the station master (a post which, at this time, existed at even relatively small stations), were supposed to provide advice on 'outings, fishing and golf and in many other ways'. Moreover, the 'campers' were enticed to make further trips on the railway with cheap tickets to other local amenities. This again was surprisingly big business. The 1955 brochure for the scheme cites 107 locations; in 1960, British Railways decided to offer an upgraded version with retired Pullman cars that offered a rather more luxurious interior, though, in truth, this was merely a clever marketing ploy. These holidays, which retained their popularity into the 1960s, were sold by British Railways until 1971, when the decline in station staff and the availability of a much wider range of holiday destinations abroad killed off the trade.

There were other curios which still existed at the time of nationalization. British Railways continued, for a time, the practice of offering 'through coaches', which enabled people to travel to little-used stations without changing trains, even when there was no regular direct service. The coaches would be hauled at the back of a train, and when a carriage reached the station where normally passengers would have to change, it was detached and then hitched to another service, allowing passengers to reach their destination. This service was very popular for people travelling with luggage or children, but was costly to provide since the interchange stations had to have a little shunting engine to effect the manoeuvre. Yet British Railways did not just retain these services, but for a time it expanded them to the extent that in the winter of 1955/6 the *Atlantic Coast Express*, which ran between London and various seaside resorts in the South-West, offered no fewer than sixty-five destinations that could be reached directly without changing carriages.

There was another version of this, which had long existed on Britain's railway network but very rarely anywhere else in the world. This was the 'slip coach', a remarkable 'one direction' concept that required extra staff. Instead of stopping at intermediate stations, an express service would consist of coaches that were uncoupled one by one from the train at some distance from a station. The detached coach would then drift in under its own momentum and stop at the platform. This was, though, difficult to operate, as it required a brakeman on each carriage that was detached, since he would have to ensure the free-rolling coach would come to a halt in the right place. The coaches, too, had to have special equipment to ensure that the brake pipes and other connections with the rest of the train could be separated easily. Moreover, slip coaches only worked one way, since to return them in the other direction required the train to stop and connect them. It is hardly surprising that few other countries adopted this method. Nevertheless, despite these complexities, this strange British phenomenon survived more than a decade under the nationalized British Railways, with the last one slipping into Bicester station off a Paddington–Birmingham express in September 1960.

All of these special services demonstrated a fundamental fact about the railway which would be eroded, slowly, over the years: there was still a belief that the railway had a duty to ensure people could travel by rail around the country whenever they needed to – and at a fare that was not exorbitant. For many people, the railway was a monopoly, their only option for many of the journeys they needed or wanted to undertake. The Labour government nationalized the railway because there were few other options available and because it fitted in with its ideology. It cannot be said, however, that the Labour government was particularly good for the railway. To some extent, the left of centre party had a vested interest against modernization. After all, the railway was the biggest customer for coal, another nationalized industry that was not faring well and one that was particularly dear to all good socialists' hearts. Moreover, diesel or electric traction would lead to a reduction in staffing, not something that was likely to please a party created by the trade unions.

The Labour administration gradually tired, and after just holding on to a majority in 1950, lost to Winston Churchill's Tories in an unnecessary general election held in October the following year. As David Henshaw concludes, under Labour, the system appeared to have experienced 'all the negative aspects of socialism without any of the benefits – a top-heavy bureaucracy, without market safeguards or a policy of integration'.[23] The Tories, oddly, proved more ready to spend money on investment, but it would come at a price and inevitably entail a re-organization. British Railways was expected to focus on cost-cutting and closing unremunerative lines. Moreover, many of those at a senior level in the organization still saw steam engines as the future.

3

New for Old

Britain's railway was vital to the war effort but, as we have seen, it was in desperate need of investment by the end of the conflict. Unfortunately, a scarcity of materials and skilled people was a barrier to change and, in any case, modernization, in terms of both technology and management techniques, is never easy in an asset-heavy industry like rail. The railway was also hampered by post-war austerity in its efforts to replace out-of-date assets that were expensive to renew. All this was compounded by the conservative instincts of those in charge of the railway, whose careers stretched back to the pre-war era when steam ruled unchallenged.

Some British Railways managers undoubtedly did try to effect change, but they faced numerous obstacles. The inexorable growth of road transport, the start of the construction of the motorway network in the 1950s and later the era of cheap flights are trends whose importance is easy to see with hindsight, but one can forgive railway managers in the immediate post-war period for failing to predict their significance.

Nevertheless, by the mid-1950s, as memories of the war began to fade and austerity was gradually relaxed, it became increasingly clear that the railway had to modernize to survive. Slow, dirty and frequently late steam trains ensured the railway lost any competitive edge over the road-based alternatives. The investment that gradually began to be made in the early 1950s undoubtedly led to improved services, but there was still a pre-war feeling to the railway in an era in which the car, television and household appliances were beginning to be the norm. Although British Railways made an operating profit until 1955, and passenger numbers increased up to 1957, both the government and railway managers realized heavy losses were inevitable unless services were improved to counter growing competition from cars and lorries.

The emphasis, as it would be for much of the existence of British Railways, was on cutting costs rather than on attracting new customers or even retaining existing ones. The Tories, who came to power in 1951 after six years of Labour government, were not interested in 'integrated transport', which had been at the heart of the idea of creating the British Transport Commission. Instead, they focused on efficiency, competition and, in particular, returning long-distance road haulage to the private sector.

The Transport Commission was slow to respond to the external trends that were so obviously moving against the railway. It was only in the spring of 1953 that the Railway Executive belatedly published a report which set out a £500 million plan to modernize the railway. It recognized that steam had probably had its day (there was still some doubt!) and focused on electrification, which took up a third of the proposed budget, along with more modest investments on signalling, stations and even diesel railcars. However, the plan's bizarre inclusion of a £40 million investment in 'helicopter terminals and services' highlighted its incoherence and its misreading of the impact of technology. It proposed that terminus stations in nine cities across the country would be adapted as combined helicopter and rail hubs, which would serve not only domestic destinations but link with Irish and even some European cities.

This off-the-wall idea was fortunately never put to the test, since the whole plan was lost in the upheaval caused by the Tories' decision to abolish the Railway Executive. This was the key change put forward in the 1953 Transport Act, which was a deliberate move away from the concept of integrated transport. Instead, the railway would be run directly by the Commission through area boards that oversaw the regions. As this short explanation of a complex series of administrative changes implies, this was a recipe for an incredibly bureaucratic process that paralysed decision-making in the industry. Whereas the Railway Executive had consisted of a few key managers, now meetings to decide railway policies were huge affairs, with large numbers of officials filling a vast new boardroom the size of a standard local authority council chamber – and as a result often failing to make any coherent decisions. The new chairman of the board, Sir Brian Robertson, was an ex-military man who ran the meetings accordingly. Michael Bonavia, who attended them, said, 'The Chairman's summing-up was always impressive but sometimes one felt that the root of the matter had not been penetrated.'[1] Indeed, Bonavia points out that any decision by a regional general manager would have to go through six layers of bureaucracy to obtain approval.

The main target of the Transport Act was to privatize the highly profitable road haulage business whose nationalization by the Attlee government had always been opposed strenuously by the Conservatives. The rather haphazard plans to improve the railway were something of an afterthought, designed to appease public anger about the state of the network. Now that eight years had passed since the end of the war, the government had belatedly recognized that not enough had been done to improve or develop the railway, both because of the lack of funds to invest but also as a result of the failure to adopt new technology. While the design of cars and lorries had improved apace compared to pre-war models, the railway, with its dirty and cumbersome locomotives, and its rundown stations and carriages, was clearly at a competitive disadvantage. It was like watching a storm brewing up without having anywhere to shelter.

In fact, the 1953 Act did nothing to properly address the problem of how to improve the railway and reflected the Tories' long-held antipathy to a nationalized rail network. David Henshaw sums it up neatly in his book on railway closures, by saying the Act's 'implementation proved a nightmare, resulting in a tangle of bureaucracy that exceeded anything imposed by the former socialist regime'. Worse, the Conservative government then restricted any rise in fares and freight rates in a vain attempt to control inflation, which proved to be 'an incredibly foolish policy that set the industry on the road to financial ruin'.[2]

The Executive's investment plan mouldered for a year or so before it was transformed into the far bigger and more ambitious Modernisation Plan published in January 1955. The Plan was costed at a staggering £1,240 million to be spent over a fifteen-year period (the sum is equivalent to about £35 billion in 2021 money, but as a proportion of the economy it represented a much greater percentage of gross domestic product than even the updated sum would today). It was the most expensive investment programme ever embarked on in the history of the railway – until HS2 – and would ultimately cost around £1,600 million. The intentions were laudable:

> The aim must be to exploit the great natural advantages of railways as bulk transporters of passengers and goods and to revolutionise the character of the services provided for both – not only by the full utilisation of a modern equipment but also by a purposeful concentration on those functions which the railways can be made to perform more efficiently than other forms of transport, whether by road, air or water.[3]

The Plan offered a transformation of all aspects of the railway, for both freight and passengers. Passenger services were to become faster and more reliable and would link Britain's major cities with regular and more frequent services. There was an assumption that, if services were improved, then passenger numbers would not decline and possibly would even rise slightly. Freight services were to be upgraded with modern wagons that would be able to run faster, thanks to improved brakes. The Plan was remarkably comprehensive, seeking to modernize the track and signalling. Old-fashioned mechanical signals would be replaced by far safer colour lights, and both stations and train carriages would be upgraded. The optimism inherent in the Plan was expressed in its opening paragraph: 'The Modernisation Plan will win traffic back from roads. Freight traffic will also return and grow.'

Unfortunately, the whole process was undermined from the start. The Plan, which had been long in gestation but finalized in a great rush at the end of 1954, was prepared by a series of committees, which failed to coordinate their findings. The urgency was prompted by ministerial concerns that something needed to be done about the railway, which still remained popular among the public. Transport was seen as crucial to economic growth and the government had just announced a £400 million roads programme that included the nation's first motorways. Therefore, as Terry Gourvish puts it, 'ministers would have found it difficult to refuse support for an industry which all recognised had suffered greatly from financial stringency in the past'.[4]

Despite the Plan's long preparation period, the final version was rushed out because of fears about an impending strike by the National Union of Railwaymen, something the Tories, with their small parliamentary majority, were keen to avoid. As Christmas 1954 approached, the annual wage round had reached a point where a possible walkout was causing great concern in the Cabinet. Railway workers had received poor wage settlements in previous years because the Commission was cash-strapped; a relatively generous settlement, therefore, aimed at buying off the workers, combined with the Modernisation Plan, offered a useful way out of the dilemma. The fact that a very expensive and rather ill-thought-out fifteen-year plan was used in this way shows how British Railways was always at the mercy of political whim. Somehow, short-termism always won out over the long-term needs of an industry that by its very nature requires strategic planning, and at least some of the Modernisation Plan's failings could have been addressed had more time been allowed to produce it.

The flaws in the Plan were deep-rooted and would prove profoundly damaging to the future of the industry. Most notably, there was no rigorous assessment of the numerous schemes and improvements hatched up by the various sub-committees which had been tasked with drawing up the lists of projects. Cost-benefit analysis, so widely used to assess projects today, might have helped in providing comparisons between the various schemes, but this technique was still a decade away from widespread use in British industry. Nor had the Treasury yet found ways of controlling the investment programmes of the nationalized industries, as no clear guidelines had been formulated. In particular, there was no attempt to predict the rate of return on a particular investment or to prioritize different elements of the Plan, which ranged from technological innovations to revising timetables. In reality, the Plan was back-of-the-envelope stuff pushed through for short-term political expediency at a time when the government was anxious to spend its way out of post-war austerity. Therefore, although both the Treasury and the Ministry of Transport were aware of these shortcomings, the Plan was waved through with remarkably little scrutiny by the Cabinet.

The Chancellor, R. A. Butler, declared that the Plan drawn up by the Commission was 'a courageous and imaginative conception'.[5] Even the press was enthusiastic, with the *Economist* chirpily pronouncing that it was 'carefully thought out' and 'a firm statement of good intentions'.[6] Gourvish concludes that 'most observers accepted the Plan as a laudable attempt to rectify a lack of investment in the industry, which stretched back to the interwar years'.[7] Sadly, this enthusiasm would soon dissipate, as all too quickly the Plan's flaws emerged.

The core idea, which would be repeated by Beeching, and by numerous subsequent reports that attempted to 'solve the railway problem', was that with the right mix of investment and cost reduction, the railway could be returned to profitability. It is ironic that the year of the publication of the Plan was the last time British Railways made an operating profit. The Plan envisaged that modernization would result in extra revenue of some £85 million annually, which would enable the railway to break even by 1961/2. In fact, there was little basis for these figures.

While the helicopter idea had, thankfully, been dropped, there was instead to be a transformation of the railway that a more rigorous analysis would have quickly revealed as a fantasy. At its heart, rightly, was the move away from steam. The battle between the traditionalists, who still saw steam as the future, and the modernizers, who favoured more modern traction methods, had been won by the latter, but not conclusively enough. While it was generally accepted by both sides that electrification was the right solution, resources were limited and a medium-term compromise was sought. The question was whether steam should continue to fill the gap in the interim, or whether there should be a big push towards diesels. Ultim-ately, the modernists won out with a recognition in the Plan that there would be no new suburban or express steam engines and that all construction of new steam locomotives would be phased out (the last one, *Evening Star*, was completed in 1960 and had a working life of barely five years). Electricity and diesel were the future, with an initial emphasis on the former.

Although the Modernisation Plan was unquestionably flawed, it was not without merit. Indeed, as Gourvish concludes, 'Many of the schemes implemented during the modernisation period were worthwhile and would have satisfied more stringent tests, had they been applied.'[8] The Plan envisaged electrification of nearly 3,000 miles on a network of around 18,000 miles, more than dou-bling the existing mileage, which was concentrated on the Southern Region and a few commuter routes. Some sub-urban lines in north and east London, routes to Kent on the Southern and the Glasgow suburban network were all earmarked for electrification. But the flagship schemes were the West Coast Main Line and later the East Coast.

However, although diesel was initially seen as a stop-gap, the huge programme of developing far too many different types of locomotives led to much wastage. One problem was that the managers of British Railways' six regions were given free rein and came up with all kinds of madcap schemes. Some 174 different designs were piloted and ultimately twenty-six different classes of diesel loco-motive were produced, many before a prototype had even been tested. As a result, British Railways had hundreds of unserviceable locomotives which broke down regularly, attracting much critical press attention. Indeed, some of the designs were so bad that the locomotives were scrapped ahead of the steam engines they were supposed to replace.

A bad situation was made worse by the decision of the Western Region to choose diesel-hydraulic locomotives, in which the engine is directly connected to the axles through a hydraulic turbine, rather than the widely adopted diesel-electrics, whose engines generate electri-city that powers motors connected to the wheels of the locomotive. In the event, the diesel-hydraulics were inconvenient as they did not generate electricity for light-ing or air conditioning, and they were soon withdrawn, some after less than a decade of service. The Western also kept on producing small tank steam locomotives for use on branch lines when it was clear that diesels were a far more efficient alternative. This was one example of why the regional managers were known as 'barons'. They saw colleagues from other regions as rivals and demanded the best for their fiefdom, disregarding the need for cost-saving standardization across the national network. They were wont to make ridiculous bids for resources, such as the London Midland, which sought to have 660 electric locomotives to run on the West Coast Main Line when 100 eventually sufficed. They also submitted projects that were clearly unnecessary, on the basis that if the region next door was introducing new equipment, why shouldn't they? Again, it was the Western Region, led by Reggie Hanks in the late 1950s, that was particularly vociferous in defending its own narrow interests, rather than the needs of the railway more generally.

The worst example of waste in the Plan was the construction of huge marshalling yards. The notion that the railway must be able to transport a wagon anywhere in the country, regardless of the number of times it needed detaching and shunting, still prevailed. This made it necessary to have marshalling yards where freight wagons for various destinations were brought in on one train and then detached and redistributed to form other trains to new destinations. Small packages of freight were crammed into wagons and sent around the network, often at snail speed, and occasionally going missing for weeks at a time. This was clearly a service that was at risk from road competition, but since the railway was still burdened with its common carrier obligation, which was not removed until 1962, the Plan envisaged modernizing the service with the unrealistic aim of making it profitable, rather than abandoning clearly uneconomic carryings. In order to make the process more efficient, huge marshalling yards would be built, allowing many small sidings to be closed.

Most were little used or quickly became redundant, as they were built decades too late or in the wrong place. According to Gerard Fiennes, a brilliant post-war railway manager who wrote a seminal book, *I Tried to Run a Railway*, some marshalling yards were located 'in the middle of nowhere', which made them difficult to operate. A fierce debate raged at BR headquarters about the siting of these yards, which were costed at £85 million in the Modernisation Plan. Fiennes believed they had to be close to where most of their business would come from, and in his capacity as BR's chief operating officer he managed to scrap plans for the most ludicrous ones. Fiennes's success was not without consequences: a flyover that had been built at Bletchley in Buckinghamshire to take the Oxford to Cambridge line over the West Coast Main Line became an expensive white elephant that was later regularly cited by opponents of the railway. The intention had been to carry freight from the nearby Swanbourne yard, but following Fiennes's reassessment of the marshalling-yard programme, that was scrapped. Instead of 2,400 freight wagons per day on the journey between the Welsh coal mines and the East Coast ports, it carried the occasional passenger train on the Varsity line between Oxford and Cambridge which, unaccountably, was closed in 1968. Fiennes was unapologetic: 'The Bletchley flyover remains a memorial to people who failed to see that railways must live by concentration and not dispersal.'[9]

Work had started slowly on the modernization of the yards and it was not until 1959 that the programme really got going, which gave Fiennes and his allies in BR time to kill off the worst excesses of the scheme. Hundreds of smaller yards were closed but around thirty of the new large yards were completed. Kingmoor in the traditional railway town of Carlisle was the biggest, with nearly forty miles of sidings, arguably making it the most modern in Europe, with the potential to sort 5,000 wagons per day. Completed in 1962, it briefly flourished before traffic reduced sharply. Similarly, Perth, which handled 1,200 wagons per day when it opened in the same year, closed six years later.

The success of the yards was also hampered by a legacy technical issue. Some wagons had vacuum brakes, others had none. This complicated matters in marshalling yards, as it was better to put the wagons with brakes together near the locomotive whose power was needed to operate them, but this required extra shunting moves. In any case, vacuum brakes, which were more suited to work with steam locomotives than diesels, were the wrong choice, and the policy of installing them throughout the wagon fleet was quietly dropped in favour of the universal installation of air brakes.

In many ways, this typified the lack of planning that undermined the Modernisation Plan and meant that, ultimately, it was fatally flawed. The harsh truth is that the Modernisation Plan was not a 'plan' at all, but rather a series of projects hastily cobbled together to give the illusion of coherence. In the short term, everyone got what they wanted. As Charles Loft explains in his account of the early years of British Railways, the British Transport

Commission 'wanted the go-ahead for modernisation, which it got; the government wanted the all clear for the strike settlement, which it got. The plan was in this sense a remarkable success.'[10] Although, of course, it wasn't, as the Commission had admitted that its financial problems could not be solved and the government had merely added to them by pushing up the wage bill by some £10 million annually. There was a fundamental dishonesty at the heart of the whole episode, based on the pretence that the railway could pay for itself and that government subsidies would not be needed when clearly the opposite was the case.

The British Transport Commission's approach to costing the Plan is revealed in a telling aside in the report itself. After carefully totting up the various elements of the Plan to reach £1,240 million, the report then adds 'say £1,200 million' – in other words, knocking off £40 million as a rounding figure. Not surprisingly, the story of the Plan was later characterized by the Treasury – by then rather more confident of its ability to police the nationalized industries – when giving evidence to a 1960 parliamentary inquiry, as 'merely a hotch-potch of the things that the Commission was saying it was desirable to try to achieve by 1970, ill-qualified and not really explainable'.[11] Ouch.

Fiennes suggests the problem was rooted in the early days of British Railways: 'It is one of the disasters about British Railways that in the years between 1947 and 1955 no one had done the basic work on what we were there for at all; what traffic should be carried by what methods in what quantities: where from and to, at what rates.' He added: 'We had made the basic error of buying our tools before doing our homework on defining the job.'[12] At the heart of the Plan were two irreconcilable objectives: the government wanted the British Transport Commission to fulfil its obligation to break even; and the public wanted a modern railway of broadly the existing size, though possibly accepting a few closures.

Just how many closures was a difficult question. Clearly, apart from generating extra revenue, the other side of the coin for reaching profitability was reducing costs and, in particular, shutting 'uneconomic' lines. But defining 'uneconomic' in a business as complex as the railway, where there are literally millions of different journeys made every day, has troubled railway managers ever since the *Rocket* was steaming out of Liverpool. Between the wars, there were some lines that were obviously redundant or that duplicated others, with the result that, in the interwar period, 240 miles of line had been closed, though around 1,000 miles more were turned over to freight-only use.

After nationalization, a Branchline Committee was quickly established. That was rather a misnomer since its function was not to improve those services but rather to shut down the ones deemed too heavily loss-making, and it was later renamed the Unremunerative Railway Committee. According to Henshaw, the 'shadowy' Branchline Committee, which was made up of senior rail managers, 'was charged with the unsavoury task of seeking out and destroying uneconomic branch lines, and a team of full-time officers set to work, putting forward a steady stream of loss-making, and generally unopposed, closure proposals'.[13]

British Railways recognized that closing a line would always cause local hardship but argued that it was necessary to do so when the service was uneconomic. Identifying basket cases was reasonably easy, as given the limited nature of the closure programme in the interwar years, there was no shortage of branches that had never been viable, but had been built because of some special interest by a railway company or were the result of strong lobbying by local grandees. There was, as yet, no concept of a social railway, one in which the benefits could not be captured through the fare box but were all too obvious to those who lived near the line. The closure programme was therefore speeded up after nationalization, but it still left a lot of services on marginal lines.

British Railways closed 301 branch lines, culling 3,618 miles out of a network of just under 20,000 route miles at nationalization, and shutting 1,800 stations and halts, before Beeching arrived at the helm in 1961 A typical example of a pre-Beeching closure was the fifteen-mile Tanat Valley Light Railway, which opened in 1904 and ran between Llanyblodwel, near Oswestry in Shropshire, to Llangynog in Powys, and had one platform and a little goods yard. Given Llangynog's population was just under 300, it was hardly surprising that the annual income of the line was a mere £252, which may seem respectable in relation to the tiny population it served, but it was understandably not sufficient to sway the Branchline Committee, which recommended its closure in 1951. Keeping this type of line open made little sense, although the savings from closing them were modest compared with the overall mounting losses being incurred by the railway. A survey at the end of the 1950s suggested that around £4.3 million annually had been saved by these early closures once the lost income from people no longer using the railway was taken into account.

Opposition to the closure programme was slow to emerge, hampered by the fact that few could defend many of the early candidates. As the Branchline Committee considered less obvious cases, more protests emerged. The statutory bodies, the local Transport Users' Consultative Committees which had been created in each region and which were supposedly independent, proved totally ineffective, since by 1955 they had rubber stamped all but two of the 118 closures proposed by the Branchline Committee. Even when the local committee rejected a closure plan, the central committee, which had the final say, tended to approve the withdrawal of services. An opposition movement, led by two new groups, the Railway Development Association (later Society) and the wonderfully named Railway Invigoration Society, began to organize protests against closures. They were hampered by a shortage of resources and, crucially, a lack of information about passenger numbers and finances for specific lines. Their key focus in the early days was the reluctance of British Railways to use new technology, which damaged the economics of these lines.

In the second half of the 1950s, the Transport Commission found it harder to push through closures; Consultative

Committee hearings began to be inundated with protesters armed with more information, helping to create a bottle-neck in the process. This was fortunate since, unknown to the opposition movement, the Commission had a wider secret agenda as it planned to begin to shut down some of the secondary regional routes that had been built at the height of the Victorian era of competition between rail companies.

In the face of this opposition, British Railways adopted a tactic that would later become almost standard practice: closure by stealth. On lines that were making modest losses, the timetable would be scaled back in order to make the service all but useless to local people and therefore render the closure inevitable. It would often start with the abolition of Sunday services, which were expensive to provide as staff were often paid time and a half for a guaranteed eight-hour day (at that time, workers could not be paid any less than the hours of a full shift even if they worked far fewer). Then, a regular service enabling people to go and come back in a day – for, say, a shopping trip in the local town – would be cut to one or two trains per day, which made such journeys impossible. Finally, affordable fares would be scrapped and the timetable adjusted to make connections with main-line services harder.

While the Tanat Valley line and other similar routes were lost causes by any measure, a few of the more useful branches closed at the time – such as those serving Dartmoor, a big tourist attraction – might have been given a new lease of life had diesel replaced steam. Diesels cost less to operate and attracted new customers because they were cleaner, more reliable and offered a smoother journey. When a diesel railcar was introduced belatedly on the Buckingham to Banbury line in 1956, passenger numbers increased threefold in the first year. It was only after the recommendations of the Modernisation Plan that diesel-powered units started to be used on some branch lines. It had taken eight years for the British Transport Commission to introduce a technology which dated back to the 1930s and, as mentioned before, was widely used on the Continent. As a result, some lines were saved and others simply earned more revenue, but this was before a certain Dr Richard Beeching took over as the head of Britain's railway in June 1961.

4

Beeching's Double Act

The failure of the Modernisation Plan caused the Treasury to distrust British Railways' financial planning for the rest of its existence. In truth, however, modernization alone could never have reversed BR's ailing fortunes. More fundamental forces were at work and the organization's growing deficit was the result of the high capital debt incurred at nationalization, rising staff costs (labour shortages were understandably exploited by well-organized unions) and, crucially, increased competition from cars and lorries which led to a decline in passenger and freight revenues.

A failure to grasp the principles of railway economics was to lead to the most infamous period in British Railways' history: the publication in 1963 of the Beeching report and its aftermath. If the Modernisation Plan was a positive outcome of the conjunction of a number of political factors, the arrival of Dr Richard Beeching at the head of British Railways was precisely the opposite. There were malign forces behind his arrival, and they were largely instigated by the appointment in 1959 of his boss, Ernest Marples, as transport minister.

There is no doubt that Marples, who held the transport brief for five years, had an agenda, and it was inimical to the railway. His role as minister of transport was compromised from the beginning, as he had made his fortune from Marples Ridgway, a civil engineering business he founded soon after the war which was in receipt of substantial government road building contracts. Marples resigned as director when he was appointed as a junior housing minister in 1951, but he retained his 80 per cent holding in the company for some time after he was made transport minister before finally passing the equity to his wife after his share ownership was revealed – there was no MPs' register of interests in those days. None of this prevented Marples Ridgway from securing a lucrative contract to build part of the M1, a project for which Marples himself had given the final go-ahead. The company also won several other large civil engineering contracts, including one to build the Hammersmith flyover in London.

Although Marples had worked for the railway briefly before he was elected MP for Wallasey on Merseyside in 1945, he was, like most transport ministers of the period, a 'roads man' rather than a railway fan. He was sympathetic to the powerful roads lobby, which actively sought a reduction in railway mileage, as the Road Haulage Association boldly stated in its house magazine:

> We should build more roads, and we should have fewer railways. This would merely be following the lesson of

history which shows a continued and continuing expansion of road transport and a corresponding contraction
in the volume of business handled by the railways . . . a
streamlined railway system could surely be had for half
the money that is now available.[1]

The editorial went on to argue that the railway had a 'long
history of failure', rather neglecting its success as the first
land-based mass-transit system.

Marples was a colourful character, rather in the Boris
Johnson mould, though his background was very different. A self-made man from humble origins with few
strongly held political views, he was an innovator with an
abundance of energy and drive. As Postmaster General,
he introduced subscriber trunk dialling – which allowed
long-distance calls to be made without going through
an operator – and, at Transport, he oversaw the introduction of parking meters, seat belts and yellow lines. He
even flirted with the idea of replacing 'boring' trains
between London and Scotland with a 'tracked hovercraft'
capable of travelling at 300 mph on a purpose-built ele-
vated line. According to Christopher Cockerell, the
inventor of the hovercraft, this would have cost only
£100 million to build (£2.5 billion in today's money), but
technically it was never viable.

Given Marples's energy, which stimulated this plethora
of schemes, it was no surprise that, in a cartoon by the
ever-sharp Vicky in the *Evening Standard* depicting the Cabinet as a football team, Marples was shown as the centre
forward. In later years, Marples nearly came unstuck when

he was caught up in a sleaze scandal that revealed his apparent fetish for being whipped by prostitutes while wearing women's clothes. According to Charles Loft's book on the Beeching years, Marples 'demonstrated a consistent carelessness towards rules that impinged on his personal convenience, which appears to have stemmed from a reckless enjoyment of flirting with political danger almost for the hell of it'.[2] He was spared by the mores of the time as Lord Denning, the eminent judge who had uncovered Marples's predilection in the course of writing a report into the Profumo affair in the early 1960s, felt it was not appropriate to name the 'minister' concerned. Nevertheless, Marples's identity was eventually revealed, and his career ended in disgrace as he had to flee to Monaco to avoid a ruinous tax bill, and he died in self-imposed exile in France in 1978. There are echoes of Boris Johnson in several aspects: his stream of ideas, his show-manship and, particularly, his cavalier attitude towards what constitutes appropriate behaviour for a minister.

David Henshaw in his book *The Great Railway Conspiracy* argues that this crucial period in British railway history was the result of a coalition of interests inside and outside government that were trying actively to do the railway down. Actually, it did not need to be a covert conspiracy. The zeitgeist was very much that the railway's time had passed and that this was the age of the internal combustion engine, given the increasingly widespread ownership of cars, which were improving year by year while remaining affordable, as well as the prospect of a network of modern motorways on the horizon. The Marples–Beeching double act ensured a major and rapid policy shift towards roads, but in truth there was already a widely held belief that the railway would decline. The only question was by how much.

Marples ensured it was a lot. He set up a rather murky 'advisory' committee under the chairmanship of the industrialist Sir Ivan Stedeford, whose background was in the motor industry, which supposedly had the remit of looking at the management of all transport across Britain. However, its true purpose was rather exposed by the fact that there were no representatives of the rail industry nor any trade unionists on the committee. The key member was Dr Richard Beeching, a scientist who at the time was an executive of ICI (Imperial Chemical Industries) and would later become chairman of British Rail. Interestingly, the Ministry of Transport was represented by David Serpell, who went on to write a report advocating rail closures even more radical than Beeching's (see Chapter 6).

The committee's findings and recommendations were never published, but they formed the basis of the 1962 Transport Act which abolished the British Transport Commission and established the British Railways Board in 1963. The recommendations were later uncovered by Chris Austin and Richard Faulkner, the authors of *Holding the Line*, an account of how Britain's railway over the years has been constantly targeted by Whitehall. They reveal that the core philosophy behind the report was that 'the concept of public service blurs the concept of a commercial enterprise'. It was just one example of the perennial failures over the years to understand the wider purpose of the railway. Austin and Faulkner comment that 'this simple sentence set the course of the rail industry for the future. We are still living with the consequences.'[3] The prevailing attitude was succinctly expressed by the notorious Conservative politician Enoch Powell, who said: 'There must be concealed . . . in our present railway system, as a sculpture is concealed in a block of marble, the railway system of the future which does pay and does correspond to the economic needs of the country'.[4] That fallacy would cloud the remainder of BR's existence.

There is no doubt that the Stedeford committee, with its unbalanced membership, had a clear, predetermined agenda. Supposedly independent, it was actually set up to give impetus to the plans that the government would have carried out anyway. As Michael Bonavia puts it, the committee believed 'that the railways could and should be run as a commercially profitable undertaking, if only the top management would shake off its "public service" mentality'.[5] This was well illustrated by a key passage in the report. The committee criticized the fact that the chairmen of the various regional consultative committees had complained that 'the majority of the cases now coming before them for the withdrawal of uneconomic railway services could have been put forward several years earlier on equally strong grounds and that, from this experience, there must be a similar number of cases not yet prepared'.[6] The conclusion of such thinking was obvious: 'We recommend that, with a view to expediting progress, a dated programme of further proposals for closure be prepared.'[7] No evidence was taken from people who might be affected by closures, nor from lobbying organizations like the Railway Development Association or the trade unions. The committee did, however, give a hearing to the Railway Conversion League, a bizarre and extreme organization which actively campaigned to turn rail lines into roads for coaches and HGVs, a notion which despite its clear impracticality was taken seriously for several decades (see Chapter 10).

The White Paper published in December 1960, which was the basis of the subsequent 1962 Transport Act, was equally unequivocal: 'The practical test for the railways, as for other transport, is how far the users are prepared to pay economic prices for the services provided . . . It is already clear that the system must be made more compact.'[8] It envisaged not only closures but a much more rigorous approach to investment. Marples wanted future projects to make a genuine return on capital. The annual deficits which had started at just £16 million in 1956 had soared to more than £100 million by 1962. Even though it was tacitly recognized that every line had some social value, as its closure would cause hardship, there was to be a hard-nosed approach to losses. Any line which did not wash its face would have to go.

Beeching had shown his hand by expressing a view to the committee which unequivocally paved the way for radical closures. He wrote in a paper for the committee that there was a need for a report on 'the size and pattern of railway system appropriate to the present and foreseeable needs of the country. The foundation of the whole investigation must be an assessment of the inherent merits of rail transport, relative to alternative forms of transport, for various forms of traffic.'[9]

It was exactly what Marples wanted to hear. He was looking for a process to make radical cuts to the rail network and needed a strong individual to front it. Marples moved quickly, terminating the contract of the chairman of the Transport Commission, Sir Brian Robertson, and announcing Beeching as the chairman-designate of the British Railways Board.

Beeching, who had shown his fierce intelligence and readiness to confront the railway establishment in his work on the Stedeford committee, was the ideal candidate. The son of a journalist, he had worked in armaments design during the Second World War and joined ICI in 1948, where he rose quickly to become technical director. A large, portly man with a small moustache, there was an element of Alfred Hitchcock about him, which can be seen in the famous picture where he theatrically holds up his infamous report. Anthony Sampson, in his influential book about the state of post-war Britain written in the 1960s, felt that Beeching, with his slow, gravelly voice, 'might be mistaken at first for one of those large phlegmatic men who tell long stories over a pint of beer in a country pub'.[10] That would be a misjudgement. Gerard Fiennes's description of him is rather more apt: 'He oppressed me vastly with his intellectual gianthood. In his presence I was tense, tongue-tied and often plumb stupid. He was as relaxed as they come.'[11] Beeching's languid demeanour as he smoked his favoured expensive cigars and listened to his interlocutors in a friendly and courteous manner hid a formidable intellect and a capacity to take on complicated issues at great speed. He was a radical who was not interested in recognized structures and demonstrated this by effectively abandoning the formal organizational set-up at the British Transport Commission, which stumbled on for eighteen months before its demise.

Beeching could not have imagined that his name would become synonymous with railway closures. His defenders argue that he was only following orders and that, in any case, closures were inevitable. Neither defence entirely exonerates him, as some of the responsibility for what proved to be a far too hasty and widespread reduction of the network lies with him, though he was also responsible for positive changes to the railway. Moreover, as those quotes from people who worked with him demonstrate, Beeching was far too strong-minded and intellectually rigorous to be simply acquiescing to Marples's demands. He knew what he was doing.

If the appointment of a man with no railway experience to head British Railways raised eyebrows, his salary dropped even more jaws. Beeching was appointed on £24,000 per year (equivalent to around half a million today and more than twice the Prime Minister's earnings at the time), matching his ICI salary, and nearly two and a half times the amount his predecessor, Sir Brian Robertson, had received for heading the far larger British Transport Commission. It was, indeed, more than the average pay of key company directors of the time; and eleven years later, a period of high inflation, Beeching's successor but one, Peter Parker, was appointed with a salary slightly less than Beeching had received. However, as *The Times* commented in an editorial, his 'exceptional salary presaged an exceptional role'.[12] Marples clearly realized that the job was something of a poisoned chalice and that Beeching's task was to shake up the railway, which required a commensurately high salary. The White Paper on nationalized industries published just before Beeching's appointment envisaged all these organizations achieving a break-even position within five years. As Terry Gourvish puts it, 'Beeching was appointed to give effect to government intentions for its largest loss-maker by a Minister bent on redirecting resources into road transport.'[13] His four-year tenure would be the most momentous period in BR's history until the decision thirty years later to privatize the railway.

Beeching, who had toured the railway as part of his work on the Stedeford committee, began writing his report soon after replacing Robertson as the head of the doomed British Transport Commission on 1 June 1961. While this was a period in which BR's deficit was increasing every year, there were also signs that the more positive aspects of the Modernisation Plan were having an impact. By 1962, there were more than 3,000 diesel locomotives on the tracks, compared to fewer than 500 in 1955 (and nearly all those were shunters used in yards). The famous Deltics, beloved of trainspotters as the most powerful diesels ever deployed – until recently – on the British rail network, started running on the East Coast Main Line in

1961 and provided a faster and more reliable service than their steam predecessors. Several electrification schemes had been introduced and, as we saw in Chapter 1, the first section of the West Coast Main Line scheme had already been implemented. Electrification was not always a smooth process – a series of fires on the newly electrified Glasgow suburban routes resulted in a temporary return to steam – but overall there were signs that the railway was edging forward by embracing new cost-cutting and efficient technologies that were improving services.

However, the vision of a gradually improving British Railways was not one that Beeching sought to convey. In fact, he would have found it difficult to present a balanced assessment of the railway even if he had wanted to, because his remit excluded the social and wider economic value of the network. As David Henshaw puts it, 'The report completely ignored [implementing] various cost-measures that had been under consideration both at home and abroad for several decades; measures that might have turned marginal lines into profitable concerns.'[14]

Indeed, in the run-up to the publication of Beeching's *Reshaping of British Railways* report on 27 March 1963, government ministers made sure that the perception of the railway as a failing industry would be the core message picked up by the media.[15] In a report to a Cabinet meeting in early March, Marples set out precisely how he wanted the Beeching report to be presented and acted upon. Speed was of the essence in implementing his plan, and basically what he considered the busybodies of the local Transport Users' Consultative Committees were neutered by limits on the amount of time they could spend considering the impact of closures. The Cabinet agreed that the British Railways Board's proposals as set out in the report should be implemented as soon as possible.

Even the fiercest critics of the report admit that it was well written – its 148 small pages were 'a model of clarity and succinctness', as Austin and Faulkner put it.[16] And some elements of it were eminently sensible, such as the necessity to move away from unprofitable wagonload and 'sundries' freight traffic. Transport planners had calculated that it was quicker, at the time, to walk across London with a parcel than to send it by rail. Beeching would later say that freight wagons averaged 'half a mile an hour from loading to unloading', as they spent so much time in marshalling yards and on trains that were held up because passenger services were given priority.[17] Instead, rather sensibly, he recommended BR should concentrate on trainloads such as coal and aggregates, and on container traffic, which was just beginning to be developed.

Beeching's most damning set of statistics framed the entire thinking behind the report and essentially justified its recommendations. Of BR's route mileage of 17,830 in 1961, one third carried just 1 per cent of total passenger miles, and 1 per cent of freight ton miles. It got worse: 96 per cent of the passenger business and 95 per cent of freight was carried on half the network. In other words, the rest had very few trains and most of those carried fresh air. At the other end of the spectrum, the busiest thirty-four stations accounted for just over a quarter of total receipts.

These bare statistics did, indeed, look compelling. But there was something of a 'back of the envelope' feel about them as they were cursory and failed to present the whole picture. The fundamental flaw was that they were based solely on a traffic survey undertaken over the space of just one week, from 16 to 23 April 1961. Moreover, as the report itself acknowledged, the overall economy in 1961 was faring badly and therefore it was not a particularly good basis for a long-term assessment of railway passenger numbers. The timing of the survey also excluded the summer traffic that was a key feature of many routes. This was deliberate. Beeching wasn't particularly interested in holidaymakers since he calculated that providing the extra 6,000 coaches used only in summer cost more than six times the amount they earned from the fare box. His report, therefore, recommended the closure of 127 stations at holiday resorts.

The methodology was also badly flawed. Revenue was counted at the departing station, which meant that a return from London to Whitby, for example, would not be counted as contributing to the branch line, but without its existence the passenger might have chosen another method of transport. This partly explains why those thirty-four busiest stations accounted for such a high proportion of revenue.

If the allocation of income was arbitrary, the way costs were calculated was even more so. They were aggregated at the regional level and there was no attempt to match them against revenue as costs were simply divided up by the mileage of each line. For the most part, rolling stock expenditure, too, was simply allocated on a pro rata basis, with a few exceptions when locomotives were permanently allocated to a route. The fact that most branch lines used second-hand rails recycled from busier routes was not taken into account in the assessment of costs. Producing a realistic balance sheet for a specific line was impossible, as railway finances are convoluted, to say the least, because the industry is full of fixed costs which have to be divided up somehow; therefore determining what was and what wasn't a loss-making line was art rather than science. Crucially, the report disregarded the fact that the railway was run as a network and disaggregating the finances was a nigh on impossible task. In other words, it was very difficult to ascertain the precise economic contribution of a particular service and, as we shall see in Chapter 10, this was recognized in the reforms of the 1980s, when British Rail managers were, for the first time, allowed to assess the impact of revenue-generating investment. The fact that these complex issues were masked in the report greatly helped win over the public to what Marples was trying to do. Closing branch lines was politically harder than, say, scrapping thousands of old freight wagons, and the *Reshaping* report went to considerable lengths to offer a simple message that branch lines were fundamentally and permanently uneconomic, rather than trying to genuinely assess the impact of their closure.

In fact, blaming branch lines for losses was far too simplistic. In any case, they were not even the main source of losses. As Austin and Faulkner point out:

More money was lost by the great urban networks where resources costs were huge, with fare income low by virtue of short distances travelled. Equally, it was here (as it still is now) where the greatest social benefit was delivered by the railways in supporting the economic needs of the cities they served and reducing traffic congestion.[18]

But there was no room for subtlety in Beeching's report, which painted a gloomy picture of declining revenues, with passengers switching to roads and, on longer routes, to the airlines. There was no assessment of how many people might be tempted to use the railway by faster, more frequent diesel and electric services. As well as branch lines, commuter services, seasonal traffic and stopping trains also came in for criticism. The report went to considerable lengths to rule out any prospects of commercial viability for these lines, dismissing any arguments that diesel multiple units, railbuses or cheaper operating methods would rescue them. He also wanted to rid the network of stopping trains on main-line routes. As Henshaw puts it: 'Once the analytical Dr Beeching had made up his mind to eradicate stopping trains, the figures were massaged in such a way as to present an overwhelming case for closure.'[19] He achieved his aim by closing intermediate stations on main-line routes, which meant that several sizeable towns and villages were left with a railway line which still ran through the built-up areas but provided no easy access to local people.

It was only after Beeching had left that BR undertook a radical overhaul of the running of branch-line services.

The system was first introduced in East Anglia, where in 1966 Gerard Fiennes devised a system that involved de-staffing stations and collecting fares on so-called 'Pay-Trains', a scheme that was extended to other regions over the next decade. Removing staff from a large number of small stations made considerable sense, and BR then tried to boost income on these surviving branch lines with a television advertising campaign.

Beeching made no meaningful attempt to assess whether a line could be made viable by trimming staff and replacing steam engines with diesel railcars. Instead, he simply calculated that passenger numbers of at least 10,000 per week on lines that also carried freight and 17,000 per week on those without were needed to make a route viable. It was a high threshold. The implication was that almost all branch lines should close, leaving swathes of the country, including Devon, Lincolnshire, North Wales and the Highlands of Scotland, without any rail services other than being crossed by a few scant regional routes. Even some of those were sacrificed on the altar of efficiency. As a child, in the early 1960s, I had travelled on the Grimsby train direct from King's Cross to Louth, a town of around 16,000 people in Lincolnshire, to spend a couple of weeks on a farm nearby. However, the line fell victim to the Beeching cuts, worsening the economic situation of an already deprived area; and indeed Louth, which had been something of a railway hub, lost its other lines as a large part of the county became a railway desert. I revisited this charming town in the summer of 2021 and realized that, had it been kept on the rail network, it would have all the potential of being a major tourist destination, with its large cathedral-sized church boasting the highest spire of any parish church in England, and attractive Georgian terraces reflecting its past prosperity based on the wool trade.

Overall, Beeching recommended that both a third of the rail network and a third of stations should be closed. His plan called for many of the surviving lines to be confined to freight use, claiming that retaining passenger traffic would cost £1,750 per mile annually to cover the additional expenditure needed for signalling, maintenance and staffing. It wasn't only branch lines that were to be axed. Several trunk routes went, most notably the Somerset & Dorset, the Waverley route between Edinburgh and Carlisle via Hawick (since partly reinstated) and, most significantly, the Great Central between London and Nottingham. This had been the last main line to have been constructed in Britain, and while it did indeed duplicate other lines, it was a well-built alternative route that was very useful as a relief track when engineering works were being carried out. The Settle–Carlisle route, one of the most scenic in the country, was also earmarked for closure but was retained after a lengthy protest campaign (see Chapter 10).

The old trope of achieving profitability was trotted out again. Beeching claimed the closures would see the annual British Railways' deficit wiped out by 1970. But, just as with the Modernisation Plan, this was pie in the sky, as it failed to understand either the cost base of the railway or the strength of the external forces changing the world of transport. Perhaps the best response to the report came from the National Union of Railwaymen, which produced a mock-up with an almost identical cover, titled *The Mis-shaping of British Railways*.

Although Beeching attracted countless detractors, some of his railway colleagues saw him as their saviour. Richard Hardy, a senior railway manger in the Beeching era, said he was 'far from being the cold, clinical, faceless tycoon who many believe him to be'. Instead, he described him as 'considerate, friendly, imperturbable, determined, courageous, and deep down very sensitive', and 'his character was strengthened by the pawky sense of humour that eased his path through life and endeared him to those that knew him'. Most importantly, according to Hardy, 'Beeching saved the railways from financial and organisational disintegration. Let us never forget it.'[20] In particular, Hardy points to two innovations for freight traffic which were originally conceived by Fiennes and put forward by Beeching in his report: 'merry-go-round' coal wagons and container traffic.

Merry-go-round was a brilliant way of reducing costs based on the simple concept of coal wagons that emptied from underneath without even having to stop. Far fewer wagons were required because they spent much less time being loaded and unloaded. Fiennes calculated that, rather than the 550 conventional wagons needed for a new power station near Edinburgh, under the merry-go-round system – a name he dreamt up while in the bath – only forty-four were required. The main barrier to introducing this system was that the terminals, which were not owned by British Railways, required considerable investment to adapt them, and therefore the concept was introduced more slowly than might otherwise have been the case.

The other innovation was the use of containers to carry freight, a service which later became known as Freightliner. Although now in use across the world, containerization was a revolutionary system in the 1960s, and was, inevitably, strongly resisted by dockworkers. The idea was that shipping containers would be transferred on to flat-bed wagons by crane and transported between a small number of terminals with the capability to handle them. Beeching liked the concept and believed it could be used on domestic routes but, in fact, the system allowed the rapid transfer of international freight to and from ships, and that was also a big boost for the railway. Beeching enthusiastically endorsed both containerization and the merry-go-round system in his report, and they became key parts of the modernization of British Railways' freight business.

Hardy's dewy-eyed depiction of Beeching, however, does not really accord with the facts. The massive closure programme was a joint endeavour between the transport minister and the head of the railway which had been decided beforehand and taken forward in a strategic way. While Marples argued that he was constrained by the White Paper and had no choice but to give the go-ahead for the cuts, Beeching claimed he was only following orders. Both claims were disingenuous and little more than a fig leaf for a scheme to undermine and cut back the railway system hatched up by the two of them working together.

The closures were planned to go ahead whatever the evidence, which, in any case, was very partial given the lack of a proper financial assessment.

Beeching, incidentally, was unrepentant. The prolific author Hunter Davies recalls visiting Lord Beeching (who was created a baron in 1965) at his East Grinstead home in 1981. Ironically, Beeching's house was next to a disused railway line that Davies was strolling down for a book he was writing about walks on old railway routes. He found Beeching was perfectly happy with his achievements and the conversation settled once and for all the argument as to whether Beeching was the innocent abroad exploited by Marples.

Moreover, Beeching told Davies he was wary of the most obvious and cost-effective way of improving the railway: electrification. Indeed, while on the Stedeford committee, he became aware of the increasing cost of the West Coast Main Line electrification and he managed to persuade Marples to delay giving the final go-ahead for the project. As a result, a junior British Railways manager was tasked with assessing the scrap value of all the electrification equipment that had already been erected! Fortunately, Sir Brian Robertson, at the British Transport Commission, managed to see off opponents of the scheme and the scrap-metal merchants left empty-handed. Despite this, Beeching continued to express doubts about electrification throughout his time as chairman of British Railways. He was interested in short-term gains, and electrification comes with a high price tag for lineside equipment and new locomotives before eventually the savings in maintenance heavily outweigh the initial expenditure. Beeching even questioned the value of having high-powered locomotives like the Deltics on the East Coast Main Line, arguing that medium-powered diesels were the most efficient form of traction. This was short-sighted, since reduced power would have made it impossible to shorten timings between major cities, which had been shown to increase revenue; but it highlighted Beeching's doubts about the long-term value of the railway. In fact, as we have seen in Chapter 1, the success of the West Coast Main Line electrification set BR on the path to a brighter future, as would the introduction of the High Speed Train in the mid-1970s (see Chapter 7).

It's perhaps not surprising, therefore, that Beeching told Davies that he thought his initial axe had not been wielded forcefully enough. In fact, had he been allowed to, Beeching could have sowed even more havoc. He wrote a second report, *The Development of the Major Railway Trunk Routes*, published in 1965 after the new Labour government had already decided not to renew his contract. The report was a blueprint for a further series of cuts, this time not to the branch lines but focused on the major secondary routes which often duplicated existing main lines. The first report had, indeed, led to some savings, but nothing like enough to cut the deficit, and it had also resulted in a loss of traffic on the main lines. Beeching had argued that people who no longer had a station on a branch line would simply drive or take a bus to the nearest main-line station, whereas, in fact, once they got in their cars, most of them never got out again until they reached their ultimate destination. Closures were often justified on the basis of 'bustitution', with new bus routes being promised to replace trains, but this was inevitably a failure. Buses were far slower and less convenient than trains, not least because many ran between disused railway stations, which were often on the edge of villages or towns. People could not take prams or heavy luggage on buses, and they didn't have toilets, a factor for many older people. Most of these poorly used bus services were scrapped once their three-year subsidy came to an end, leaving large parts of the country with no public transport at all.

Beeching's second report envisaged a smaller but more efficient network of trunk routes with fast and frequent services. While this seemed a positive step, with recommendations of investment in key routes, it was underpinned by a further round of savage cuts. The report suggested focusing on just 3,000 of the existing 7,500 route miles between major centres of population and industry, and saving large amounts of money on the rest. The saving would be achieved either by closing lines or cutting maintenance, often by reducing the number of tracks – four-track lines, for example, would be reduced to two, and some two-track ones would be singled. While, at the time, Beeching and British Railways denied this was a plan to bring about a second major series of cuts, Beeching told Davies that he had wanted to stay on as chairman to implement the second plan, and he was very clear that too many lines had survived his first cull. He questioned why there were several routes between London and Birmingham when one would do, and regretted that his second report was never implemented: 'We have today 8,000 miles of trunk railway – and they carry around ten per cent of the nation's trunk freight, while 3,000 miles of roads carry the other ninety percent. Something is still wrong. We've got too many lines.'[21]

Harold Wilson's Labour government, which had come to power in October 1964, tried to stop the publication of this second report early in 1965 through fear of further outrage over rail closures. But, ironically, the Wilson administration on taking office had appeared even more assiduous in cutting back the rail network than its Conservative predecessor.

When Beeching's first report was published, Labour – then in opposition – savaged it, and appeared intent on stopping and even reversing the closure programme once in office. A resolution passed at a massive party and union rally at Central Hall, Westminster, in June 1963 attacked 'the folly of a policy which attempts to direct the future development of the railways solely on the basis of profit consideration'. Harold Wilson, at the time the leader of the opposition, picked up the cudgels and suggested that most of Beeching's cuts would not be made: 'We shall halt the main programme of rail closures allowing . . . individual closures to take place in one or two cases pending a national transport survey.'[22]

In fact, no such assessment emerged until well after most of the closures had been completed. Indeed, on closer inspection, it could be argued that Wilson's statement with its weasel words didn't really propose halting

the closures at all. On the day Beeching's report was published, Labour MP George Strauss, supposedly the
opposition transport spokesman, was far more effusive
about the report than several of Marples's backbenchers
who spoke out against it in the debate. Strauss congratu-
lated Beeching, calling the report 'lucid, comprehensive
and well-argued' in setting out 'how best the railways
could be reshaped to fit modern conditions and above all
what steps should be taken to make them remunerative'.[23]

Once in office, Labour implemented the closure programme with an enthusiasm that reflected Strauss's
statement. Tom Fraser, who was the minister of transport in Wilson's first government, was keen to push
forward the cuts rapidly but realized this would have to be
done surreptitiously as there were already signs of a public backlash. In March 1965, the Cabinet secretly endorsed
a deceitful strategy devised by Fraser in which he suggested that a small number of closure 'proposals should
be brought forward for rejection', allowing ministers to
claim that they had saved certain lines, while waving the
vast majority through.[24] As Austin and Faulkner report,
'with astonishing cynicism, the Cabinet minutes asserted
that "proposals of this kind, when submitted, should
provide the minister with an opportunity to demonstrate
the Government's readiness to reject closures which were
incompatible with regional transport plans"'.[25]

In the event, the Labour government clearly reneged on
its pre-election commitment to halt major closures and,
when challenged, deployed the specious argument that
ministers were unable to stop the process because of the

requirements of the 1962 Transport Act. This was untrue, because Fraser could have intervened at any point. A key principle of British government is that no new administration is bound by the decisions of its predecessors. Indeed, a private member's bill to that effect had been tabled by the indefatigable rail supporter Sir Alexander Spearman, the Conservative MP for Scarborough and Whitby; but the Cabinet, after discussing the idea, failed to back it. No wonder, then, that whereas only 940 route miles were closed in the two-year period to the end of 1963, in each of the following three years, when, from October 1964, Labour was in power, more than 1,000 miles were axed. No wonder that subsequent generations of railway managers were suspicious of government plans and promises.

Beeching's second report, which was published despite the Labour government's concerns and with far less fanfare than the first one, was in some respects even more damaging to the future of the railway. Although it was never fully implemented, it resulted in reduced capacity on many important lines by removing some tracks or closing diversionary routes, with promises of substantial investment for key surviving services that was either delayed or never materialized.

Beeching himself, however, was quickly put to the sword by the Wilson government. His very name had become toxic, and he was the symbol of an unpopular policy which Labour had continued to implement even while ensuring that his tenure was not renewed. He left at the end of his contract in May 1965 with the usual fudge as the government claimed it was voluntary whereas it was clear that Labour did not want to be associated with his name. He returned to ICI and later turned down what must be one of the most bizarre job offers ever for a former rail manager. After the untimely death of Brian Epstein, the legendary manager of the Beatles, in August 1967, a suggestion was made to John Lennon that Beeching should be brought in to sort out their financial affairs, which were in a parlous state. Lennon took the idea seriously and approached Beeching, who rather sensibly said 'no'.

Beeching could be excused for the fact that the timing of the publication of his first report was unfortunate. The Modernisation Plan and his *Reshaping of British Railways* had been produced in the wrong order. It would have been far more logical to first subject the railway to the kind of close scrutiny in Beeching's report and then select those elements where investment should be focused. Unfortunately, history does not work as neatly as politics, and happenstance all too often dictates the pace of change. In reality, neither the Modernisation Plan nor Beeching's closure programme could ever have achieved the aim of reversing the trend of growing deficits.

The Beeching episode may not have been an overt conspiracy, but it was the result of a strong coalition of interests working together. Marples's attitude to transport was well summed up by a remark he made in a parliamentary debate when he said, 'Traffic is going onto the roads because the people wish it to go on the roads. I am not forcing it.'[26] All his instincts and efforts were to promote motor transport rather than the railway, and the

Beeching–Marples axis succeeded in that respect. Even critics of Beeching such as Henshaw recognize that swathes of railway lines made no sense in a motorized age; but, in a detailed analysis of the cuts, he argues that at least 1,200 miles of the passenger lines closed by Beeching 'should never even have been *contemplated* for closure'.[27]

By the time of the 1966 general election, won decisively by Labour, it was clear that cuts would never achieve the goal of wiping out the railway's deficit. Yes, it had been reduced somewhat, but predictions suggested it would rise again as more and more people bought cars. The haphazard pattern of closures had inevitably led to all kinds of anomalies which remain to this day. Some major towns like Dudley and Mansfield in the Midlands were left without a railway station, while tiny halts dotted around the country were still being served by regular train services. The railway network had been battered by Beeching and British Railways was a much diminished organization. However, at the same time, it was beginning to establish a new identity, one that was more befitting the modern age. British Railways was the past – British Rail the future.

PART TWO
British Rail

5

Establishing an Identity

The story of Beeching and the way his first report was implemented is important in understanding the subsequent history of what would soon become British Rail. The persistent fear of another round of Beeching-style cuts coloured the organization's behaviour over the ensuing decades. There was a constant stream of inquiries and reports into the railway until the very end of BR's existence, some of which proposed levels of cuts that would have made even Beeching blanch.

Beeching is, of course, best remembered for axing lines, but during his four-year tenure heading BR, he lifted every stone in the organization. They couldn't be put back without dealing with what had been discovered underneath. While it is impossible to demonstrate unequivocally the precise point at which the fortunes of British Railways began to be turned around, the period of Beeching's chairmanship after the publication of his first report is the best candidate. Away from the scenes of devastation on the fringes of the network, where thousands of miles of lines were being closed and stations left to the mercy of the elements, there were many positive developments, several of which had been initiated by Beeching. The instant success of the West Coast Main Line electrification showed that, when the railway was treated as a business, it could earn a good return on the right sort of investment. That way of looking at BR's finances was not yet accepted in the mid-1960s, nor indeed was it feasible given the lack of financial information available at the time; but under Beeching there was, at least, a recognition of the need for a more commercial approach. The dilemma was: if parts of the railway were never going to pay their way, should they be retained and, if so, how should they be paid for? And to what extent could organizational change achieve a financial turnaround that would make more of the railway viable? Those questions would not be tackled until after Beeching's departure.

In the meantime, there was progress on several fronts. The new Euston station was utilitarian and characterless but it was making a statement about the railway's intent to be relevant in the late twentieth century and, indeed, further into the future. If it looked like an airport lounge, that was precisely the intent. Airports, after all, were modern, forward-looking and exciting, everything the railway had not been. Not only was it part of a conscious fightback against new rival modes of transport, but also it showed the worth of a key aspect of the British Railways Board's modernization strategy: the use of branding and the development of a clear design language for all aspects of the railway.

Beeching deserves much of the credit for this. A Design Panel had been set up by the Transport Commission to develop a unified look for the railway. The aim, according to David Lawrence, the author of the history of BR design, was 'to move the railway away from a fragmented version of a heroic and romantic, sentimental and picturesque Victorian plurality, away from the patchy application of regional colours, to a clean and coherent, sober and rational emblem of progress'.[1] It was an immense and laudable task which became enduringly successful and was to prove essential in changing the public perception of Britain's railway.

The Design Panel, which at first was only advisory and voluntary, tried to bring a modicum of order into the appearance of the eclectic mix of styles on locomotives, carriages, stations, and public spaces on railway property. Beeching ensured that the concept of corporate identity became ingrained, and consequently beefed up the Design Panel, incorporating it into the organization's remit when the British Railways Board was established, and appointing one of its members, George Williams, as Director of Industrial Design. With this new-found permanent status, the panel was able to hire professional design consultants, a role given to the pioneering Design Research Unit, which had been established soon after the Second World War as the first such design agency in the UK.

The only previous example of a major public transport organization adopting such a coherent image was London Transport which, ever since its inception in 1933, had employed a clear design language based on a number of key elements: the roundel, red buses, the Harry Beck map of the Underground and the Johnston typeface, all of which have survived to this day. Williams realized that British Railways needed to follow London Transport's example. He was a visionary, who sought to blend engineering and aesthetics, and wanted his fellow railwaymen to share his vision. Andrew Haig, a designer who wrote an assessment of the BR design innovations, said that 'Williams realized the urgency of needing to create a strong visual image in order to convince the public British Railways was a modern industry. He persisted with single-minded determination in his attempt to get the idea of a corporate image accepted, if only in principle.'[2] Williams, who died in 1965, before much of his work came to fruition, deserves the credit for creating a recognizable BR brand, the importance of which cannot be exaggerated. The railway needed to be reinvented, and while overall the Modernisation Plan was a failure, some of its key features convinced many people that the organization did have a future, even if the mainstay of its technology, the steam engine, had to go.

The transformation of BR's image was radical and swift. Out went the heraldry with the lions, wheels and badges, which seemed passé in the post-war world, and in their place there was to be a series of entirely new design features with four key elements: a symbol, a typeface, a style for station nameplates, and house colours. This was representative of a time when Britain was emerging from the long years of post-war austerity into a far more exciting period characterized by the modern clean lines of the furniture in Terence Conran's Habitat, Alec Issigonis's Mini, the compact car for the masses, and Mary Quant's miniskirt. According to the *Beauty of Transport* website: 'Beeching understood that turning around British Railways would require not only better financial management and business practices, but also a corporate identity that focused it on the future, instead of the past. Unlike previous chairmen, he was an unapologetic moderniser, no fan of the heraldic devices and steam railway colour schemes British Railways used for its trains.'[3] So while Beeching's name is synonymous with line closures and abandonment, the most lasting symbols of the railway, such as the logo, a raft of successful design features and even the name of the organization, owe much to his business acumen.

The most noteworthy aspect of the design overhaul was the 'corporate identity symbol' (the word 'logo' had not yet acquired common currency) of the famous 'double arrow'. Its simplicity is deceptive: try drawing it freehand from memory! But during a lengthy process it was selected over many other less notable suggestions. One had the letters 'BR' struck through with white stripes to give the appearance of the union flag; another resembled a noughts and crosses grid with an up arrow on the left and a down arrow on the right. But eventually it was Gerry Barney's brilliantly simple design that triumphed. Initially, it was not without its critics, with some likening it to a piece of barbed wire or a bolt of lightning, though that was not necessarily a criticism given the push for electrification. But BR persevered and quickly started using the logo across the network, a unifying factor which, crucially, cut across the regions. In fact, within a couple of years, research by BR revealed Barney's logo was as widely recognized as the Michelin Man, the ubiquitous comic-strip style mascot of the French tyre company. The success and durability of the double arrow logo are demonstrated by the fact that it survived rail privatization and is used today on Google maps to show the location of railway stations.

The new font was another success. Rail Alphabet, a sans serif typeface based on the Swiss Helvetica lettering, was created by Jock Kinneir and Margaret Calvert. The two designers were also responsible for the font used on the much clearer road signage that was being introduced around the same time, as well as the now-famous NHS lozenge logo. The design was quickly adopted on new, bigger signs at stations, which replaced the old BR 'totem' ones, a pleasant but somewhat fussy cylindrical design with sans serif lettering that had been introduced on the creation of BR in 1948 and had been used for all stations in different colours according to the region. The totem signs were relatively small, and the upper case lettering made them rather difficult to read quickly. Much thought had gone into ensuring Rail Alphabet's letters were sensitively crafted and precisely spaced, in both upper and lower case, in order to facilitate legibility even when the train was whizzing through a station (I, like many other people, still struggle to read them in these circumstances). The new font was also used throughout the BR network, including on the organization's road vehicles, hovercraft and ships, and notably on the new automatic departure boards where its great simplicity and readability were vital for people anxiously searching for the right platform for their train.

One of the most far-reaching changes, made at Beeching's behest, was the name switch from the old-fashioned sounding British Railways to British Rail. In fact, British Railways remained the official name and continued to be used in legal documents and for the name of the Board, but the shorter version was for public consumption and publicity. It was, again, a conscious move away from the past and from the industry's heritage as there was no room for sentimentality in the new BR.

The emphasis on design was well ahead of its time, as in the 1960s few organizations, private or public, had developed such a sophisticated understanding of corporate identity. The comprehensive design scheme was presented at a large exhibition at London's Design Centre in early 1965, the culmination of a decade's work by the Design Panel. Visitors received a leaflet promising 'everything seen and used frequently by the public, every station, every sign, every piece of printed matter will be given an instantly recognised family likeness'. All the design requirements were set out in the corporate identity manual which was given to staff across the organization. It would have a lasting influence, as the history of BR's design stresses: 'Many parts of the business adhered closely to the corporate identity for twenty years.'[4]

It is no exaggeration to say that 'BR's "rail blue"

corporate identity . . . was one of the most comprehensive ever adopted by any British transport company, and indeed probably any transport company'.[5] It was the all-encompassing nature of the design requirements that was so radical, as the Beauty of Transport website emphasizes:

> Everything that might possibly be touched by a British Rail employee or customer got the treatment, it seemed. From windows to wine glasses, serviettes to signs, trains to trucks, cutlery to carpets, the corporate identity ranged over all. Most modern British companies are content to buy in at least some standard sundries. Not British Rail. Everything was bespoke to some extent, and everything had to conform.[6]

The detailed design code even went as far as specifying the look of clock faces and antimacassars.

BR's entire corporate identity programme became a benchmark in industrial design across the world and preceded the now much more famous Swiss railway's unitary design, which did not emerge until 1980, more than a decade later. From having lagged behind the airlines in terms of branding, British Rail was now far ahead of them, and remarkably seemed more forward-looking and modern than its aviation rivals and even the space industry. British Railways' corporate identity manual actually came out several years before NASA, the American space agency, produced a similarly iconic branding handbook.

Indeed, BR's manual attracted so much interest from the public that it was published as a coffee-table book and became a design classic. Cleverly, the manual was produced for staff in a series of four ring binders which made it easy to update. It was so comprehensive that the documentation filled a whole room at British Railways' headquarters in Marylebone. Its specifications were rigorous bordering on authoritarian. It mandated 'the look and position of all wording, signs and symbols, on all posters, leaflets, documents, stationery, buildings, vehicles (road and rail), and ships'.[7] Indeed, the level of detailed consideration was such that, on the funnels of the Sealink ferries owned and operated by BR, the standard symbol was used on the starboard side, with a mirror image on the port side. This was in line with a maritime tradition which dictates that ships have a definite front and back and therefore the logo on the funnels should always have the top arrow facing towards the bow of the ship. Flags, too, had the logo in reverse on the back to ensure that the arrow at the top always pointed towards the flagpole. Such subtleties have long been lost, and rogue versions of the symbol can now be found across the country on road signs and maps.

The colour scheme was rather less successful. It was never fully introduced because of the difficulty of retrofitting the vast array of different locomotives and carriages in the British Rail fleet. The dull greens and maroons, as well as the famous plum and spilt milk livery of the old London & North Western had to go. There was a narrow palette of permitted colours: Rail Grey, which was very light; a dark Rail Blue; and Rail Red, which was very bright, but ended up being little used. The descriptions of these colours further demonstrates the care that went into the process. The blue, for example, 'belonged to a hue group called Monastral Blue, or Phthalocyanine [*sic*] Blue, a durable fade resistant blue green which looked powerful without being bright and carried dirt well'.[8] Every existing colour was assessed for its suitability: 'black was too dark, green too dull, red too much associated with the London Midland Region . . . yellow might be upbeat but it was hard to select a shade which would not show the dirt or look insipid'.[9] Eventually, blue was chosen for the locomotives, and a grey and blue livery for coaches. Suburban and provincial coaches were, however, painted in all-over blue for ease of cleaning. Later on, the pattern was changed somewhat, and the blue and grey livery became the norm, apart from on a few diesel multiple units.

Coach interiors were also brought into line. There was a new colour scheme: 'Second class for smokers was upholstered in yellow, grey and blue wool textiles, and that for non-smoking in blue and green. English cherry or Rio rosewood veneer lined some wall surfaces', while aluminium fittings were satin gold or silver'.[10] There were well-thought-through improvements such as bigger windows, improved lighting, more space for luggage and better toilet compartments, which were assembled from prefabricated plastic parts, though as yet nothing for people with disabilities, who had to travel – along with bicycles – in guards' vans without sanitary facilities, or, in many instances, heating.

The front ends of many trains were painted yellow at this time to comply with safety regulations rather than to meet the design brief, which rather detracted from the strictures of the corporate image. Although the yellow was out of keeping with the BR colour scheme, the blue had been deliberately chosen to blend in with other colours, as Lawrence, the author of a book on BR design explains: 'Choosing a combination of two colours had to be informed by the need for the contrast between them to be perceived in any lighting conditions, and for the colours to be so distinct as to complement each other.'[11] The detailed thinking behind the introduction of these standard colours was such that printed material used slightly different blue and red shades as they reproduced better on paper.

Many stations were given a makeover, too. As well as the easier-to-read new station signs, there were other changes, notably lots of paint in the new colours. But not all the changes were good news. As the demolition of Euston had shown, there was little respect for heritage and many pleasing but inconvenient buildings which were difficult to maintain were demolished. During this period of rapid change, British Rail was so focused on the need to modernize its image that there was a general presumption that old railway stations should be swept away. This was the period in BR's history when there was the least consideration of the railway's traditions and heritage. The railway was following a wider trend in society, where there was an almost venal approach to history, with town centres being torn down to make way for ugly office buildings and grey pedestrianized precincts, and ring roads being driven through hitherto peaceful suburbs. Therefore, it was in keeping with the zeitgeist that the railway paid little heed to the structures that had built up in almost a century and a half of history in its quest to modernize and present a forward-looking image. John Betjeman, in the introduction to his short book on London's railway stations written in 1972, was in despair. He suggested that it was likely to be only of historic interest because 'the architects of British Rail never cease to destroy their heritage of stone, brick, cast iron and wood, and replace it with windy wastes of concrete'.[12] Thankfully, Betjeman's prediction proved to be unduly pessimistic. The destruction of Euston and the subsequent successful campaign to save St Pancras from a similar fate changed the mood both within BR and in the wider public, and, as we shall see in Chapter 9, the organization developed a far more sensitive approach to its culture.

In the iconoclastic 1960s and 70s, prefabrication was the order of the day. Architects on the London Midland Region used a system called 'Mod-X' in which, 'around a steel frame, wood, glass and vitreous enamelled metal were assembled to form a regular grid of wall units'.[13] The result was as insubstantial as the description suggests, and few of those structures survive today. On the Southern, there was even more extensive use of a system called CLASP (which rather oddly stood for Consortium of Local Authorities Special Programme), which had been developed as a way of rapidly constructing public buildings such as schools and hospitals in order to speed up the massive post-war rebuilding programme. The claim was that with CLASP 'soot-grimed brick and brake-grained timber ... [would be] superseded by vitreous enamelled [again] steel, pre-cast concrete panels, plate glass and neo-prene [synthetic rubber]'.[14] The result, though, was just as ugly as the system's name suggests. Since CLASP was not designed specifically for railways and crucially required 'no design work before it appeared on site', the results were simply out of keeping with the railway vernacular. More than 100 stations were scheduled to be given the CLASP treatment but fortunately only thirty were ever completed.

All relation to heritage and, indeed, the railway was lost. These boxes could have been installed anywhere and their very anonymity was the intention. Only the station name and British Rail symbol indicated the building's function: the interiors were planned as simple prefab-ricated square spaces – ticket office, waiting room, toilets – using standard CLASP partitions of glass and plastic laminate linings, or plasterboard and tiling. Few remain today. Notionally, they had a sixty-year design life, but they proved unpopular and many had to be removed as they contained large amounts of asbestos, raising public safety concerns.

This cavalier approach to stations was rather out of keeping with the desire to create an up-to-date image that was pleasing and popular. While the aim of the programme was clearly efficiency and cheapness over aesthetics, those carrying it out thought it more important to dispense with the old even if the new was not as good. Lawrence puts it rather cruelly but accurately when referring to the 1960s: 'As funding receded towards the end of the decade, new buildings of lesser quality replaced existing stations, simply because the existing structures cost more to staff and maintain, and were redolent of a past age.'[15] That last point was the sin of all sins, as far as the brash new BR was concerned.

Across the network, similar changes were being made. As staff were removed from little-used stations, many buildings were shut and cosy waiting rooms that previously boasted a coal fire and a few elegant benches were boarded up and replaced with stark, transparent plastic shelters that offered only partial protection from the elements. Many abandoned stations were left to decay, though some in busier locations were turned into offices and a lucky few became private homes or holiday cottages.

There were instances of more substantial station rebuilds in the modernist style, most notably at Coventry, which was made to look like a mini-Euston: all glass and slippery mock-marble floors, beneath a huge concrete roof. The new station at Harlow at least had the saving grace of blending in with the architecture of the rapidly expanding New Town. There was the occasional success, such as Broxbourne, now a Grade II listed building, and Folkestone Central, which, with its see-through clock tower and its heavy concrete roof, was an attempt to create a distinctive style that moved away from the railway's origins, though it attracted a lot of complaints from townspeople at the time.

Simon Jenkins, in his book on Britain's 100 best railway stations, sums up this period of British Rail station modernization: 'Victorian architecture was unfashionable, especially where it fell into the category of industrial archaeology. The 1960s and 1970s were to be dire for historic architecture generally, and there was little opposition to what became a systematic eradication of the railway's heritage.'[16]

Inevitably, the modernization and redesign also required railway staff to undergo a makeover. A comprehensive range of uniforms was created for men and the growing number of women who were, at last, being employed in roles beyond the customary cleaning and catering jobs. There was a long tradition of uniforms in railways, not least because the workforce was often treated with military-style discipline in the early days of the industry. The new logo, of course, replaced the heraldic badges on caps, except for station masters, who retained the old style. Jacket lapels were reduced in size and the rather untidy porters' smocks were swapped for smarter waistcoats with matching trousers that had a single line of red piping to indicate their role. Uniforms for female 'hostesses' employed on rail–air link and hovercraft services were modelled on those worn by airline cabin crew, except, of course, they were in British Rail colours. Most remarkably, moulded synthetic uniforms with drainpipe trousers for the men and very short skirts for the women were used to promote British Rail internationally as a future-thinking organization.

Oddly, the tradition of locomotive naming didn't fit in with the new design programme, although existing names were allowed to remain. Once the last steam engine had been scrapped, however, nameplates disappeared until

1977, when BR's public relations team realized they were missing a trick. From then on, diesel and electric express locomotives were allowed to be given names again in recognition of the publicity value, and this honour was bestowed on the great and the good.

There were other changes initiated in this period, such as fares reform, and the beginnings of market pricing – in other words, charging more for peak trains and reductions for off peak. The government still controlled fares in the 1960s, but BR was allowed to introduce innovations, such as the first discounted advance tickets in 1963. Unlike today's version, which normally must be bought at least a day in advance, these inaugural advance purchase tickets could only be obtained an hour before travel. The aim, based on the concept of airline standby tickets, was to fill empty seats at the last moment. It was also the first attempt by British Rail to woo passengers away from other types of transport. This was, at last, an indication that BR recognized it had to look beyond its traditional captive customers and make its product more attractive in order to increase market share.

The backdrop of this innovation and modernization was the phasing out of steam, the most momentous technical change in railway history. This had been presaged in the 1955 Modernisation Plan with predictions that there might still be some steam locomotives in use in 1990. In fact, once the programme of replacement started, it was carried out remarkably quickly, and all had disappeared long before that projected date.

As we have seen, the hasty and haphazard introduction

of different types of diesel locomotives resulted in far too many models being trialled, but at least it led to the rapid replacement of many steam engines. Sensibly, the initial focus was on the mass production of diesel railcars, which were perfect for suburban and secondary routes, and by the end of 1958 there were nearly 2,500 of these vehicles in service. The drive to replace steam locomotives with diesels got off to a slower start but soon accelerated. The total of 16,100 steam locomotives still running on the tracks in 1958 was reduced to a quarter of that total by 1965 and three years later all had gone.

Because so much of the railway was now operated by electric or diesel multiple units, the reduction in the overall number of locomotives was remarkable and demonstrated the crucial improvements in efficiency that the new technologies made possible. In 1957, there had been 18,200 locomotives, nearly all steam engines. Just fifteen years later, there was a total of just 4,100 locomotives, all diesel, except for 318 electric engines. This rapid pace of change was thought by some to be too fast. Undoubtedly, there was some waste because of the undue haste, but it was not solely about the technology and the improvement in efficiency. BR was changing its image and wanted to achieve that as fast as possible. This explains why there was a deliberate policy of prioritizing the replacement of steam engines on passenger rather than freight traffic. By 1964, fewer than 15 per cent of passenger trains were headed by steam engines, whereas more than half of freight services were still hauled by them.

The scrapyards filled up rapidly and there was despair

among train enthusiasts, anxious to see their beloved favour-
ites one last time before they were sent on a one-way journey.
The most notorious yard, Woodham's in Barry in South
Wales, became a shrine for trainspotters ('gricers', as they
are known in the UK, or 'foamers' in the US) as hundreds
of steam engines were broken up there and it was the last
chance for people to see them.

The numerous railway magazines of the time could
barely keep pace with the cull, and their headlines reflected
the sombre mood of their readers. These magazines also
featured numerous photographs of a network suffering
from decades of neglect, with weed-strewn platforms,
buddleia growing on tracks, peeling paintwork and shabby
stations bereft of people and, indeed, hope. As mentioned previously, the last steam locomotive to be built,
Evening Star, rolled out of Swindon works in March 1960.
Five years later, its working life on the main line was over,
and it eventually ended up in the National Railway
Museum in York.

There was fierce competition between the regions to
see which could dispense with steam first, and it was the
Western Region which triumphed in March 1966. The last
ever BR steam train in normal service ran on 3 August
1968 from Euston to Preston. When it arrived in Preston,
men in funeral attire marched along the platform, bearing
a coffin on their shoulders adorned with slogans bemoan-
ing the end of steam. A week later, BR ran a 'goodbye to
steam' special excursion, which was hauled by four different locomotives. The service, from Liverpool Lime Street
to Settle via Manchester and Carlisle, passed over the

famous Ribblehead viaduct. BR showed its commercial acuity by charging a stunning fifteen guineas for the ride (equivalent to almost £300 in 2021 prices) and every seat was filled. Thousands more lined platforms on the route to watch the train pass through. In one of those quirky asides loved by pub quizzers, steam did in fact survive after 1968, as British Rail operated a passenger service on the Vale of Rheidol railway until the 1980s, which was hauled by little locomotives that became the only steam engines ever to sport the new Rail Blue colour along with the double arrow logo, but this was on a narrow-gauge railway and therefore was a weird anomaly.

Getting rid of steam in a hurry was seen by British Rail as a way to cement its new modern image. When steam was scrapped on the Continent, it was done at a considerably slower pace. For example, in France, where electrification was embraced with far more enthusiasm, the last steam locomotive was built in 1952 but not withdrawn until 1974; in West Germany, steam survived until 1977. While the switch to electric and, in particular, diesel power in Britain could be seen as a positive move, the speed with which it was achieved led to significant amounts of equipment being withdrawn before its shelf life had expired. The rush to modernize, however, overrode all other considerations.

The changeover from steam to diesel was a much more complex process than simply swapping one type of locomotive for another. Quite apart from their different fuel sources, they both had other very distinctive characteristics. Steam engines required two people to operate them, since the fireman played an essential role; whereas, technically, diesels could be operated by one person. Initially, the powerful railway unions insisted on retaining a second man – there were no female drivers until 1978 – because of various negotiated requirements, such as a limit on single-manned mileage and the need to control the steam heating apparatus on some diesel locomotives. Night-time driving always required a second person in the cab. Gradually, though, in the mid-1960s most of these restrictions were negotiated away, resulting in enormous savings for British Rail.

The move away from steam resulted in significant job losses: firemen, engine cleaners and fitters were all made redundant. But a new set of skills was required. Being at the controls of a diesel locomotive was undoubtedly an easier task than driving a steam engine, but it still required experience, route knowledge – which involves training on every line that the driver will operate on – and, crucially, some understanding of engineering. In the early days, many diesel locomotives failed and required 'rescuing' because their drivers lacked a basic understanding of how they worked and were reluctant to do the equivalent of 'opening up the bonnet' of a car, which might have enabled them, for instance, to isolate a defective part and continue safely. BR feared that a little knowledge might be a bad thing and lead to enginemen tinkering with delicate parts. But over time drivers were encouraged to gain a basic understanding of their new kit and the result was improved reliability.

A source of frustration and embarrassment for BR

was the poor state of track and signalling. Neither had kept pace with traction improvements, making it a challenge to reduce journey times. There were implications for the timetable, too, which had been designed with steam engines in mind. Steam locomotives required a lot of preparation time, which had to be built into the schedule to allow them to be filled with water and coal, steamed up and checked over. When diesels replaced them, theoretically there was an opportunity to use them far more intensively as they started up at the flick of a switch. However, it took time to adjust timetables, especially when the type of traction might change from day to day. Only when a particular service switched entirely to diesel could the timetable be speeded up. Because so many diesel types had been introduced, many of them unreliable, delays caused by 'teething problems' were commonplace, and in terms of frustration for passengers these were the equivalent of today's 'leaves on the line' announcements. The reason for this was that new diesels were effectively being trialled in service rather than on the test track.

As a result of its traditional independent spirit and the lack of standardization across BR, the Western Region had been allowed to develop a range of diesel-hydraulic locomotives which proved to be an endless source of trouble. Their engines ran at far more revolutions per minute than the diesel-electrics used throughout the rest of the network and consequently were more unreliable and expensive to operate. Many of the Western's locomotives started failing within three or four years of introduction and required far more costly maintenance than other diesels. Although the Western was eventually forced to fall into line with the other regions, this was an illustration of the power of the old regional barons which needed to be challenged in order to bring about BR's modernization (see Chapter 10).

It was not just the Western's locomotives that were unreliable, as across the network there were other teething problems which attracted public attention and consequent negative press coverage. According to railway author Geoffrey Freeman Allen:

> For the first two or three years of the diesel traction takeover . . . the public began to feel it had been sold a false prospectus; dieselisation seemed to mean nothing more than changing one kind of traction, which had gone out of fashion, for another which happened to be in vogue, purely to satisfy some managerial whim.[17]

The perception therefore was that neither the passenger nor the railway was benefitting, though, in truth, the savings were considerable and services did, after a while, improve immeasurably.

Other savings were made through the introduction of innovative technology, including new tamping machines that could level and consolidate the ballast under the tracks, which previously had been done by platemen wielding picks and shovels. Operated by a single person, the machine could cover a quarter of a mile of track in a six-hour night shift, work that would have taken a five-man gang a fortnight. Manually operated signal boxes, too, were being replaced by new electrically powered centres, each of which could replace many older boxes.

While in 1962, according to Simon Bradley in his history of Britain's railway, there were still 'well-staffed country stations served by steam-hauled carriages of pre-war design, with goods yards equipped to handle wagons full of anything from coal to cattle, by 1968 there were no such stations or trains left . . . an entire working world had disappeared'.[18] So, on the one hand, it was out with the old with the loss of much of the old British Railways, and, on the other, it was a modern British Rail with its confident logo and elegant typography creating a completely renewed organization that offered so much more for its passengers: new stations, cleaner trains, more frequent and faster services. In its importance as a turning point in British history, this transformation was likened by Bradley to 'the dissolution of the monasteries, though without the martyrdom'.[19]

Overall, the new corporate image had given BR a much-needed bright and forward-looking identity that was to stand it in good stead for many years. In some respects, this was well deserved, as radical changes, such as abandoning steam, had been made; but there were still numerous throwbacks to when the railway was a ubiquitous form of transport carrying both passengers and goods and, in many respects, a monopoly.

That world was fast disappearing, but there were many leftovers from that era. There were still, for example, parcel offices and coal depots. At many of the surviving stations, horses still hauled carts in the yard and tickets were little changed from those devised by the pioneering

Thomas Edmondson in the mid-nineteenth century, while services, even expresses, were slowed by the poor state of the track, an enduring legacy of the war.

British Rail still had a long way to go to become the modern, purposeful organization it aspired to be. Nevertheless, the BR of 1965 was a very different organization in almost every respect from that of 1955. The Modernisation Plan never achieved its goal of financial self-sufficiency but it had, with the help of Beeching's radicalism, enabled a transformation to take place. The biggest immediate problem was money, as even a relatively high-spending Labour government was reluctant to lavish too much on keeping the railway going. It needed a more coherent and sustainable approach to funding in the face of growing public concern about a never-ending cycle of cuts. And the value of services needed a more sophisticated measure than the fare box. After allowing so many closures to go ahead, Harold Wilson was anxious to sort out the railway and he made one of his boldest ever appointments, putting Barbara Castle in charge of the Ministry of Transport, the first ever woman to hold that post. More change was afoot.

6

War on Rail

If Marples is an obvious villain in this story, then Barbara
Castle, his successor but one as minister of transport, can
take her place high among the roster of heroes. She was
definitely a railway 'lass', in contrast to the 'roads men'
who had preceded her. She hadn't sought the job, but
once in post she set about shifting transport policy in
favour of the railway.

Castle had enormously enjoyed being the first ever
head of the Ministry of Overseas Development, a department created by the new Prime Minister, Harold Wilson,
in October 1964. She was reluctant to move to the frac-
tious Ministry of Transport, but Wilson gave her no
option. He then reneged on his promise to allow her to
sack the existing Permanent Secretary, Sir Thomas Padmore, who had worked under her predecessor and was
opposed to many of the changes she wanted to make.
She was the first woman transport minister, a role that up
till then had been seen as a male preserve for boys to play
with their toys. The fact that this was a significant break
through the glass ceiling was well illustrated on her first

day, when she discovered there was no women's toilet on the same floor as her office, necessitating the rapid conversion of one for her use. Not surprisingly, the ministry as a whole and the wider transport industry were male-dominated. Policy, meanwhile, was skewed towards roads, which Castle, as a non-driver, was determined to change.

Wilson had appointed her knowing that she was a formidable politician who would seek to shift policy in a very different direction from both Marples and Tom Fraser, her immediate, lacklustre predecessor, who had never shown any interest in the role and had merely gone along with traditional road-oriented transport policies. He had allowed civil servants to dictate the agenda and continue the programme of rail cuts unhindered by ministerial intervention. Wilson, though, realized that with the rail unions on his back over his pre-election commitment to rein back on the closures, a change in tack with the appointment of a heavy hitter like Castle was essential. As Charles Loft put it in his book on the aftermath of Beeching, 'Wilson's overriding transport policy objective was to make sure transport policy was not a problem and it was Castle's job to deliver that objective.'[1] It wasn't an easy task. Put simply, Wilson wanted her to deliver the manifesto commitment to create an integrated transport network and develop a distinct Labour transport policy, a task Fraser had failed to achieve.

Castle arrived at the ministry just before Christmas 1965. She was a remarkably quick learner and soon got to grips with her brief, as she noted in her diaries: 'It was no use trying to turn back the clock. I refused to be a King

Canute trying to force people onto railways which could not take them where they wanted to go.' But she knew what needed to be done to bring stability. 'In the first place, we had to decide what size railway system we wanted in the new situation, how to subsidize it and how to get more traffic from road to rail.'[2] To encourage freight to switch to rail, she supported the strategy initiated by Beeching of moving towards container traffic, which she realized was far more efficient than carrying small consignments in wagons.

Castle faced an uphill task not least because of the continued strength of the roads lobby, which sought to portray public transport as the enemy of the motorist in its attempts to influence popular opinion in its favour. The depth of the antagonism to the railway can be gauged by the intervention of the Automobile Association. In the spring of 1967, the inaugural edition of *Drive*, a magazine the AA sent out to its 3.75 million members every quarter, the director-general, Alexander Durie, claimed motoring was the life blood of the nation's economy 'and perhaps the most significant explanation for the great advance in living standards in the last decade'. That was why, he said, 'the AA is speaking out strongly against any attempt from any quarter to thrust *inferior, inconvenient and inflexible mass transport* on a society which is so determined to use the *superior, flexible, transport of the motor car*' (my emphasis).[3] In the same magazine, a year later, Durie reprised his argument, warning readers of the 'sinister threat to prohibit the driver using his car in the centres of towns and cities', which represented 'dangerous thinking' that would force people to travel by public transport, 'an outmoded system they have so plainly rejected'.[4]

Castle, like Marples, was an innovator, as can be seen in her efforts to improve road safety. In the mid-1960s, around 8,000 people a year were killed in traffic accidents, nearly five times the figure in 2019, despite the fact the number of cars on the road was a third of today's levels. The breathalyser, a 70 mph speed limit, tachographs on trucks and compulsory seat belts were all introduced on her initiative, which stimulated much media outrage with accusations of hypocrisy because she had never possessed a driving licence. She realized that attracting more people to the railway was a matter of both carrots and sticks, and she tried to weight things more in favour of rail by improving road haulage safety standards, such as limiting drivers' hours, and by having road hauliers soak up more of the expense they imposed on the roads through higher taxation. There was, though, something of a lost opportunity in that she did not attempt to halt the existing programme of rail closures, which might have been politically rewarding and prevented some of the most damaging cuts, because she was convinced that cutting uneconomic lines would help railway finances. Instead, she sought, as she wrote in her autobiography, not 'to allow the motor car to destroy the railway system and other forms of public transport on which people without a car depended for their mobility'. Her task was not made easier by her civil servants, who, she felt, were 'temperamentally inclined to accept the Beeching cuts', nor by the fact that British Rail's annual deficit had grown to £159 million.[5]

Castle asked Stanley Raymond, Beeching's replacement as chairman of British Railways, who was an old-time railwayman and had worked his way up from a childhood in a Barnardo's orphanage to the top job in BR, to assess the optimum size of the rail network. Beeching's second report would have reduced the network to 8,000 miles, which she deemed unacceptable, not least because such a radical closure programme was, by this time, out of kilter with public opinion. While the paring back of the network under Beeching had not caused a major outcry, there were already signs that further extensive cuts would have led to widespread protest. Although Castle didn't trust Raymond to modernize BR, on this occasion she did concur with him that around 11,000 miles would be a viable network.

Having come to an agreement with Raymond, she had to win over the unions. She succeeded by stressing that this was a much better outcome than if the second Beeching report had been implemented. She also promised that anyone made redundant would be well treated, a crucial red line for the unions. Despite some public protests from the unions, behind the scenes they were willing to go along with her plan. Although reluctant to close railway lines, Castle accepted sixty new proposals to axe short branch lines, accounting for around 600 miles, and did not stand in the way of most of the closures that were already going through. She did step in to prevent a few closures, such as the branch lines to Looe and St Ives in Cornwall and the Exeter to Exmouth route, which today is a particularly busy commuter and leisure railway known as the Avocet line. York to Harrogate, Manchester to Buxton in the Peak District and Oxenholme to Windermere in the Lake District were also spared. Given that all these thrive today, it does suggest that several of the branches discarded so readily by Beeching might well have been worth preserving. Indeed, some 600 miles of line have been added to the network since the Beeching closures, and there have been 400 reopened or new stations.

The last significant closure – which occurred under the Labour administration – was the Woodhead route between Sheffield and Manchester. It was not only a well-used freight route providing a crucial east–west link, its importance was such that it had even been electrified in 1955. Unfortunately, this was before the 25 kV alternating-current system became standard on BR, and it had been fitted with a 1,500 V direct-current system that meant its trains could not be used elsewhere on the network, a fact that contributed to its closure. The line was shut to passenger traffic in January 1970, although Beeching had recommended that another trans-Pennine route, the Hope Valley line, be closed instead. However, because of a perceived social need, the latter was retained and took all the Manchester–Sheffield passenger traffic. While freight continued to use the three-mile-long Woodhead tunnel, a downturn in coal carryings led to the complete closure of the line in July 1981. It was one of the biggest mistakes of the Beeching era, and Labour should have reversed the decision, as it is much regretted today given the road and rail congestion on all the east–west transport routes in the Midlands and North.

The quid pro quo of these continued closures was that Castle created a system to regularize the subsidy required by loss-making lines, which was set out in her 1968 Transport Act. At 281 pages this all-encompassing bill was, at the time, the longest piece of legislation ever passed by Parliament and it had significant long-term impact on railway economics. The Act's immediate effect was to wipe out the historic British Railways capital debt, which had been a burden on the organization's finances since nationalization. To provide stability for BR, there was to be a complete separation between the 'commercial' and 'social' railways. A group of independent experts would determine which lines were loss-making and how much subsidy would be needed to maintain individual routes. The onus was on British Rail to show that loss-making lines were worth keeping open for wider social or economic reasons. The experts, though, had their work cut out, as BR did not have the data to demonstrate conclusively the revenue generated by a particular line and the costs that should be allocated to it. Broad figures of average costs were inappropriate because, for example, a branch line might use older rolling stock and tracks recycled from the main line, and require less intensive maintenance than a busy main line. British Rail had never previously attempted to break down the figures into such granular detail. Nevertheless, £61 million was paid out in the first full year the system operated, which meant every grant-aided line remained open.

A lasting legacy of the 1968 Act was the creation of Passenger Transport Executives in city regions such as Merseyside, Greater Manchester, Tyne & Wear and the West Midlands, centred around the major conurbations in each area. These PTEs were in line with the Labour party's policy of 'integrated transport', as they ran local buses as well as suburban train services. This enabled them to coordinate routes so that, for example, a bus could deliver passengers to a railhead in time to connect with a particular train service. In what was a rare example in Britain of genuine devolution, the Executives could subsidize loss-making bus and rail services under their control and invest in new ones, such as the Tyne & Wear Metro and a new two-mile circular rail tunnel in Liverpool. They didn't get everything they wanted, however, as investment required central government support. In Manchester, for example, a plan to build a city centre underground line, which would have made Barbara Castle's cross-town journey when travelling between Parliament and her Blackburn constituency considerably easier, was abandoned on cost grounds.

Castle was unwillingly moved to another ministry in early 1968 while her bill was still going through Parliament, and she was replaced by Richard Marsh, who would later become BR chairman. Castle's departure might explain why Manchester's underground railway didn't get off the drawing board and, indeed, why eventually the most extensive tram system in the UK has now been created as a cheaper alternative. Nevertheless, the ability of the PTEs to work with British Rail to integrate local train and bus networks was a great success. Suburban rail networks thrived in the PTE regions, in sharp contrast to other major conurbations such as Bristol and Nottingham, which lost all their local services as there was no mechanism to support, let alone expand, them.

The 1968 Transport Act also saw the creation of the National Freight Corporation, which took over much of BR's loss-making small-consignment traffic and transferred it to the roads which were undoubtedly better equipped to handle that type of business. Controversially, the National Freight Corporation was given a majority shareholding in Freightliner, BR's recently created container business, which was very much seen as the best way of ensuring that at least some freight would still be carried by rail.

An unexpected consequence of the 1968 Act, which was to have a beneficial effect on the quality and frequency of services offered by British Rail on many lines, was that it encouraged the paring back of capacity deemed surplus by reducing double-tracked sections of line to a single one. This method of saving on maintenance was widely used in many parts of the network over the next couple of decades, but it had the disadvantage of constraining the ability to expand the railway once passenger numbers started soaring in the 1990s. Chris Austin, who later became BR's parliamentary affairs manager, explained how, when he worked for the Southern Region, he was responsible for 'singling' the non-electrified route from Ashford in Kent to Hastings on the Sussex coast:

The line was in a terrible state of neglect and there was an estimated £1.5 million worth of trackwork and renewals to be done. That would never have been agreed by the Board. So basically, we kept the good bits and got rid of the rest. It saved all that money and, indeed, the line which may otherwise have been closed.[6]

The Ashford–Hastings project also involved replacing a dozen manually operated level crossings with automatic barriers, a job that involved considerable expenditure – Austin reckons £100,000 per crossing – but which saved on employing a small army of relief signalmen who had been well paid for their shift work. This, too, was a common feature of BR's desire to cut costs, combining a reduction in service quality with reducing staffing levels through the use of technology.

The big irony is that, after all the fuss over closures, ultimately they had little impact on the overall economics of the organization. The fact that an operating surplus of nearly £50 million was achieved in 1969 resulted from a series of factors in which the mass closures played only a small part. The biggest savings were made through a remarkable reduction in the number of staff, down from 476,000 employees in 1962 to just 250,000 by 1970. BR closed half of its thirty-two major workshops in that period and, as we have seen, steam disappeared from the network. These two factors were much more instrumental in bringing about what proved to be a temporary move into the black by British Rail than the branch-line closure process.

After 1968, the emphasis was on keeping subsidy to a minimum, rather than further closures. Consequently, as mentioned above, BR received its £61 million subsidy in 1969 in order to recoup losses on some 300 lines. The payments covered not just the sort of basket cases that would have been slated for closure, but also many commuter lines which, although heavily used, were expensive to operate because demand was concentrated in the peaks. Some main lines, too, received grants, an illustration of the fact that huge swathes of the railway were uneconomic. Yet the social benefits of rail, such as providing a vital transport link for areas badly served by the road network or helping to cut traffic congestion, were invariably still overlooked in the discussions on the viability of a particular line. There was still no recognition of the fact that the railway delivered so many other benefits beyond the income from the fare box, and still no method of assessing the value to society at large of a particular train service. Consequently, battles with the Treasury were being fought on an almost daily basis. Roy Jenkins, the Chancellor of the Exchequer at the time, had, with the usual Treasury instincts, unsuccessfully tried to block these grants. However, there remained a principal flaw in the system, which was that the money was only available for one three-year period, after which new applications had to be made, putting constant pressure on BR to consider potential closures. There was also an ongoing risk of political interference, which explains why the Mid-Wales line, which ran through six marginal constituencies, escaped closure, while the Varsity line from Oxford to

Cambridge was axed even though it had not originally been on Beeching's list and would have served the burgeoning New Town of Milton Keynes.

Ominously, at the start of the 1970s British Rail was back in the red with a growing operating deficit. Ted Heath's Tory government, which had surprisingly won the 1970 general election, initially sought to pursue a radical programme of continued closures, as concern grew over mounting losses. Before the election, Heath had been keen to ensure the railway's deficit was reduced as part of wider programme to cut back on what the Tories perceived as 'lame duck' industries. Indeed, the thinking was that the very concept of maintaining the rural railway network was anomalous since most locals, especially those voting Tory, would long ago have forsaken the trains for cars.

The new Tory government elected in 1970 therefore set up a working party to look at a selection of potential future scenarios for the railway, the most extreme being closing them entirely, though 'this was probably for comparative purposes rather than a serious suggestion', according to Charles Loft in his book on Beeching's cuts.[7] More realistically, a list of 110 lines that apparently failed to cover even their short-term operating costs was presented to ministers in the new Department of the Environment, which now included transport. The working party's view was that twenty closures per year were needed to prevent the deficit growing, but even this limited programme ultimately proved impossible to deliver.

This was a strange period in the history of BR. The organization was working with officials at the transport department to close more lines even though it was obvious public opinion was against further cuts to the network. The chairman of the committee to save the Broad Street line, which ran across north London covering many suburbs not served by the Underground, captured the mood in a letter to *The Times*: 'Beeching caught the country unprepared but there is now scarcely one threatened line that is not forearmed with a defence committee,' he wrote.[8] Many MPs, including some prominent Tories, were also prepared to go to the barricades to defend their local services. Opponents were adopting more sophisticated tactics: QCs briefed by campaigners would suddenly turn up at hearings into closures, and academics and transport professionals were often called as expert witnesses.

John Peyton, Heath's transport minister, was more sympathetic to the railway than Marples and much less willing to embark on a Beeching Mark 2. When he began to consult on the list of failing lines, he came under pressure from both the Welsh and Scottish Secretaries who warned against any more cuts in their respective countries, arguing that Beeching's cuts had gone far enough. In Scotland, for example, the proposal to close the Far North line running through the sparsely populated Highlands was seen as politically very damaging, particularly as a swathe of rural lines in the north-east of Scotland had already been closed. Similarly, in Wales, many small towns had lost their rail connections and further cuts would have wiped large parts of the country off the rail map. It

would hardly have been good politics to focus all the closures on England and therefore Peyton was stymied,
although that did not stop continued efforts within his
department to make further cuts to the rail network.

Richard Marsh, whose tenure at the Ministry of Transport had been brief, left Parliament to become chairman
of the British Railways Board in the summer of 1971, and
realized quickly that it was not worth pursuing the search
for the notional profitable network. Having asked his
officials to provide information on the financial situation
of railways across the world, he found that 'as far as we
could see, there was only one passenger railway system, as
opposed to long-haul freight, which was even breaking
even, and that was the Swiss railways', though, as he then
added, 'the following year they joined the club and went
into the red'.[9] Indeed, his team found that, other than
Switzerland, the railway systems of the world, from Japan
and Germany to the United States, had built up substantial amounts of debt. Marsh told Peyton that it was
inconceivable that all railway managers were incompetent
across the world and therefore concluded:

> There was clearly something very special and fundamen-
> tal about passenger railways. I had long conversations
> with John Peyton and told him I wanted to keep his pol-
> itical colleagues off my back to give me an opportunity to
> see if I could find out what the root cause of the prob-
> lem was, whether it was possible to run a railway at a
> profit or even break even.[10]

Peyton, who had shown his openness to different ideas

GWR · LMS ▪ LNER · SR

The establishment of British Railways in 1948 brought together the four companies that had run the trains in the interwar period, each of which was fiercely proud of their traditions and trains. They ran a very wide variety of services, including many branch lines, such as this one (*below*) in Wales.

THE WORLD FAMOUS FORTH BRIDGE

SCOTLAND FOR YOUR HOLIDAYS

Services and fares from BRITISH RAILWAYS stations, offices and agencies

British Railways produced a series of memorable advertisements covering every region of the country. This one shows a record-breaking Pacific Class locomotive crossing the Forth Bridge.

At the time of its creation, British Railways was almost entirely operated by steam engines, but in 1960 introduced the Blue Pullman, a luxury diesel service and the first of a new generation of modern trains that proved to be hugely popular.

British Railways organized its own package holidays to various UK destinations and also promoted them with colourful brochures.

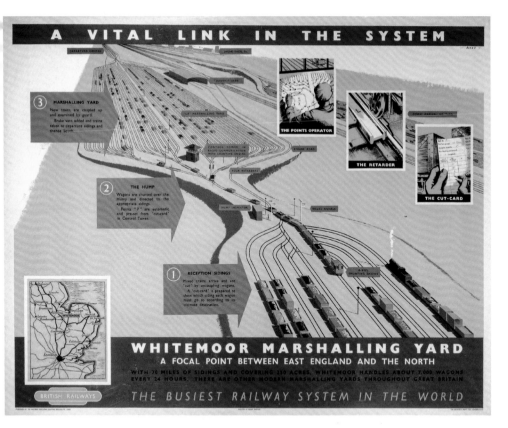

The 1955 Modernisation Plan brought significant investment to British Railways, some of which, such as this vast marshalling yard in Cumbria, was largely wasted as it was never fully used and soon closed.

Other initiatives born of the Plan, like the electrification of the West Coast Main Line, were far more successful.

Working practices, such as those shown on this electrification project in the 1960s, paid little heed to modern standards of health and safety.

Until the early 1960s, British Railways ran special trains for the thousands of Londoners who spent the summer as hop pickers in the Kent countryside.

Richard Beeching, the chairman of British Railways, at the press launch of his infamous report, *The Reshaping of British Railways*, which recommended drastic cuts to the rail network and the closure of thousands of stations.

Once the decision had been made to introduce diesel and electric traction, the old locomotives were phased out very quickly, with the last steam-operated service, seen here at Carlisle, attracting huge crowds on 3 August 1968, a mere eight years after the last one, *Evening Star*, went into service.

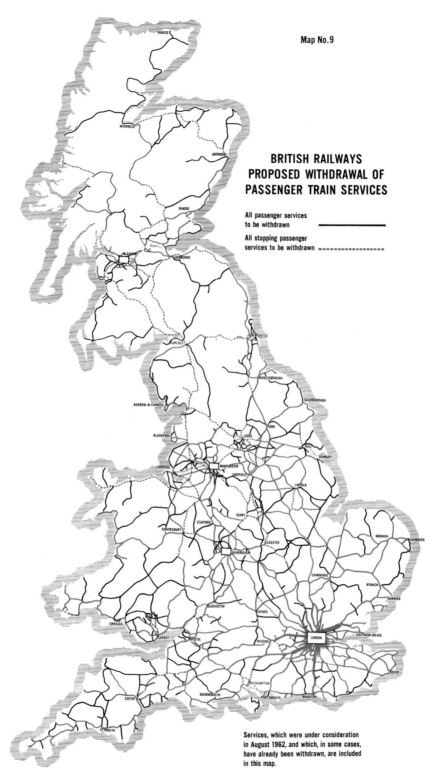

Map No.9

BRITISH RAILWAYS
PROPOSED WITHDRAWAL OF
PASSENGER TRAIN SERVICES

All passenger services
to be withdrawn ———————

All stopping passenger
services to be withdrawn ====================

Services, which were under consideration
in August 1962, and which, in some cases,
have already been withdrawn, are included
in this map.

This contemporary map of Beeching's cuts gives a clear idea of just how much of the network would be lost and of the parts of the country, like Wales, Cornwall, Cumbria or the Highlands, that would have been almost abandoned by the railways.

In 1965, British Rail, as it then became known, revealed its now iconic new logo. A thick, ring-bound corporate identity manual was produced, specifying how the branding should be applied to every aspect of the company, from signage and the colour of trains to the design of food packaging, and from uniforms to timetables. It was to become a bestseller and was reprinted in 2016. It represented a landmark piece of corporate branding that has proved enduring and influential.

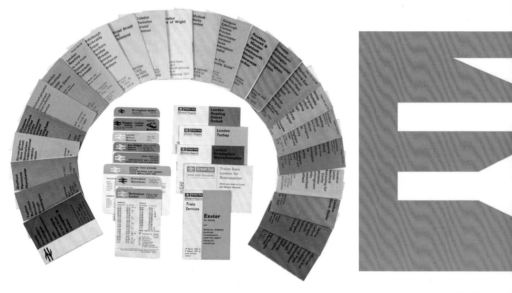

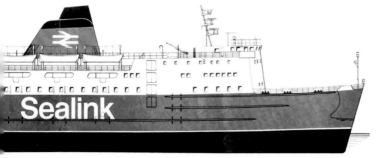

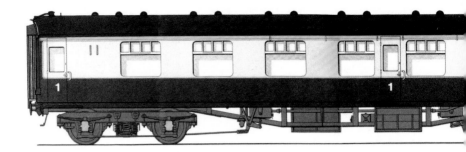

Train Driver

The material of the Train Driver's uniform is a worsted serge in blue-grey. Cap badge and buttons are in gold but otherwise this uniform is without lapel symbols or cuff rings. A blue sleeved vest with zip fastener down the front and a dual purpose overcoat in navy blue are also issued. The train crew Secondman has an identical uniform but in worsted/woollen serge and with silver cap badge and buttons.

≷ Property Board

Arch premises

To Let

First line where 3 lines
Second line where 3 lines
Last line where 3 lines

01- 585 6052

**A quarter bottle
of wine
will make your meal**

	Quarter bottles	
BORDEAUX RED	Medoc	4/-
BORDEAUX WHITE	Graves	4/-
BURGUNDY RED	Macon	4/-
HOCK	Liebfraumilch	4/-
CHAMPAGNE	George Goulet NV	10 -

You will find our full range in ⅓ bottles, ½ bottles and bottles in the wine list which also carries a varied selection of Aperitifs, Spirits, Beers and Soft drinks.

Buffet Pack

KEEP
BRITAIN
TIDY

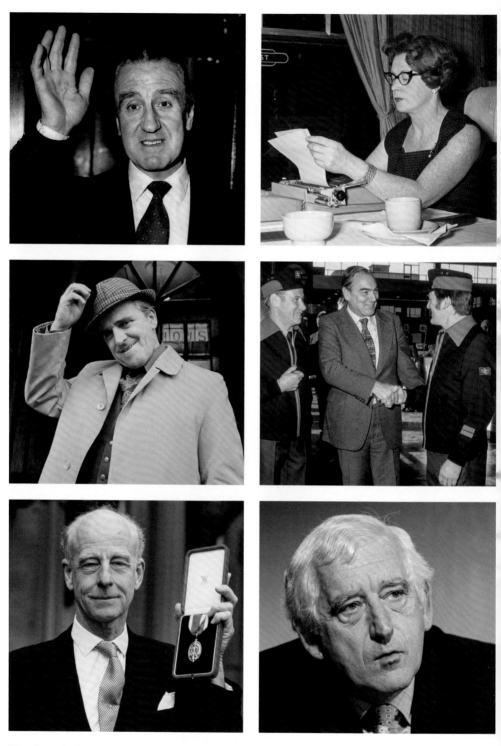

Key players in the story of British Rail included (*from top to bottom and left to right*) Ernest Marples, minister of transport (1957–1964); Barbara Castle, the first female transport minister (1965–1968); Sid Weighell, general secretary of the National Union of Railwaymen (1975–1983); Peter Parker, chairman of British Railways (1976–1983); Sir Robert Reid, the first chairman of that name in British Railways (1983–1990); and Chris Green (who headed successively Scotrail, Network SouthEast and InterCity between 1984 and 1994).

by employing a former Labour minister to run BR efficiently, gave up on pursuing closures. According to
Charles Loft, 'by early 1972 ministers had effectively
placed a political moratorium on closures'.[11] But many of
Peyton's officials were not on message. Some senior civil
servants in the department, together with the British Railways Board, continued to work on a study to find the
optimum size network for commercial viability. It was,
yet again, the search for the Holy Grail of a profitable
railway, which clearly Beeching had not found – although
he would claim he was not allowed to continue the search.

The proposals in the 61-page consultative document,
termed a Blue Paper, were devastating. Overall, mileage
would be reduced from 11,600 by almost half to 6,700
and large areas of the country, including west of Plymouth and north of Perth, would be left without any
railway lines. In Wales, only the main lines to Holyhead in
the north and Fishguard in the south for ferry connections to Ireland would survive. Large regional centres
such as Middlesbrough, Canterbury, Stratford-upon-
Avon, Blackburn and Salisbury would be removed from
the rail network.

Marsh later recalled how he had helped to kill the proposals with 'a slightly underhand political trick'. He had
asked for an overlay of the Blue Paper's railway map on
transparent paper with the Conservative and Labour seats
depicted in their respective party colours, which showed
unequivocally how all the lines earmarked for closure
were in rural areas with Tory seats. When Peyton saw this,
he told Marsh: 'Well I don't know why you didn't show

me that at the beginning, and why we wasted all that time this morning.'[12] Nevertheless, the report, which had been entirely drawn up by officials with no ministerial involvement, was still being worked on when the draft was leaked to the *Sunday Times*. There was a huge outcry and an inquiry into the leak, which for a time threatened to result in the arrest of Harold Evans, the paper's editor. Peyton claimed the proposals were not policy, but merely the result of some preliminary brainstorming. He was forced to ditch the report and bring down the curtain on the Heath government's attempts to push through a closure agenda.

Even then, the lesson had still not been learnt. There were continued attempts to close large swathes of the railway throughout British Rail's tenure despite the obvious political difficulties in carrying out such a programme. Consequently, as soon as there was a change of government back to Labour with Heath's defeat in February 1974, the whole process was kickstarted yet again.

Labour was supposed to be more supportive of the railway than the Conservatives, but there was a faction within the new government that was hostile towards the industry. It was led by Tony Crosland, who took over at the Department of the Environment when Wilson regained power in March 1974. Crosland's view of the railway was influenced by train journeys in first class to his Grimsby constituency, on which he discovered that his fellow passengers were as middle class as him, and he felt this relatively affluent group were not only benefitting from subsidies but also quite capable of paying higher fares. His argument was that since most users of the railway were business people and London commuters, support for rail services was a regressive tax paid by people less affluent than rail passengers. Chris Austin and Richard Faulkner, the authors of *Holding the Line*, which examines the hostile relationship between government and the railway, suggest that this view was widespread and deeply damaging to the railway: 'While this classic Whitehall view of the railway was clearly wrong, it has remained in the consciousness of opinion formers ever since and is still trotted out when rail fares are discussed.'[13] Yet, as the authors point out, this supposed bias towards well-heeled rail travellers was never true of the railway as a whole, and it was particularly not relevant to the local and regional lines which were the subject of potential closures and served poorer communities, where many people had little access to other forms of transport. And Crosland's fellow first-class travellers were hardly a random sample on which to base railway policy.

Nevertheless, the upshot was that Crosland embarked on yet another go at closing lines to make savings at BR. He produced a consultation document, known as the 'orange paper' because of the colour of its cover, which reiterated his notion that rail passengers were a privileged bunch who were not in need of support from the state because 'higher subsidies could be paid only at the expense of other vital programmes and would not be socially justified'.[14] The orange paper argued that the railway should concentrate on what it did best – bulk freight haulage, fast intercity services and densely used commuter ones.

But astonishingly the last were not to have any government support and commuters would be given five years to adjust to sharp fare increases that would allow subsidies to be wiped out. This was supposedly long enough for them 'to make any adjustments in their way of life with the minimum of inconvenience'.[15] In other words, these rich bastards should fend for themselves, a quite extraordinary lack of recognition for the part played by railways in reducing congestion and enabling office work to be concentrated in town centres, producing what economists call 'agglomeration benefits'. Bustitution reared its ugly head again, even though Crosland was aware that it hadn't worked previously after the Beeching cuts because the service was invariably simply inferior to that offered by trains. Crosland vowed it would be different this time, without explaining how, apart from promises of extra funding for buses.

The paper provoked a strong reaction from both British Rail and the public at large. Sid Weighell, the general secretary of the National Union of Railwaymen, was aghast, arguing: 'If it had been produced by one of the road lobby pressure groups, I would have recognised the prejudice and accepted it as such, but this document was supposed to represent the balanced view of the Government.'[16] The unions, along with various community groups and railway supporters, launched a well-funded 'No Rail Cuts' campaign which held large mass meetings and clearly worried Labour MPs minded to back closures.

While some of his junior managers had clearly

connived in the production of the report by providing information, an exasperated Marsh stood firm. He remained convinced that the railway would never earn a commercial return on its capital investment. His view was that closing more branch lines would reduce income and weaken the trunk lines served by branches. Consequently, BR issued a robust and highly critical response to the paper: 'The Board finds little evidence of a systematic approach to the complex problems involved.'[17] In fact, the whole tone of the orange paper was out of place with Labour thinking, as was pointed out by the party's official response to the consultation process: 'Labour Party policy is quite contrary to the suggestions contained in the Government's paper.'[18]

The government's anti-rail sentiment was strange, given that one of the first new laws it passed when Labour returned to power in 1974 was a rail-friendly Transport Act. The Act simplified the arrangement by which grants for uneconomic lines were paid, lumping them together in what became known as the 'Public Service Obligation', obviating the need to itemize every individual line's payment and widening their eligibility as they became available for Inter-City and freight services. Although this was apparently a recognition that rail subsidies were essential, the White Paper still portrayed the rail industry as a burden on public finances. Its tone implied that the search would go on for lines that could be axed and for ways of reining back investment. The contradiction between this negative view of the railway and ministerial support, in public at least, for the industry derived from the existence within the civil service of a group of officials hostile to rail who were intent on keeping up their campaign for closures. They were supported by politicians, like Crosland and Marples, who were publicly prepared to push for further closures. BR was forced to bear this cross throughout its existence.

In the run-up to the publication of the White Paper, a secret conference was held at the Sunningdale Civil Service Staff College in Surrey, where a group of senior civil servants discussed the future of the railway with further closures in mind. The main paper, presented by Peter Baldwin, the Permanent Secretary at the Department of Transport, stated unequivocally: 'We [by which he meant his fellow officials] believe it to be most important that closures should become possible again in time to have substantial results within the next five years.'[19] Remarkably, he identified some 5,000 miles of lines as candidates for closure and had prepared a package by which the unions would be bought off with extra bus services and a favourable deal for the road haulage industry.

Given this kind of briefing from senior officials, it was not surprising that the White Paper was couched in terms of a need for further closures and restrictions in investment. Crosland had tried to keep the momentum in his rail-closure campaign by asking to present the White Paper to Parliament and the press, even though by then he had been moved on to another department. Bill Rodgers, his successor, declined his cheeky request and ensured that the tone of the Paper was more favourable to the railway than Crosland would have wanted. Nevertheless, the Paper presented the rail industry as a drain on taxpayers which had to be kept to a minimum. In an annex to the Paper, Rodgers recognized that it was impossible 'to maintain the present network indefinitely, without a substantial increase in provision for investment and subsidy, and the difficulty, under present procedures of making any significant progress on closures'.[20] In the White Paper itself, he was even more explicit when referring to what were called 'local lines': 'To retain them indefinitely within the national system would place an ever increasing burden of support on the Exchequer, and drain investment from the major national network.'[21] In other words, further closures were inevitable and desirable.

The cunning element in the plan was devolution. The idea was to allocate only 75 per cent of the money currently being paid to support local lines, thereby forcing the local authorities to make tough decisions about whether to make up the difference or operate buses instead. This was despite the fact that most of the bus services which had replaced lines closed by Beeching had by then been either partly or completely abandoned. Most councils, it was thought, would choose to fund buses rather than more expensive rail services, given that after the intervention of the International Monetary Fund in 1976 to rescue the British economy, local authorities were being required to make drastic cuts to their spending.

In the event, the proposed legislation never saw the light of day. Labour's parliamentary majority had disappeared by the time the White Paper was published in 1977 and although the government, now led by Jim Callaghan, who had replaced Wilson, survived thanks to being propped up by the Liberals, there was no chance of pushing through contentious legislation.

When Margaret Thatcher swept to power in 1979, it seemed certain that the work of pushing for further closures initiated by Crosland and Baldwin would continue, especially as, famously, she hardly ever travelled by train. There was, though, initially a period of quiet as the Conservative administration dealt with a series of crises, notably soaring inflation and unemployment, and later the Falklands War, which meant that the railway was not considered a priority for reform.

However, towards the end of Mrs Thatcher's first term in office, there was an attempt to impose cuts on the network that even Crosland would not have dared suggest. Oddly, it was initiated by Peter Parker, who had taken over from Richard Marsh in 1976 and who was a great friend of the railway and who wanted to see it modernized and thriving. However, he mistakenly chose the retired civil servant Sir David Serpell, who had been a member of the Stedeford committee set up by Marples, as chairman of the committee and the result was a near disaster.

Parker, like Beeching, had been recruited from industry, but he was a very different type of BR chairman, with roots in the Labour party and a great reputation for championing the railway. A witty, charming and engaging man, who had been a very successful amateur actor while at Oxford, he was a far cry from some of his dull predecessors and right from the start he was impressed by the quality of his fellow railway managers, something which greatly endeared him to them. On the back of his very entertaining autobiography, *For Starters*, he sets out ten rules for good management, which range from 'eating and drinking less, and laughing more', to 'hiring people who are cleverer than you are and delegating more than you think is good for you'. It was a philosophy that he embraced at British Rail.

Having joined BR in 1976, Parker had his feet well under the table by 1980 and was foolhardy enough to ask the government to set up a review of the Board's objectives. Helped by sharp, soaring price rises caused by inflation and uncertainty in the Middle East that were hurting motorists, the railway had reversed the long-term decline in passenger numbers and Parker had continued its programme of making savings, particularly by cutting back on staffing. As a result, there was a brief period when BR was out of the red for the first time since the mid-1950s. However, by the time the Serpell review was commissioned in May 1982, the situation had significantly worsened, due to the lengthy flexible-rostering dispute (described in Chapter 8) and a reversion to declining passenger numbers as a result of the economic recession.

Parker believed Sir David Serpell, who had been on the Stedeford working party in 1960, would deliver a thorough and considered assessment of what the railway needed to do. He was wrong. Parker, who rather mistakenly called Serpell an 'outstanding friend of the railways', had wanted a blueprint for modernization and improvement.[22] Instead, Serpell and his committee decided to play with fire and their proposals made Beeching's efforts look tame. The first part of the report, published in 1983, was a rather bland assessment of the railway's finances, with criticism of the management and the suggestion that fares would have to rise massively to make British Rail pay its way. Oddly, far from producing a series of recommendations, the report put forward a series of options – always, in PR terms, a bad idea – that were in direct conflict with one another. For example, it recommended boosting freight services on lines that elsewhere it sought to close and suggested shutting the line between Spalding and March, which had already fallen foul of the Beeching axe. The *Guardian* did not hold back, calling it 'a really rotten report'.[23]

It was the second part, which considered a series of options for cuts, that would ensure the report would soon be consigned to the dustbin of history and put Serpell up there with Beeching and Marples in a list of trainspotters' hate figures. Seven options were presented, with the most radical, Option A, resulting in a reduction of the rail network by 84 per cent to a mere 1,630 miles – essentially leaving only the main lines from the capital to Birmingham, Manchester, Leeds, Newcastle and the two main Scottish cities, and a few London commuter services. The second option was slightly more generous, suggesting the retention of 2,220 route miles. While the report avoided recommending either alternative, the authors noted pointedly that these options were the only ones which would deliver a commercial railway that would pay for itself in the long term. The others would require annual subsidies in the order of £500 million to £800 million.

The report, however, was couched very negatively, with the assumption that this high level of funding would never be made available by government and all but the option requiring the most subsidy would also need substantial cutbacks to the network.

The infamous Option A was the sort of idea that a more astute chairman than Serpell would never have allowed to be considered, given the political impossibility of pushing through such a plan. In fact, Option A was used cannily by British Rail to ensure that the Serpell report was smothered at birth. At the instigation of Parker, a BR executive, John Prideaux, had called in the eminent rail journalist Richard Hope for a briefing the day before the official launch and had shown him the report. Hope was aghast to find that it consisted of two volumes and was 178 pages long, with lots of diagrams and maps. There was no executive summary or press release. Hope recounts how he told Prideaux, 'I can't digest this overnight and nor will the media be able to digest it.' Prideaux accepted that and instead provided him with a few dozen copies of the map of Option A. Hope rang round the newsrooms and 'by 10.30 a.m. next day I had already done 13 radio and TV interviews finishing up on Jimmy Young's [Radio 2] programme'. At the subsequent press conference, there was only a Department of Transport official, who stonewalled, merely stating that it was all 'a matter for the Secretary of State'. So instead Hope handed out the photocopies, saying, 'forget the rest, that's your story'; and, as he put it, '24 hours after this farce, the Serpell Report was a dead duck'.[24]

Parker, unlike many of his predecessors, understood the importance of media relations and, crucially, of public affairs – essentially the fancy name for lobbying government – having appointed the first person to hold the post in BR. He had genuinely wanted to have positive advice on the future of rail from Serpell, but instead the report had totally failed to address ways of improving the railway and had focused entirely, yet again, on how to wreck the network. Parker was dismayed and furious, saying that the Board had been forced to counter-attack promptly by challenging the methodology and limitations of the report as well as killing it through the clever selective leak: 'It gave no consideration to the quality of services, only to economies. It made no adequate reference to the study of international comparisons [in which BR performed well]. It failed to acknowledge the pace of changes already in hand: we had been shedding jobs at the rate of 1,000 per month for two years.'[25]

After BR's brilliantly effective sabotaging of the report, the government, two months before an election, quietly forgot the whole exercise. Riding the wave of post-Falklands euphoria and facing a weak and divided opposition, Thatcher's government wanted to avoid a row over Britain's (mostly) beloved railway. The minister who had commissioned it, David Howell, soon found himself out in the cold after Thatcher's second general election victory. Her adviser (later Sir) Alfred Sherman, no lover of the railway or of nationalized industries generally, had written to her about how Parker had run rings around Howell by leaking 'a distorted version to the press in order to whip up feelings against the report for weeks before it appeared, by which time, no one really troubled to read it'.[26] Sherman was deeply disappointed, as he had wanted to stop the railway haemorrhaging money. Parker was able to claim what he called a 'second class victory' for BR after a 'first class row'.

By overreaching themselves, Serpell and his committee had inadvertently put a stop to any further discussion of radical closures. A few were attempted, notably the Settle to Carlisle line (see Chapter 10), but there were no further attempts to hack out large sections of the network, as simply a mention of 'Beeching' in the media response to any such plans would put paid to them. Therefore, by the mid-1970s, the map of British Rail looked much the same as it does today, half a century later. The closures had petered out with 275 miles in 1970, then 108 miles over the next three years, and finally none in 1974. This termination of the closure programme was in part because it was far easier for opponents to argue against shutting lines in the 1970s, when faith in the car as the universal solution to transport problems had begun to fade. The Arab–Israeli conflict of 1967, and the use of oil as a weapon in global politics by the Organization of the Petroleum Exporting Countries (OPEC), led to sharp increases in fuel prices and a recognition that alternative modes of transport, which were often cheaper, needed to be retained. Since then, apart from the closure of many freight-only branch lines to depots and factories that were no longer using rail, the network has remained the same size, at just over 10,000 route miles.

Nevertheless, while there were no drastic closures on the scale of Beeching, British Rail managers still felt they were up against it. That's because, frankly, they were. BR managers were often defensive because they were constantly under attack and lived in permanent fear that drastic cuts promoted by the enemy within were in the offing. This would colour many of the decisions that BR made during the second half of its existence and at times limited its scope in making improvements. As Austin and Faulkner suggest in *Disconnected!*, 'had Department of Transport officials found a way of closing lines without involving their ministers in the process, and eliminating their accountability for closure decisions, they would have done so'.[27]

Marsh rightly blamed the pro-road bias among many Ministry of Transport officials for the attacks on British Rail during his tenure, as he wittily described in a valedictory interview when he left British Rail in 1976: 'Some civil servants are so anti-railways that I can only assume that something nasty happened to their mothers in a steam train.'[28] This hostile climate in Whitehall continued long after Marsh stepped down as chairman and was entrenched by the balance – or rather lack of it – in staff working on transport. At the time the Blue Paper was produced in 1972, for example, there were just seventy civil servants working on railways and public transport, compared with 1,700 who spent their time on highway planning. No wonder there were continued attempts to divert funds dedicated to railways, which were protected by Barbara Castle's Transport Act, to roads.

In fact, the continued attempts to pursue a closure

programme were based on flimsy evidence. British Rail was still not making any clear overall assessment of the value of a particular line, except in the very basic terms of considering the revenue from the stations on the route and then making a very crude calculation of costs based on average figures across the network. Yet a more sophisticated method, cost-benefit analysis, whereby costs are calculated more accurately and set against wider social benefits, such as the impact on the local economy and on road congestion, had become available. In 1963, this new method of assessing transport schemes provided a positive answer to the question of whether the Victoria Line, the first new Underground line since the initial decade of the twentieth century, should be built, which otherwise might not have been the case (which in retrospect, given that pre-pandemic 200 million passenger journeys were made on the line annually, demonstrates all too clearly that there was a desperate need to find new ways to appraise the validity of schemes).

The new methodology was slow to take off, however, and it was not until 1971 that BR asked Christopher Foster, the economist who became a legendary figure in government circles, to carry out a cost-benefit analysis on two suburban lines in Manchester slated for closure. They passed and were saved, but BR remained reluctant to apply this technique to other lines, partly because of the difficulty of obtaining accurate data, but also because there was still a feeling among many of its managers that further cuts were necessary. However, while the internal battles over closures and economies were still being waged, British Rail was changing radically.

7

The Changing Shape of the Train

Away from these battles being waged over closures and the nagging anxiety about an increasing deficit, the railway was evolving, most notably in changes to its rolling stock. The traditional train formation, with a locomotive hauling a set of disparate coaches and a guard's van attached at the back, was fast disappearing. On country routes, as we have seen, diesel multiple units, with engines underneath the carriages, were helping to cut costs and improve timetables.

However, it was not until 1960 that the concept of multiple units was tried on long-distance main-line routes, many years after this type of train was commonplace on the Continent. Blue Pullmans were the pioneers, running between major British towns and cities with a permanently fixed formation of either six or eight cars. They had a maximum speed of 90 mph, a lot faster than most of the old locomotive-hauled trains they replaced, and as they provided only a limited-stop service, they operated on much shorter journey times. The loss of flexibility from the fixed formation, which meant that carriages could not be added or removed at peak or slack times, was outweighed by the far greater simplicity of the process of reversing trains at terminus stations, as they could be driven from either end. No longer would there be a locomotive stuck at the buffer stops until another one hauled the train out for its next journey. This may seem like a purely technical change, but in fact it saved vast amounts of money as both less rolling stock and fewer operating staff were required.

In what was a groundbreaking innovation for British Railways, the Blue Pullman coaches were fitted with air conditioning and soundproofing throughout, and each window had an individually controlled venetian blind, another novelty for the time. As the Pullman brand suggested, these brightly coloured trains were aimed at business travellers and were marketed as a kind of plane on rails, with table-service meals and a hostess service for every passenger. The focus on the business market meant the service ran from Mondays to Fridays only, principally on the London Paddington to Birmingham and London St Pancras to Manchester routes. Their introduction was initially delayed because the National Union of Railwaymen had objected to the employment of Pullman staff, who were paid slightly less than their BR equivalents, but after lengthy negotiations BR managers caved in and took on the staff directly. There were technical difficulties, too, which eventually contributed to the short lifespan of these elegant trains. The ride quality was not as good as on conventional services because the bogies – the wheel sets underneath the train – had originally been designed for a lighter type of train and consequently the passengers, given they were mostly a demanding set of business customers, complained of the bumpiness and excessive vibration at high speeds.

Originally, the Blue Pullmans were planned to be introduced on various other routes, but several of the all-powerful and traditionally conservative BR regional bosses – the so-called barons – refused to take them, preferring to stick with their traditional locomotives and coaches. Therefore a mere ten sets were produced, and they lasted only until 1973, as the technical problems were difficult to resolve without a major refit and they were expensive to operate.

Nevertheless, the trailblazing Pullmans played an important role in demonstrating the potential of modern trains as well as confirming that there was a profitable market for exclusive services aimed at those prepared to pay a premium fare. This was particularly significant as competition from air was a growing threat at a time when scanners and other security checks at airports were non-existent, making getting on a plane as easy as ... well, hopping on a train! Geoffrey Freeman Allen wrote in 1965 that 'internal air services are making deeper inroads by the year. Their speed is the selling-point with business travellers ... it is possible to leave London Airport at 8 a.m., spend two hours in central Glasgow and be back in their London office by 2.45 p.m.'[1] Standby airline tickets were available at a heavy discount as an added inducement to take the plane.

The Blue Pullmans ensured BR moved away from its preference for locomotive-hauled trains and proved to be the inspiration for the hugely successful High Speed Train (HST) developed in the late 1970s, which became synonymous with the Inter-City brand. However, it was not a simple linear path to get there and it was, in fact, the Inter-City brand that was established first rather than the train.

The first mention of the term 'inter-city' (*sic*) to describe the long-distance rail network was in Beeching's *Reshaping of British Railways*, and later the concept was elaborated in BR's 1964 annual report, which suggested that the Board would establish 'a planned national pattern of inter-city services between major centres providing regular high-speed passenger services on all main routes'. This was a marked departure from the established pattern on BR's main lines, which had a mix of infrequent and relatively slow trains and a few named trains that offered a faster and more luxurious service. The key decision by the British Railways Board was to develop Inter-City (as previously mentioned, the name later morphed into the modern but illiterate InterCity) as a brand encompassing services across the network which would be both fast and timed at regular intervals. The electric trains introduced on the West Coast Main Line were used to trial this new concept, with the idea that a similar service would be launched on all main lines across the network, with London as the hub.

British Railways had already been inching forward in that direction. On most main lines, both frequency and speed had been increased. Often a rather unfair comparison was made between the fastest pre-war and post-war trains, suggesting there was very little difference. While that was true of the fastest services, the key point was that there were many more fast trains compared with the pre-war period, with five times as many services averaging more than 60 mph in 1965 compared with 1939, largely thanks to the introduction of diesel and, on the West Coast, electric traction. There was, for example, a train every hour from 8 a.m. to 6 p.m. in each direction between London and Newcastle when, at the time, 'no other railway system in the world operates such an intensive, day-long service over 250 miles'.[2] Regular interval timetabling – 'clock-face', as it is known in the industry – with trains departing at the same time past the hour throughout the day was being introduced on a succession of main lines out of London. This was innovatory since even today there are parts of the network in Europe where clock-face timetabling is still not standard.

The success of the West Coast Main Line improvements, covered in Chapter 1, was the spur to introducing Inter-City services across the network. And, unlike the Blue Pullmans, Inter-City was for everyone, with first-class and second-class seats offered without any Pullman-type premium payment. There were still Pullman services on a number of routes, and designated trains such as the *Flying Scotsman* were retained, but the overall focus had shifted firmly away from 'elite' trains for the few towards a general improvement in the service for all.

This new populist ethos put paid to the idea of providing 'lounge first' cars for first-class travellers where business people could conduct meetings 'on the go', as can be found on many trains on the Continent. Three test coaches were fitted with large compartments in which swivel-chairs were provided in the middle, along with the usual seats on either side, so that business meetings could take place. 'Lounge first' compartments were advertised with great fanfare and a short film which demonstrated the chair with a young woman sporting a tiny miniskirt swivelling around between a lot of important-looking men sitting on the seats around her. However, BR eventually rejected the concept on the basis that it did not fit with its strategy of trying to keep the weight of trains down to a minimum in order to allow faster acceleration and operation, as well as concerns that it would be perceived as being too elitist.

The Inter-City brand was the subject of BR's first television advertising campaign which was deliberately intended to reach out beyond the existing passenger base of commuters, business travellers and holidaymakers. The idea was to encourage people who would not normally consider long-distance rail journeys to use the train for leisure travel. The initial advertisements featured 'Monica', an elegantly dressed woman in her twenties whose presence was intended to show that rail travel could be for the young and glamorous. The initial slogan was the rather banal 'City to city – Heart to heart'; but later ones, such as 'This is the Age of the Train' and 'Let the train take the strain', caught on (and remain in my head to this day). The focus on mass appeal was exemplified by the choice of Jimmy Savile, the DJ and children's TV presenter, to front the 'Age of the Train' campaign, and the advertisements featuring Savile attracted huge publicity and coverage in the tabloids. Savile was a remarkably popular figure at the time and his extensive criminal sexual activity was only revealed after his death in 2011. Peter Parker needed some persuasion, but after seeing a screen test was won over by the Rolls-Royce driving and cigar smoking celebrity: 'Jimmy came up trumps because of people's perception that he would only do what he believed in, whatever the money.'[3] Parker was not the only one to fail to spot that there was a dark side to the now disgraced late entertainer's jolly public demeanour.

The Inter-City brand would become synonymous with the HST 125s, the streamlined diesel trains that would roar up and down Britain's main lines at a maximum speed of 125 mph for more than thirty years. But they were a backstop to another train, whose development was, unfortunately, stillborn. The Advanced Passenger Train had been slated to become the emblematic symbol of BR's modernization. It would run at speeds of 150 mph by using a tilting mechanism that allowed it to negotiate curves at much faster speeds than conventional trains. This was crucial on Britain's rail network, which had been built by the Victorians using much tighter and more frequent curves than other European railways, where it had been possible to iron out many of these bends. In the UK, curves accounted for 50 per cent of the mileage of the system, so that straightening was considered far too expensive and extensive to be worthwhile. Britain was also reckoned to be too small to accommodate a network of new dedicated high-speed routes, which had been built in Japan and was being planned in France. Therefore, rather than modernizing the infrastructure, it was the rolling stock which had to be adapted to fit Britain's ageing railway system.

The initial prototype was a gas-turbine powered train that used a revolutionary gyroscopic control to enable the train to tilt round curves, similar to the way motorcyclists ease into the bends on a racetrack. The APT-E (Advanced Passenger Train – Experimental) was first proposed by the Advanced Projects Group in the British Railways Research and Development Division in 1966. This was part of the Railway Technical Centre, which had been created by BR to give priority to rail research; it was eventually centralized at Derby, a traditional railway town.

After two years of discussion, the Ministry of Transport agreed to jointly fund the project with BR to develop a train that would have a design speed of 155 mph. This was a futuristic and genuinely groundbreaking project, which was much more than the development of a new train design based on existing models. It was more akin to space research, as instead of the traditional rail industry tinkering with adjustments to designs that had developed organically over the past 150 years, the aim was to develop a completely new concept for a train. It was a remarkable departure for BR, as the APT concept was based on a programme of fundamental research into railway vehicle dynamics that was intended to revolutionize rail travel.

According to Stephen Potter in his book *On the Right Lines?* this 'required the solution of several theoretical problems which until then had been poorly understood by railway engineers'.[4] The development of the train involved fundamental research into wheel–rail dynamics and rail bogie design through a scientific approach involving modelling, simulation and considerable laboratory work. This was pure science rather than mere engineering, a fact that did not endear the project to traditional engineers in BR's powerful Chief Mechanical and Electrical Engineer's Department, who viewed the APT as impractical and did not want to see their precious research resources squandered on such an outlandish venture. Despite being led by a highly rated British Railways executive, Sydney Jones, the innovative Director of Research, 'there was a very real awareness among the project team that every mistake would be carefully observed and, if they were not careful, exploited by the "cut-and-try" school', with the threat that the project could be axed at any point.[5] The project was nothing if not ambitious, with simultaneous aims that were remarkably demanding: seeking to allow trains to travel at over 150 mph on unimproved British Rail tracks, and with the existing signalling, while reducing energy consumption, as well as aiming at more minor targets, such as keeping noise levels down and achieving a similar cost per mile as existing trains. As Potter concludes, it 'represented the most radical jump in rail technology ever attempted'.[6]

It was not just the tilting mechanism that was revolutionary. The weight of the train was drastically reduced by using aerospace technology to design its aluminium frame, and the engines were both powerful and light. The lower weight, in turn, allowed the number of wheels to be reduced, thus minimizing friction. There were also two different braking systems, including a novel concept, 'hydrokinetic' brakes – which work by pumping water between fixed and rotating vanes inside an axle to slow a vehicle down. These were much lighter than older brake designs.

The innovative tilting mechanism, initially developed in the USA just before the Second World War, had been in use in Spain in a simpler 'passive' system. The British system, however, used jacks to create something more intricate and 'active', but its complexity led to technical difficulties. The tilting mechanism on each carriage operated independently, meaning that if it failed on a particular coach, the entire train would be unable to tilt.

There was another physical constraint resulting from the age of the British rail network. The British loading gauge – the maximum possible height and width of a train to fit in a tunnel – is smaller in the UK than on the Continent, even though the width between the rails, the standard gauge of 4 ft 8½ in, is the same. This puts a limit either on the amount of tilt, which reduces maximum speed, or on the size of the carriages, which means the tilting results in less space for passengers. With the decision to allow for the high level of tilt of 15 degrees, in order to enable the trains to travel 40 per cent faster through curves, the space available for passengers had to be reduced. Incidentally, this remains true today, as the Avanti (formerly Virgin) Pendolino tilting trains on the West Coast Main Line have a far more cramped feel than the non-tilting trains on other main-line routes.

Initial progress on the project was rapid. The thirty-strong design team built the APT-E from scratch within three years, a remarkable achievement, and the prototype made its first test run in July 1972. Unfortunately, at that point, the programme was held up by the drivers' union ASLEF: there was only one seat in the driving cab and the union was demanding double manning. While that was necessary with steam engines, one person was able to operate a modern diesel or electric train. After a year's negotiations, the union relented; but this delay, added to technical difficulties, slowed progress on the APT's development and caused a loss of momentum on the project.

When trials did begin, the APT-E performed promisingly. On the Great Western Main Line, which has very long stretches of straight track thanks to Brunel's remarkable vision for the railway, it was given special permission to run fast, and in August 1975 it achieved a new British railway speed record of 152 mph, between Swindon and Reading. The 'E' part of its name was no accident – it was only conceived as an experimental train to test the concept rather than being a prototype for a production line, and as such it was successful, running on various parts of the network for nearly four years until, after 23,500 miles, it was retired to the National Railway Museum in April 1976.

It was just at the point when BR had proved the basic viability of the APT concept that unfortunately the project became mired in internal politics. The plan for gas turbine engines to provide the power for the traction was jettisoned and replaced with electricity, which limited where the trains could run. Diesel was unsuitable because its power to weight ratio decreases dramatically at high speeds, which would have ruled out the planned maximum speed of 155 mph. BR's board prevaricated until finally, in 1974, two years after the trials began, it announced plans to build eighty APTs, although it was still unclear which design would be used.

To make a start, BR ordered four electrically powered prototypes of the APT-P. Immediately there was a problem which would result in an unhappy compromise and damage the prospect of this new version being introduced widely. The power would be supplied by overhead wires using the 25 kV system, but in order to produce the speed and acceleration needed, two power cars were required, one at each end. That became impossible due to various technical issues, notably that having raised pantographs (the apparatus on top of the trains that makes the connection with the wires) so far apart on the trains would cause a wave effect at high speeds that would lead to wire breakages. Therefore the power cars were put next to each other in the middle of the train, and since passengers could not walk through them, the twelve-car trains effectively became two separate six-car units that both required catering and ticket inspectors, thereby increasing the operating costs.

Development of the ATP-P was further delayed by an internal reorganization, when responsibility was transferred from BR's Research Division to its Engineering Department. It wasn't until the middle of 1977 when the first power car was produced. Testing started two years later, and the train soon bettered the speed record set by its predecessor with a run on the West Coast Main Line on the Scottish border reaching 162 mph in December 1979. The trains worked well until one was involved in a high-speed derailment caused by an axle problem in April 1980 (BR's vice-chairman, Ian Campbell, who was responsible for research and development, was on board). The train stayed upright on the ballast and thankfully no one was hurt, but the derailment demonstrated the risks from the technical complexities of the new train.

Under pressure to show results from this long development process, British Rail made the mistake of introducing the trains into revenue-earning service prematurely. The first scheduled service, which set out from Glasgow to London Euston early on the morning of 7 December 1981, was a triumph. The train arrived a minute ahead of schedule, completing the journey in just under four and a quarter hours, almost ninety minutes quicker than the regular timetable, and had hit 137 mph, a new speed record for a train in passenger service. But already there were some concerns about the ride quality. The stewardess Marie Docherty achieved instant fame by explaining to the *Guardian* how she coped with the bumpy ride: 'I just stand there with my legs open.'[7]

It got worse. On the return journey to Scotland, the driver allowed the train to enter a bend too fast and consequently a safety device disconnected all the tilt mechanisms. For the rest of the route, the train had to slow down for bends which meant it arrived late, though the trip was still faster than conventional services. Unfortunately, the journalists, ever eager for a freebie, were present in force on both legs of the journey and the coverage was merciless. Under the headline 'The super train hits trouble', the *Daily Mail* reporter wrote that the tilt failure resulted in 'sending food across the table, spilling drinks and jamming electric doors', and the train was dubbed the 'queasy rider', a reference to the hit movie *Easy Rider*.[8] There was some truth in this criticism. Even in his academic book on the subject, Stephen Potter mentions the problem, and indeed the high degree of tilt on the Pendolino trains has often made me feel rather queasy as they pound the tracks at full speed north-west of Rugby on the West Coast Main Line.

On the third journey, the perils of running an experimental train in the midst of one of the coldest winters on record were cruelly exposed. The APT set off from Glasgow with the temperature dipping well below freezing point. It soon came to a halt, when a safety mechanism on the brakes failed in the Arctic conditions while travelling through the uplands of southern Scotland. Essentially the train froze up and had to limp back to Glasgow. There was a second try, but the train only reached Crewe, where it broke down again. Numerous other train services encountered similar difficulties that day because of the exceptional cold, but it was the unfortunate APT that made the headlines. Peter Parker, in his memoirs, says he never forgot the 'awful, accurate' *Private Eye* front cover which cruelly depicted the train with the caption 'Welcome aboard the APT, stopping for repairs at Penrith, Crewe, Glasgow, Penrith, Crewe . . .' Within a couple of weeks, the APT trains were taken out of service, with the intention of returning them within a few months; but apart from the odd run as relief trains in the summer peaks and to replace broken-down sets, they never saw regular service and were finally withdrawn in early 1985.

What should have been a new era of British rail engineering expertise failed because of a series of crucial errors. One key mistake was the ill-thought-out specification of a 155 mph maximum speed, even though British Rail knew that its signalling system was designed for a top speed of 125 mph. Beyond that speed, a train's stopping distance increases so much that for the APT to have run safely a *fifth* phase would have had to be added to lineside signals at a prohibitive cost (unlike road traffic lights, Britain's railways have four phases, green, double yellow, yellow and red, with the single yellow always indicating that the next signal is red). The time saved by having a top speed of 155 mph instead of 125 mph amounted to just a few minutes on a 400-mile journey. In fact, there were only a few occasions when the maximum speed was achievable, given the state of the tracks, and even with the train's powerful engines it took a long time to accelerate up to the top speed. Moreover, given that much of the railway is just two tracks, the APT would have had to reduce speed when slower local services or freight trains were ahead. This is all very basic railway operating knowledge, and therefore the emphasis on 155 mph does suggest a fundamental failure of communication within BR between the traditional engineers responsible for operating and maintaining the track and the APT team with its focus on innovation and breaking the mould. In reality, therefore, there was never any likelihood of the train running at more than 125 mph, which, incidentally, remains the maximum speed on conventional lines today. The requirement to enable it to do so not only added costs but contributed to the complexity of the design process. The emphasis on speed was, in any case, misplaced. Other factors, such as comfort, regularity of timetables, catering facilities and, crucially, pricing of tickets, were actually far more important in attracting passengers to rail.

The ill-fated press trips and the technical problems which they revealed did not actually spell the end of the APT concept, as is commonly thought. Efforts were still made to rescue the project, including jettisoning the 155 mph requirement. These became the basis of the InterCity 225 that was later introduced on the East Coast Main Line, as explained in Chapter 11. However, Parker accepted that the hopes of making the APT the core of the Inter-City rail network could no longer be realized. The research programme was drastically scaled back and the order for eighty trains never materialized.

What makes the APT episode so tragic is that its ambitions were thwarted by a failure of imagination and a lack of courage on the part of government and BR rather than by the technical difficulties, which could have been overcome. This should have been – indeed in many respects was – a fantastic British innovation. If it had succeeded, the technology would have been exported worldwide; but instead the APT became a sadly typical heroic failure, which was the subject of ridicule rather than pride through the mishandling of the public relations. There is no doubt there were technical problems, and the stop-go development process was damaging. However, the concept was viable and had already attracted widespread interest from overseas railways.

Parker reckoned the PR disaster was not the main issue behind the failure, but rather it was due to a lack of belief, which meant that there were never sufficient funds to complete the research needed for such a novel idea: 'The total development costs were £37 million. If it had received a fraction of the funds that went into Concorde the saga would surely have ended differently.'[9] And the rail system would have looked very different today. Parker, in fact, was spot on. Fear of repeating the mistakes of Concorde – which proved vastly more expensive than originally envisaged and ultimately was a total commercial failure, with only the partners in the project, France and Britain, ever buying any planes – undermined the APT project. In fact, the amount spent on the APT pales into insignificance by comparison, given that the failed aviation project ended up costing the taxpayers of Britain and France £2 billion during its fifteen-year development. A mere fraction of this sum would likely have delivered a viable APT. Indeed, the tilting system continued to be worked on, notably by Fiat, which developed its Pendolino design into the most successful type of tilting train. More than 500 of these trains have been produced for the European market, including a set of fifty-seven ordered by Virgin when it won the West Coast franchise and they began carrying passengers in 2002.

Of course, there were other reasons for the failure of the APT. The reorganization of the project team halfway through, a lack of support from engineers entrenched in the BR hierarchy and jealous of the amounts being spent on the APT, and the sheer ambitious nature of the concept, which had to cope with the inadequacies of an old railway network, were all contributing factors. Parker was in no doubt that the whole process had been deeply damaging for BR and that his hand had been forced by the ongoing technical issues:

> The APT had been too long in gestation, too ambitious in a thousand innovations, and steadily under-resourced. The technical lessons of advanced design were no doubt valuable ... but this was a defeat, all the more bitter because I had overexposed the promise of the APT. Its failure winded BR at the wrong time, just as we were rebuilding our fortunes.[10]

British Rail had no choice but to refocus on the High Speed Train. It had been fortuitous – or, in fact, a clever bit of planning – that the development of the diesel-powered HST 125 had been authorized as a trial at the same time as the APT programme was given the green light. The HST's development could not have been more different from the APT project. It was a conventional railway research scheme, building on the past while making some improvements with the help of modern technology. This was not revolution, but rather evolution, the classic 'cut-and-try' method of rail technological development and a way of working that was familiar and comfortable for

BR's Engineering Department. Unfortunately, the steady progress on the HST project undermined the continued work on the APT programme, especially justifying the engineers' scepticism about what they saw as a 'pie in the sky' concept.

Arguably, the HST could be seen as the revenge of the engineers, as its genesis was the desire of the Chief Mechanical and Electrical Engineer's Department to develop a high-speed diesel train. In May 1970, the British Railways Board granted £70,000 as seed funding for the project – an indication that there were already concerns about the failings of the APT project, although the small amount suggested there were also still doubts about whether diesel traction was the solution for a new long-distance train design. The initiative had come from the chief engineer, Terry Miller, who had worked on the great steam engines of the interwar years developed by Nigel Gresley for the London & North Eastern Railway. But he had turned his skills to diesel locomotives and, according to Roger Ford, the technology editor of *Modern Railways*, he was the right man for the job: 'He had the vision to see that conventional technology could build on the successes already experienced on the East and West Coast routes and he had the leadership ability to make major change happen, and quickly.'[11] Miller promised the Board that his team would produce a working prototype of the train in just twenty-two months and soon substantial further funds were made available by the BR board.

At the instigation of the Engineering Department, the British Railways Board issued a document, *A Strategy for*

High Speed, which set out a plan to progress both with the APT and with the rapid development of the HST, with the latter being seen as an insurance policy should the APT fail.

Miller was fortunate that he could make use of the innovations developed for the APT project. British Railways had long tried to develop a diesel train capable of 125 mph, but technical glitches, such as vibrations caused by 'hunting' (the steady increase in the oscillation of the wheels, resulting in a swaying movement which in extreme cases can cause derailment) and the excessive track wear resulting from high speed, were difficult to overcome. The wheel set developed for the ATP had solved this particular problem as it was lighter and made higher operational speeds possible.

Ironically, therefore, although the HST was an overtly conventional train, it could never have been built and put into service so quickly without the know-how gained from the APT project. The initial design was based on the original APT-E concept and, as with the APT, there were power cars at both ends of what was intended to be a seven or eight coach train. It would become the fastest diesel train in the world, powered by an engine which was remarkably light for the very impressive 2,250 horsepower it produced, and made by a British firm, Paxman Engineering. The low weight was important in reducing damage to the track, and the power was sufficient to ensure the seven coaches and two power cars could easily achieve a steady 125 mph for long stretches.

The prototype High Speed Diesel Train, as it was

known at the time, was successfully delivered within Miller's timeframe. That was a fantastic achievement, but unfortunately, as with the APT, a year's testing was lost because the unions objected to the fact that there was only a single seat in the driver's cab, from which they inferred, correctly, that it would be single manned – though, in the event, in the early days of revenue service there was some double manning following the cab's redesign.

The dispute with the unions had a silver lining, as it resulted in a fortuitous and beneficial design change – the decision to dispense with buffers, a standard part of locomotive design since the very earliest days of the railway. The design consultant Kenneth Grange, tasked with trying to find the space for a second seat in the driver's cab, had mused aloud in a conversation with Miller about why the train had buffers, given that it was in fixed formation and did not require any shunting movements. To Grange's surprise, Miller told him that there was not much need for buffers, and they were dispensed with. Grange reported that 'the result was a more stylish appearance, sounder aerodynamics, and an effective modern image for Britain's railways'.[12] And it made it easier to fit in the second seat, even though that largely proved superfluous.

In fact, the unions did have further influence on the eventual design, suggesting some improvements. When a prototype was demonstrated at Derby, the union representatives made several suggestions, such as reducing the excessive noise, increasing the size of the front windscreen and better siting of the handbrake, speedometer and intercom, most of which were adopted, demonstrating the readiness of BR to negotiate with its workforce over such matters.

Once the train started test runs, it was an amazing technical success, as the railway writer Roger Ford reported:

> Its performance exceeded all expectations. For example, its disc brakes stopped it in 1,930 yards compared with the 2,200 yards allowed for a train travelling at 100 mph. In addition, its acceleration was better than hoped for and later on in its development it would be discovered that the train's aerodynamics were so good that another coach could be added to the original seven car formation without having to increase the output of the two power cars.[13]

The brakes, however, emitted a very characteristic – and not entirely unpleasant – acrid burning smell into the coaches, because they were too near the intakes for the air conditioning. This was to become a feature of travelling on HSTs to which passengers became accustomed, as it took some fifteen years before this fault was cured and the smell eradicated.

There was a high standard of comfort, too. The buffet car service was much improved compared to previous offerings, and for many people air conditioning was a welcome novelty. Ford, a frequent critic of modern rolling stock, was unequivocal in his praise for the new trains, noting how different the HST, with its specially designed coaches, was to the ill-fated and poorly designed Blue Pullmans: 'The Mark III coach, the cheapest and lightest steel-built air-conditioned coach in Europe, gives a quality of ride, even on poor track, that later designs struggled to emulate.'[14]

Other lessons had been gained from the Blue Pullman experience, particularly the realization that, in order to get the best out of new trains, the condition of the track had to be improved. Cutting out curves meant that there were sufficient high-speed stretches to ensure timings were improved enough to transform the service. It was not just the elimination of curves. Radical measures were needed to make good the damage caused by wear and tear on the ageing railway, much of which was nearing 150 years old. On the Great Western, for example, Brunel had built a largely straight railway in the 1830s, but in many places its trackbed needed completely relaying and many slight curves needed to be eliminated. In 1975, British Rail took the radical step of closing the section between Swindon and Bristol Parkway – which is on the route to Wales – for five months in order to relay the entire line. As a result, the speed limit was increased to 125 mph on nearly 100 miles of the 112-mile route between London and Bristol Parkway station. Faster trains with better acceleration combined to reduce timings, resulting in a new and improved timetable on the main lines of the Great Western.

In October 1976, when sufficient train sets were available, British Rail started running this quicker and more comfortable new Inter-City service. The journey time between London and Cardiff was reduced by twenty-three minutes while London–Bristol was fifteen minutes faster. Later, as BR became more adept at squeezing HST services in between stopping trains and freight services, journey times were cut still further. Bristol Parkway could be reached from London in just seventy minutes, twenty minutes faster than before. The impact was immediate, with passenger numbers rising by a third over the first two years, thanks both to the improved timings and to the greatly increased frequency of service – for instance, whereas there were fifteen trains each way between London and Birmingham in 1967, by 1978 that had increased to twenty-eight, and for Bristol the number had jumped from fourteen to twenty-four in the same period.

BR devised an appropriate slogan to go with the new, modern-looking trains which were such a contrast to the steam engines that had thundered up and down the track at a mere 70 mph less than two decades previously: 'It's the changing shape of rail' – although a more accurate description might have been 'the changing shape of the train'. Indeed, what became known as 'the nose cone effect' was observed across the networks as HSTs were introduced on other non-electrified lines.

A lot of thought by BR managers went into working out how to attract people on to the new trains. Car ownership was rising rapidly in this period and railways had to sell themselves as never before. British Rail allocated unprecedented resources to a marketing strategy appropriate for this new, far more competitive world. Such was the improvement in the railway that it took a while for the public to understand that these faster, sleeker HSTs were actually available for all passengers, even those in second class. They offered a level of service that previously would not have been available even in first class (it was not until 1987 that second class was renamed 'standard'). These new trains were not just for the business passenger – they were for everyone. As Ford explains, 'Selling HST as the people's train meant playing down some of its features. Speed for speed's sake was out as were images of luxury travel.'[15] Instead, the marketing – itself a relatively new concept for BR – emphasized shorter journey times, greater comfort and improved on-board service.

Ninety-five HSTs, including 197 power cars, were eventually built by British Rail's subsidiary company BREL (British Railways Engineering Ltd) in Crewe between 1976 and 1982. BR had, in fact, wanted more, but its plans were blocked by the Treasury. What the Treasury failed to understand was that because introducing faster trains with greater acceleration cut journey times, it saved money by enabling BR to reduce the amount of rolling stock required to run a particular frequency of service. As the trains reached their destination more quickly, they could be turned around – which of course was also easier with HSTs, as they could be driven from either end – and complete more journeys than their predecessors. Therefore, the overall stock of trains could be reduced, saving on other costs such as depots and maintenance.

As the rollout gathered pace, the combination of the HST 125 and the strong Inter-City branding led to further rapid rises in passenger numbers. The 'nose cone effect' proved ubiquitous. On the East Coast Main Line, when the trains started being introduced in 1978 – two years after the Great Western – there was once again an immediate impact, even though production delays meant the new trains shared the track with older stock. In fact, BR managers noted that people were willing to stand on board the HSTs in order to enjoy their speed and comfort, even when there were spare seats on slower diesel-locomotive-hauled coaches.

On the East Coast Main Line, track improvement work was undertaken differently than on the Great Western. Instead of one major extensive closure, incremental improvements were made over a long period, starting in the early 1960s. One reason was that the British Railways Board wanted to disguise the true extent of the spending. Big ticket items such as lengthy closures to improve a large section of track were more likely to attract the attention of ministers and, particularly, the Treasury. So it was a policy of 'improvement by stealth' – cutting out a curve here, taking out a permanent speed restriction there, each of which could save a minute or so over the length of the journey between London and stops on the route such as Doncaster, Leeds, York, Newcastle and Edinburgh. (Similar subterfuge was used to get major road improvement schemes through without attracting too much attention from the bean counters.) Curves which only a few years before BR had decided were not worth straightening, because of the imminent arrival of the Advanced Passenger Train, were now being removed. Every minute saved boosted revenue as train timings became more attractive, although this fact eluded the Treasury, which saw things only in terms of expenditure and never revenue. By smoothing out the curves, the maximum speed on many sections of track was increased to 100 mph, and for several years the powerful Deltic diesels, which from 1961 had hauled the passenger trains, made use of these improvements to reduce timings. The full introduction of HST 125s in 1979 on the East Coast Main Line saw the journey time from London to Newcastle reduced to three hours. That was deemed by transport economists at the time to be the cut-off point beyond which people would prefer to take the plane; today, with the encumbrance of added airport security, it is thought to be four hours. As a result of all these improvements, the new Inter-City services quickly captured market share from domestic aviation. The air service between Heathrow and Teesside was scrapped and a plan to build an airport at Sheffield was abandoned.

The HSTs were introduced on several other routes, notably the Midland Main Line, and became the workhorse for Cross Country services, the express routes that bypass London to connect regional centres. The success of the HST 125 was even noticed in Australia, where there was a strong public clamour for improved railway services. As a result, the railways Down Under bought nineteen power cars and sixty coaches of a slightly modified HST, known as the XPT, which at the time of writing in 2021 are still in use on regional networks.

In the UK, the HSTs had a working life of more than forty years on several main lines until their replacement in the late 2010s and early 2020s, mainly by the Department for Transport-commissioned Hitachi IEP (InterCity

Express Project), known as Azuma on the East Coast Main Line. A few refurbished and re-engined HST sets are still in use in Scotland and on Cross Country and lesser-used Great Western services.

The HSTs were by no means perfect in terms of their engineering, as they suffered from cracking of their aluminium gearbox housing, leaks of coolants and weak brake discs, as well as the famous acrid smell, but these were the sort of problems that any class of rail vehicle might suffer. By and large, they were a triumph and provided an efficient and reliable service for four decades. The HST 125 soon become synonymous with the InterCity brand and the swallow that became its logo, and was crucial to the creation of a separate business in 1982, when BR began the process of breaking itself up into five component sectors, which is covered in Chapter 9.

8

All Change

Despite all these overt signs of modernization and the beginnings of a more business-type approach by the Board, much of the old railway survived. British Rail was still a behemoth, with many facets and practices that were rooted in the nineteenth century rather than in the final quarter of the twentieth. Nowhere was this more true than in its industrial relations.

Even after the Beeching cuts, British Rail was still a very large organization which carried out many tasks not undertaken by today's railway, such as constructing trains, running hotels and operating ferries. This was a period when car ownership was soaring and motorway construction had just begun in earnest. In a thirty-year period starting in the mid-1950s, 2,200 miles of motorways were completed, along with five times that length of improved trunk roads. In 1958, just 23 per cent of households had a car, but by 1975 this had more than doubled to 57 per cent. Bigger lorries, able to carry larger loads, dominated freight haulage.

BR had survived the competition, but was not

unscathed. While BR had been battered by cuts and political meddling, the railway was still a considerable force. After its size had stabilized in the mid-1970s, there were still 16,000 passenger trains and 2,000 freight services every day on its 10,000-mile network. A 250,000-strong workforce placed British Rail in the nation's top five employers, although cost-cutting meant numbers continued to decline rapidly. There were still 2,350 stations left open, just over a third of the total in the aftermath of the war, but a small number of very busy large stations handled the vast majority of traffic. However, even though many little-used stations survived, vast savings were still made as they were being 'de-staffed' (in the jargon of the day), which involved closing ticket offices and removing any permanent staff. This concept, called 'open stations', was crucial to increasing productivity, although fare dodgers inevitably took advantage.

During his tenure as chairman of BR, Peter Parker focused on promoting the railway and maintaining its standing in the public eye. His emphasis on public relations and lobbying of parliamentarians definitely helped change the public perception of the organization. At receptions and parties, he would have a notepad and pen ready to hand as soon as his interlocutors began to relate their inevitable complaints about British Rail, and he would ask them to jot down the precise details and timing of the particular incident. As he put it in his hugely entertaining and elegantly written autobiography, the culture he found on his arrival had to be changed: 'BR had to break out from this narrowing view of its fate. We had to recreate the public's confidence and goodwill towards rail. This would be good for sales and would also better our political chances when inevitably the big investment decisions were brought before any government to be judged.'[1] In appointing the organization's first public affairs manager (code for lobbyist) and a director of environment, another innovation, he was ensuring that BR was connecting with its 'many publics', which he listed as 'Parliament and local government, Whitehall, employers, institutions, the trades unions and TUC, environmentalists, people in education and the media'.[2] In other words, he tried to force an inward-looking organization to step out of its comfort zone, even if that meant, at times, having to confront its failings.

Mrs Thatcher's arrival in Downing Street saw him redouble his efforts to show the industry in a good light. He took a personal interest in every advertisement, vetting the copy line by line and even determining the format in which it would appear. Every advertisement carried a paragraph explaining its purpose: 'An industry as much in the limelight [sic] as ours has a duty to address itself to a wider audience which needs to be well-informed if it is to play its part in helping to form public opinion.' Parker had prepared the ground for this campaign and was able to play a trump card that proved highly influential. In 1977, he had commissioned a survey of the eight biggest European railways by economists at Leeds University to make up for the lack of comparative data on their relative performance. Armed with this evidence, Parker was confident that BR would be able to rebut the frequent accusations that Britain's railway was much worse than its European counterparts. Thankfully for Parker, the findings showed BR in a good light, though one suspects that, had they not, then the survey would never have been published. They revealed that overall productivity compared well with European railways. Output per employee was above the average of the other countries except in relation to its engineering subsidiary, BREL. Wages were low, and hours worked were long in comparison with other countries. Moreover, BR's rate of improvement came out top, as it was modernizing its rolling stock, both for freight and passengers. However, overall, BR's investment levels were far lower than those of other countries. In other words, it was getting value for money.

The survey also revealed that Britain had the highest fares in Europe, largely because the railway here received the lowest subsidy, with just 27 per cent of its income coming from taxpayers, compared with around 40 per cent in France and Germany, and nearly 70 per cent in Italy. Parker was delighted when the *Financial Times* described this level of support as 'mean'. The high fares in Britain were to some extent mitigated by BR having the widest and most imaginative range of discounted tickets, using methods such as railcards for students and senior citizens, cheap returns and market pricing. BR also faced fiercer competition from other modes of transport as car taxation was lower than in any of the other countries apart from Sweden, and according to the report 'the licensing system for bus and coach services also affords less protection to BR than to any of the other railways except DSB [Danish railways]'.[3] This imbalance would be exacerbated by the deregulation and privatization of bus and coach services in the UK in the mid-1980s.

Parker seized upon the research and put it at the heart of BR's first major corporate advertising campaign. It was headlined 'How long can we go on running the most cost-effective major railway in Europe?' and gave a comprehensive analysis of the report on the European rail networks. It was the sort of detailed and dull advertising, with lots of text on whole pages of newspapers, that today would be confined to obscure dictatorships trying to demonstrate their democratic credentials.

But it worked. Public perception of the railway improved, although Parker was told that members of the Cabinet, including the Secretary of State for Transport, Norman Fowler, were angered by BR's self-aggrandizing. While the Tories remained sceptical about the value of the railway and, as we shall see in the next chapter, forced the sale of many subsidiaries, Parker's campaign was important in beginning to make the public – and even some politicians – understand that subsidy was just part of the price of having an effective railway system. As he wrote in his autobiography: 'We quoted independent research to make the case that there was nothing freakish about BR's dependence on public payment for the social railway element of the business.'[4]

Parker was, however, swimming against the tide. Passenger numbers were falling – down to 600 million in 1982, an all-time low – and less freight was carried, although this was partly due to the strategy of cutting unprofitable services. The lucrative parts of the rail freight business, which included coal, aggregates, oil and steel, represented all but 10 per cent of its business measured by tonnage. The remainder was, in any case, increasingly switching from rail to road. Parcels and small packages were the Cinderella business of British Rail and would have disappeared entirely had it not been for the establishment of Red Star in the mid-1960s. This was effectively a rival to the registered mail service run by the Post Office, with customers taking their parcels to a railway station, from where they were then carried by rail to a destination station for collection. This was BR making good use of the efficient part of its service – the ability to run fast and frequent trains between major urban centres – in order to carry small but usually high-value packages speedily over long distances.

BR abandoned its loss-making comprehensive parcel collection in 1981 but Red Star, focused solely on a few major stations, was both successful and profitable. In fact, BR created a subsidiary, City Link, which used vans to connect all the stations in London with a regular timetable, allowing Red Star to establish a fully national service. City Link also offered to pick up and deliver from major Red Star offices, and this combined service became very popular, even though it was expensive. As former railway worker Mark Walker, whose first job was at Bedford station, recalls: 'The maximum weight was something like 100 kilos so we could take massive amounts of stuff. There was an engineering company in Bedford which supplied the oil industry, and we would put the load on a train to St Pancras, City Link would transfer it to King's Cross next door and it would get to Aberdeen on the same day.'[5]

In those pre-email and fax times, the service was also popular with graphic designers and printers. Because it was used to transport a wide range of goods, Red Star was for a while rather like the old common carrier service that BR had been relieved of in 1962. Walker remembers 'on the early shift, the first sound that greeted me was the chirping of hundreds of chicks being delivered to an egg plant, but we also took racing pigeons and I even recall being asked to quote for a corpse, but fortunately that offer was not taken up. There were also the huge trunks sent three times a year for public school boarders.'[6]

The Serpell report, as we saw in Chapter 6, had not come out of the blue but was a response to the difficulties British Rail found itself in at the time Mrs Thatcher was first elected as Prime Minister in 1979. Despite the success of the burgeoning Inter-City services, there was constant pressure to meet the spending limits imposed by government, which were set at the whim of the Treasury. The railway was the prisoner of two acronyms, EFL, the External Financing Limit (the money the government allowed BR to borrow to invest and to make up for losses) and PSO, the Public Service Obligation (the amount given to BR to provide uneconomic services). British Rail under Peter Parker saw the provision of better services as a way of improving the organization's finances, but ministers tended to focus on the bottom line and saw cutting costs as the only way of reducing the need for public support. Improving productivity would have made a difference, but the strength of the trade unions had customarily made this difficult. Now the issue was about to come to a head.

Railway workers had always been relatively poorly paid as an unspoken acknowledgement of the benefit of effectively having a job for life. Ray Knight, a trade union activist who spent nearly half a century on the railway, was typical. He joined in 1974, initially as a cleaner, thanks to the recommendation of a relative, but quickly became a clerk monitoring train movements at Bounds Green train depot in north London. Although he had not initially seen the railway as a career, most of his colleagues at the time did:

> You felt you had joined a family, and many would be there for life. There were a lot of single men who worked there and for them it was a home from home with canteens on the stations so they could get fed and they would wear uniforms all day. They probably did not know how to cook for themselves.

Knight much later got a job at King's Cross dispensing uniforms and recollects a lot of these same men, by then retired, coming back and asking for redundant shirts and trousers 'because they had never shopped for themselves. They would put a few quid in the tin. It was corrupt but hardly very much . . . one bloke was so grateful he turned up with a big pumpkin from his garden every year.' Knight observed that there was a clear demarcation in roles along racial lines: 'Most of the staff were white except for the carriage cleaners. They were predominantly West Indian, both the men and the women. It was the first time I had engaged with black people.'[7]

This suggests that even a decade after the landmark case involving black people's employment with British Rail, there were still covert discriminatory practices within the organization. The case had arisen out of the passing of the Race Relations Act in 1965, which outlawed discrimination in 'public places' such as bars and hotels, but the legislation failed to include employment and therefore victims of racism at work had no recourse to law. It took the courage of a railway employee, Asquith Xavier, to expose the fact that both unions and management were complicit in excluding black people from the better jobs in the organization. Xavier, a Dominican who was part of the Windrush generation of immigrants from the Caribbean, had worked for nearly a decade at Marylebone station, first as a porter and then as a guard on freight trains. However, when his depot closed, he had to seek another role. In May 1966, he applied to transfer to Euston, where the pay was £10 per week more than he had been getting. His application was rejected by the local staff committee in a letter which left no doubt that the reason was a long-standing colour bar at the station. While the management were not bound by the recommendations of the staff committee, they did not challenge it.

Xavier, however, did. He took up the matter with the branch secretary of his union and the issue eventually came to the attention of Barbara Castle, who was the transport minister at the time, and also to the notice of the media. During the subsequent outcry, it emerged that similar discriminatory practices were entrenched at other London stations, notably Broad Street. It's worth noting, too, that the Metropolitan Police did not take on a black constable until Norwell Roberts, who had emigrated from Anguilla as a child, was appointed in 1967.

Under pressure from Castle, British Rail rescinded the staff committee's decision and in August 1966 Xavier was finally given a job at Euston amid much publicity. At a subsequent press conference, a BR press officer, Leslie Leppington, suggested that it had not been management policy but rather the unions which had instigated a colour bar out of a desire to protect jobs. When Xavier, who had been on sick leave, was able to start work at Euston, he needed a police escort, and he later received hate mail and even death threats. His campaign helped lead to the passing of the Race Relations Act of 1968, which made it illegal to refuse housing, employment or public services to people because of their ethnic background. British Rail tried to ensure that such racist practices were ended elsewhere in the organization, but Ray Knight's account suggests that it took some time to ensure all jobs were open to everyone and that black people were not confined to lower-paid posts such as cleaning.

The Xavier case, which was by no means unique, and only became known because of his obduracy in not accepting the refusal to transfer him, reflected the racist nature of the unions at the time. The three main unions represented different categories of workers and had long resisted amalgamation, which would have added to their strength. The most powerful was ASLEF – the Amalgamated Society of Locomotive Engineers and Firemen – which was exclusively, as its name suggests, for train drivers and, in the days of steam, firemen. The largest of the three was the National Union of Railwaymen (NUR – now the RMT, the national union of Rail, Maritime and Transport workers) which represented station and operating staff, such as guards, porters, despatchers and catering workers, as well as a few train drivers. Finally, the Transport Salaried Staffs' Association (TSSA) represented white-collar workers, principally ticket-office clerks but also lower levels of management. As well as having racist tendencies, borne of their conservative and defensive nature, the unions were also deeply sexist; they were reluctant to allow women to carry out what were seen as men's jobs, even though many of these tasks had been carried out by females during the two world wars. Indeed, after both wars the unions were actively opposed to women retaining their wartime roles, and British Railways was complicit in this regard by ensuring many jobs were only open to men. In fact, it was only in 1978 that the first female train driver, Karen Harrison, broke the mould.

ASLEF had a long tradition of being the most militant of the three unions, emboldened by its ability to shut down the railway simply by instructing its drivers to withhold their labour. ASLEF's militancy had led to a two-week strike in 1955 that brought most of the railway to a standstill. The ostensible cause was pay, but in reality it was more about the desire of ASLEF, which defined itself as a 'craft union', to retain wage differentials compared with other railworkers, who were considered to be less skilled.

For the most part, though, the unions were rather unambitious and did not always represent the interests of their members well. Their main approach was essentially defensive, as jobs were lost to the industry at the average rate of 10,000 per year from 1948, when British Railways was created, to its eventual dismemberment half a century later. Therefore, in every discussion with management, in every dispute and in every negotiation, the fundamental aim was always to preserve jobs, usually by trying to hold on to traditional, labour-intensive ways of working. For ASLEF, which saw itself as representing the crème de la crème of British Rail's workforce, there was the need to defend its interests to ensure that the status of its members was always recognized in negotiations. For all three unions, the annual pay bargaining round was the main event. In general, they did not ask for too much, but were always seeking to ensure their members' wages could at least keep pace with inflation.

At times they just about achieved their aim. The phase of industrial strife in the mid-1950s – the NUR called a strike just before ASLEF, but soon admitted defeat – followed a period in which wages had fallen in real terms. The unions subsequently managed to obtain real (above inflation) increases, largely because the government was worried about the impact of a strike on the economy, and that fear dictated industrial relations policy. Indeed, at the time, and right through to the 1980s, industrial disputes on the railway were often resolved by the intervention of the Cabinet or even the Prime Minister. These disputes were seen as matters of national importance that were front-page news, often for days at a time. Therefore, while the 1955 ASLEF strike gained little immediately for the union, as it accepted pretty much the same deal that had been originally offered, successive governments were anxious to avoid the chaos caused by railwaymen walking out. The government resorted to the usual way of postponing hard decisions: it launched an inquiry into how railway workers' pay compared with that in other industries, chaired by Claude Guillebaud, an economist and industrial relations expert.

Following a two-year investigation, the report confirmed that railway workers had fallen behind their peers in other industries, and the government consequently allowed BR to offer increases of 8–10 per cent across the board in order to restore pay parity for the railworkers. The context is that this was a period of full employment and labour shortages which were being only partly alleviated through immigration, and therefore the government was ready to accede to demands for higher pay to prevent too many railway workers leaving the industry. Beeching, perhaps surprisingly, allowed for rather generous settlements, too, but only in return for a clear commitment to increased productivity and a cutback on staffing levels. There was by then wider recognition that comparability needed to be the basis on which wage levels were set, but the fact that the railway lost money and was dependent on government subsidy meant it was always difficult for the managers in the rail industry to agree to more generous deals. This was despite the fact that the more forward-looking managers, like Beeching and most of his fellow directors on both the Transport Commission and, subsequently, at the British Railways Board, accepted that above-inflation awards were needed to retain staff.

Beeching was also right to emphasize the need to improve productivity, which had barely risen in terms of output per worker since the mid-1950s, and he was prepared to buy out jobs through generous redundancy payments, which meant the extra costs in the short term were more than matched by savings from increased efficiency in the longer term. The NUR, which stood to suffer most from job losses, was relatively sanguine about the reduction in numbers so long as its members, many of whom were very long serving, received a generous pay-off. The resulting high level of redundancy payments undoubtedly made it easier for British Railways to shed jobs, which was made possible by the rapid adoption of new technology.

The Beeching period and its aftermath was a time of rapid change. Philip Bagwell, the historian of the National Union of Railwaymen, put it starkly in 1982:

> In the third quarter of the twentieth century, British railways underwent a technical revolution whose range and significance was far greater than any changes that had taken place in the industry in the preceding hundred years. The effect of the introduction of new technologies on the working lives of railwaymen has often been traumatic.[8]

Indeed, in virtually every aspect of railway working there was rapid change which had an impact on workforce numbers. The old system of permanent-way gangs who looked after a section of track mostly at night from a small shed or depot by the side of the line was being replaced by machinery. Moreover, the widespread introduction of continuous welded rail – instead of short sections of rail attached to each other by fishplates (connecting sections of steel, usually with four holes for bolts, two for each rail) – meant far fewer P-way (permanent way) men were needed to maintain the track.

Signalling was the same. The numbers of signallers – signalmen, as they were known at the time, since it was an entirely male preserve – decreased by nearly three quarters between 1950 and 1979. This dramatic fall was partly a reflection of the fact that almost half the route mileage of the railway closed in that period, but more significantly the adoption of new technology allowed a major reduction in the number of signal boxes. The old manual boxes where the signallers pulled levers connected directly by metal bars to the points had to be very close to the section of line they controlled. This was no longer the case when the old semaphore signals were replaced by colour light systems and the points were controlled electrically rather than manually. Many of the remote boxes were scrapped, and by the end of the 1970s there were just 2,250 boxes left, compared with the approximately 10,000 in operation when the railway was nationalized in 1948. Just to give one example, the resignalling plan for the

London Midland Region in 1967 saw three modern control centres replace 175 manually operated boxes.

Freight wasn't spared big reductions in staff, either.
There was a very sharp and rapid decline in the number
of freight wagons, from 860,000 in 1962 to just 140,000 in
1979, and fewer than 10 per cent of the 5,000 freight stations and depots remained by then. This reflected the fact
that many old-fashioned wagons inherited by British Railways were rather belatedly being scrapped and BR was no
longer required to take on unprofitable small consignments at virtually every station on the network. As the
need to shunt goods wagons was reduced, since more
and more trains were in fixed formations and the 'sundries' traffic of small consignments was largely abandoned,
the number of people working on freight declined markedly, too. Again, the remaining work was increasingly
mechanized in ever smaller numbers of depots. As more
freight trains were fully braked throughout, the old system of having a guard's van at the back with a brakeman
was no longer necessary. However, it took many years of
negotiation with the unions for British Rail to be allowed
to operate these trains without a second person on board.

Station and platform staff didn't escape the drive for
improved productivity either. Station porters who carried
bags on their trolleys were disappearing rapidly as light-
weight trolleys were provided free to passengers (nowadays,
of course, most of us have wheelie bags, an invention
that surprisingly did not become widely used until the
turn of the twenty-first century). Even a manual task
like cleaning platforms was mechanized through the

introduction of an electric sweeping machine which could do the job far faster.

There was an occasional exception to this pattern of job losses as some tasks connected with the new technology, such as servicing the new overhead line equipment or looking after the increasingly sophisticated signalling systems, required additional staff. Overall, though, there was a shift towards mechanization and away from the labour-intensive heavy manual jobs that required brawn. At the same time, there was also the beginnings of computerization, which would sweep away a further tranche of jobs. British Railways was an early adopter of computers, first hiring one from J. Lyons, the catering company, as early as in 1958 in order to determine the shortest distance between all 4,000 local groups of freight terminals, a task which otherwise would have taken 250 'person years' to calculate manually. Later that year, BR bought its own computer to produce the payroll for 11,000 employees at its Swindon works.

Computer technology was further adopted by BR in the late 1950s for issuing tickets, but only at major stations. When a machine called the Multiprinter Major, which could print tickets to 1,188 destinations across the UK, was installed at the two main Cardiff stations in 1959, it was the largest system of its kind in Britain, according to the magazine *Transport Age*. Although this led to a reduction in the number of booking clerks, Bagwell suggests that, in terms of job threats, these new machines played a minor role in what was a far more extensive process of adopting new technology: 'From the point of view of the decline in demand for railway labour, the spread of the computer into railway offices was far more important than the extended use of Multiprinter machines.'⁹

The most effective early computerization took place in 1971, when British Rail courageously agreed to adopt a programme called TOPS (Total Operating Processing System!) which had been pioneered by the Southern Pacific Railroad in the USA to control all freight movements. Every wagon was logged into a system operated at the 152 main freight centres so that it was possible to precisely identify the location of each one – thereby ending the previous chaotic manual system, which was infamous because so many wagons simply disappeared, only to be found somewhere completely unexpected a few weeks later. No longer was the system reliant on railway workers scrawling the right information on bits of paper attached to the wagons which could fly off or become illegible in the rain. Remarkably, although aspects of TOPS have been modernized and supplanted, the system's core was still in use in the early 2020s.

As all these developments demonstrate, the Beeching era and its aftermath represented much more than the closure of a large part of the railway. Just as significantly, the culture of the entire rail industry changed irrevocably. Signallers, for example, had worked in small boxes to which they walked or cycled from their railway-provided home. They would spend long periods alone, brewing up their tea and eating the sandwiches they brought with them, waving to drivers in local trains or freight services whom they probably knew by name, and phoning their colleagues at the box up the line to alert them that a train was on its way. They would know intimately every inch of the sector of railway over which they had control and were familiar with the local P-way teams who maintained the track. All that disappeared in a very short period of time. Now the signallers worked in remote boxes, out of direct view of the track, in shift patterns that were less predictable, and with a far more diverse group of colleagues. They had to process much more information than before, which they would obtain through teleprinters and computers rather than from chats with fellow signallers. As Bagwell put it, 'the mental strain associated with the job is intensified at the same time as the physical strain is substantially lessened'.[10] In this new environment, there was little chance to brew up, and the hotplate had been replaced by an electric kettle. And rather than grabbing a sandwich between passing trains, the meal-break timing had to be strictly observed.

This was just one example of how the winds of change blew rapidly through the whole organization. The phasing out of steam marked the end of a career structure that had traditionally started with the filthy and exhausting job of engine cleaner. From there a man (it was always a man at the time) would gradually progress to become a 'passed cleaner' and then on to the backbreaking job of fireman, which could mean shovelling as much as six tons of coal into the furnace in a single shift. Only then could he ascend to the top of the career ladder and become a train driver. On the trains themselves, as we have seen, diesel and electric locomotives needed only one driver, instead of the two on the footplate of a steam engine, which by itself represented a major reduction in manpower. But even more significantly, the whole paraphernalia of maintaining steam engines, ensuring they were cleaned out and in steam ready for the day's work ahead was no longer needed.

Bagwell lists the various jobs from the staff census that disappeared in engine sheds as steam was phased out:

Engine cleaners and engine cleaners' chargemen
boiler washers and boiler washer chargemen
coalmen
fire-droppers
steamraisers
locomotive shunters
cranemen
shedmen
storekeepers
timekeepers
hydraulic and pumping-engine staff
and the water-softening plant attendants.[11]

In 1950, the sizeable army carrying out this truly amazing array of tasks consisted of 18,000 men and boys, all of whom would be made redundant with the ending of steam less than two decades later. They would be replaced by the far smaller number of fitters and technicians needed to keep the diesel engines going.

Many British Railways workshops closed in this period, and even in those that survived, the number of jobs decreased, as many tasks were no longer undertaken. Again, there was far less need for the strong men of the past who worked in the foundry or blacksmiths' shop, where only the most muscular with sufficient stamina could stand the heat. With the disappearance of steam, the trades of riveting, blacksmithing and coppersmithing became obsolete, and there was even little role for the skilled carpenters on BR's books as the use of plastic and light metals replaced wood. While some of those hired to undertake these new tasks were in lower grades than their more-skilled predecessors, many of the roles required knowledge of electronics, computing and project management, which ensured they were well rewarded in a competitive jobs market. Essentially, heavy engineering was being replaced by light engineering, which was less labour intensive.

In the 1960s alone, the workforce of British Railways was almost halved, from 514,500 to 273,000. The changes affected railway workers across the network, as in many respects it was the end of the old railway and many of its traditions. As well as the reduction in numbers, the long-established status of railworkers declined in this period. Bagwell describes this period as the end of an era, encapsulated in how the railway had changed during the Beeching regime and its aftermath: 'Some of the long-established characteristics of railway employment virtually disappeared. Through the nineteenth century and, indeed, until the outbreak of the Second World War, a job on the railway was highly prized since it was a job for life, while many other employments were insecure.' Bagwell argues

that it wasn't just the security of the job that had gone: 'It
was work which brought that sense of satisfaction which
accompanies participation in an essential public service.
There was a tradition of railway employment running in
families. Second- and even third-generation railwaymen
were numerous.' Now though, he argued, the rapid
changes in both the size of the railway workforce and the
type of jobs that were undertaken had destroyed much of
that job security and undermined the pride that many felt
was part of the reward of working in a relatively low-paid
industry. Bagwell contends that the new-found emphasis
on commercial viability rather than the maintenance of a
public service undermined the railway workers' self-
esteem. Moreover, as the 1960s and 1970s was mostly a
period of low unemployment, many people left the industry to take up jobs elsewhere that were better paid and
where they did not have to endure such unsocial hours,
greatly increasing railway staff turnover. No longer was it
seen as a job for life: 'Thousands of men and women did
not stay in the job long enough for them to develop a
sense of real involvement in the industry.'[12] In other
words, the world of Ray Knight's single men ensconced
for ever in a job that gave them security as well as clothed
and fed them was disappearing rapidly.

These fundamental changes to employment practices
had another side effect. Railwaymen had long used the
security of their position to take on other tasks in the
community, such as sitting on the bench as lay magis-
trates, being elected to the local council – Wigan NUR
branch in 1962 supplied twenty-nine local councillors

alone – or becoming active in the lower rungs of the Labour party, a possible path to Parliament. The shift pattern of the jobs, and the benign approach of management towards such activities, meant that many railway workers were pillars of their local communities. However, with the Beeching closures and radical job cuts, many towns were left with no railway service and these links were lost. Union activity was also hit. Many branches were forced to close, which resulted in remaining members travelling long distances to meetings. The loss of connection between communities and the railway was reflected in the increase in hooliganism on the network, and Bagwell notes how attacks on the railway and its staff became more frequent, observing that an 'unpleasant development of the later 1970s was the increase in cases of vandalism and of assaults on railway staff. For drivers, the greatest threat came from missiles thrown at the cab windscreens of passing trains from bridges crossing the railway.'[13] As a result, high resistant glass screens became the norm in locomotive cabs.

Not all of the traditional culture described by Bagwell was, however, benign. He notes that until the major changes to the organization in the 1980s, there had been a significant growth in the number of disciplinary and accident cases whose immediate cause was alcohol. According to management, the cause of a shocking 17 per cent of accidents – both fatal and less serious – was drunkenness. Indeed, many people who worked in the industry at the time recall that alcohol abuse was rife. Chris Randall, who joined BR in Croydon in the mid-1970s, was surprised by the extent of the drinking culture. It was not unknown, for example, for a train driver to down a quick pint or two during a turnaround at a terminus station like Victoria or Waterloo, whereas today there is zero tolerance of alcohol throughout the industry. Randall started his railway career in human resources, which was 'quite sober'. But when he briefly transferred to the stores department he was astonished that excessive alcohol consumption in working hours was accepted as normal: 'Every Friday the office would empty at about midday as people headed to the pub. Most would return to their desks about 3 p.m., but so little work was done they might as well have carried on drinking.' Randall recalls one middle manager coming back to his desk after a particularly heavy session and promptly falling asleep:

> Incredibly, people tiptoed around taking great care not to wake him. When the clock ticked round to 4.30 p.m., an underling gently nudged his slumbering boss to alert him that his train home was due in fifteen minutes. With that he rose unsteadily, grabbed his briefcase and exited stage left. It was remarkable, but far from unusual.

Strange as it seems today, it was almost impossible to sack people for such behaviour. The workforce was protected by a remarkably complex structure of committees and rules through which industrial relations were carried out. The main purpose was to avoid strikes, which it mostly did, but at the cost of a bureaucracy that was at times stifling. There were, though, a series of petty, local disputes, and a cumbersome and almost infinitely bureaucratic negotiating process that was a stumbling block to progress. It was a sea of acronyms mired in an unfathomable structure, all designed to ensure that any official strike action could only take place after prolonged arbitration procedures. There was the RSJC, the RSNC and the RSNT – the Railway Staff Joint Committee, National Council and National Tribunal respectively. The Joint Council, which had representatives of both unions and management, was the first port of call for complainants about management decisions, and then potentially the issue could go up two further levels, with the final decision being made by a tribunal which had been set up by a national agreement in 1956.

Whereas the disputes that went through this procedure were generally resolved by negotiation, there were still wildcat strikes in parts of the network where local industrial relations were fraught. While these instant strikes, organized without a formal ballot, could be triggered by minor issues, they often resulted in major disruption to services when other employees walked out in solidarity. When Gordon Pettitt, who joined the railway in 1950 and served in a wide variety of jobs, including running the Southern Region, became divisional manager at Liverpool Street in 1979, he found himself up against a group of workers who were all too ready to call a strike:

> When I arrived, there was a lot of disillusion among managers because of the frequency of strikes over petty issues. The whole machinery allowed the unions to escalate disputes so I realized we had to cut it off at the

beginning before things could escalate. The trouble was that the unions were very canny and all their people had been on courses to learn the rules and regs, while the managers were not as familiar with them as they had not been trained.

Strikes called at very short notice were often 'unofficial' – in other words, not sanctioned by the higher echelons of the union. Those taking part, however, knew there was unlikely to be any comeback and usually they didn't even lose wages as it was too difficult to work out precisely who had been involved and for how long they had been out.

Pettitt recalls how:

The guards at Southend would go on strike about some issue in the middle of the day, once the commuters had been delivered to London. Usually it would be some minor issue about rostering or anything. It was always the NUR, and the management would give in so that the commuters would be able to get home that evening.

Pettitt relates how one day a train went off without a guard by mistake and an off-duty supervisor took over the role. The next day, all the guards went out on strike and said this must never happen again. Pettitt stood firm. There was chaos on the concourse at Liverpool Street that evening as there were few trains, but the next day the union caved in: 'We had called their bluff. We never had trouble again. And surprisingly we did not get many complaints from the commuters. They understood.'[14]

Mark Walker, who worked for the NUR for most of the final two decades of the twentieth century, recalls there was a rule book with all the terms and conditions of service, some of which dated back to the lengthy and successful rail strike just after the First World War: 'The "Conditions of Service" was a kind of prayer book of all the agreements that had been recorded since 1919. The machinery of negotiation was your map and the combination of these things was supposed to enable you to resolve any dispute without the need for industrial action.'

The most trivial issues sometimes took the most time to resolve. Walker cites a case he was involved in where a railwayman – let's call him Charlie – was overlooked for a Sunday shift to replace a colleague who was sick. Charlie filed a grievance complaint because he was more senior than the man who was brought in to fill the shift and therefore should have had first refusal for the extra work. The dispute went to a 'sectional council', where management and unions tried to resolve disputes. But Charlie was not satisfied, went back to his branch, which then filed his complaint to the Railway Staff Joint Committee at BR headquarters. Walker takes up the story: 'If it was a matter of principle, it would then go to the National Council and even then, possibly, to the Tribunal. So the whole rail industry was built on this machinery of negotiation, and usually it worked, and consequently, mostly, there was relatively peaceful industrial relations.'

While this was byzantine, there was an upside according to Walker:

It was a two-way process as the employers could use this mechanism to suggest changes, just as the unions could submit claims to management. The introduction of dieselization, electrification, colour light signalling, mechanized track renewals and all sorts of other technological changes sweeping the industry could be negotiated through by making changes to the grading structure and pay rates.[15]

That explains why these radical and transformative changes had, until the 1980s, passed off without a major dispute with the unions. The leadership of the main union affected, the National Union of Railwaymen, largely accepted that if generous compensation payments were available, it would allow the changes without industrial action. ASLEF's members were less affected, apart from the single-manning issue. Initially, this had been the subject of a deal which satisfied most of the membership, but gradually the arrangement was eroded over time. There was a perception, too, among the union leadership that there was a genuine quid pro quo – there might in the end be fewer workers, but those that were left would be better remunerated.

This tacit agreement enabled a long period of relative industrial peace in the 1960s and 1970s, in stark contrast to BR's first decade, which had seen a seventeen-day walkout by ASLEF in 1955. The peace, however, could not last for ever. There was, in fact, underlying dissatisfaction on both sides. BR managers were constantly seeking ways of improving productivity to fund pay rises demanded by the unions who, in turn, were always looking for ways to catch up with the pay levels in comparable industries. The tension came to a head in 1980/81 thanks to a combination of several issues. First, the arrival of Mrs Thatcher as Prime Minister brought to an end the era of beer and sandwiches in Number Ten that had characterized Wilson's Labour government. Secondly, as we have seen, BR's chairman Peter Parker was trying to address the question of what the railway was for and rather inadvertently launched the process that culminated with the Serpell report (covered in Chapter 6). Thirdly, BR wanted to improve productivity and introduce new technology, but it was under pressure from a right-wing anti-union government while having to cope with mounting losses caused by the recession and high inflation that marked the early days of the Thatcher government. All these events combined to create a crisis in industrial relations on the railway and were the setting for the worst industrial dispute of the British Rail period.

After catching up with comparable industries in the 1960s, railway workers' pay declined relatively again, particularly in the period of very high inflation in the second half of the 1970s. A report by the Low Pay Unit in 1980 found that the average earnings of British Rail manual workers were lower relative to the national average than in the 1960s and had fallen markedly in real terms since 1975. These lower than inflation wage rises and pressure from British Rail managers to improve productivity brought the unions and management into a conflict which would result in a decisive swing in the balance of power towards the bosses – but only after a deeply bitter and protracted dispute.

The annual pay round was the immediate trigger for the dispute, but there were several other changes that had long been sought by the management: unstaffed or, as they were called, 'open stations', leaving tickets to be sold and checked on board trains; driver only operation, dispensing with the guard, which was made possible by the introduction of sliding doors; and flexible or variable rostering.

There was not much dispute over the 'open stations' concept, though in many ways this was an own goal as even quite large stations dispensed with ticket checks, which made fare evasion far easier. The 'driver only operation' (DOO) concept was seen by the unions as the thin end of the wedge, and it became a major source of dispute with the drivers later in the 1980s, when new electric trains were introduced on Bedford to London St Pancras services, now part of Thameslink, and which the headline writers invariably called 'the BedPan line'. However, it was flexible rostering that was to become the *casus belli* for BR's worst ever dispute, which resulted in numerous strike days and a fundamental breakdown in industrial relations. By and large, shift workers on the railway worked midnight to 8 a.m., or 8 a.m. to 4 p.m., or 4 p.m. to midnight. The BR board wanted to introduce flexible shifts of varying lengths from six to twelve hours, although in the face of pressure from the unions this was changed to seven to nine hours.

The dispute started with the rejection of a 7 per cent

pay increase in 1980, a year when inflation was hovering around 20 per cent. The offer was increased to 8 per cent plus 3 per cent to be granted later in the year, after negotiations at the newly created Advisory, Conciliation and Arbitration Service (ACAS). The BR board, however, infuriated the unions by initially refusing to pay the 3 per cent. The pay settlement was eventually agreed, with a proviso that the 3 per cent would be delivered on condition that the other issues in the dispute would be resolved later, at various specific dates in 1981 and 1982.

Negotiations were so protracted that they became embroiled in the 1982 pay round, at which point the NUR made a fateful tactical mistake by calling for an all-out indefinite strike starting on 28 June that year. The strike was principally over pay but also anger at British Rail's threat to impose new rosters without union agreement. BR decided on taking a strong line on the pay negotiations by insisting that any increase was contingent on productivity agreements, but behind the scenes there was another reason for its new, tougher stance. The Tory ministers now in Westminster were insistent that the money earmarked for BR's investment plans for new trains and upgraded lines would only be made available if productivity improved. Parker, who was generally sympathetic to the unions, felt the future of the railway was at stake because without the extra investment there would be no modernization and the industry would wither away and die.

Rather than using normal union channels, Parker, who often talked to train drivers and was in regular contact with frontline workers, took the unusual step of sending a letter by post to every individual NUR employee. His personally addressed missive started with the words: 'It is one minute to midnight. Make no mistake. If there is a strike, you may well have no job to come back to.'

It did not take much for the NUR to realize it was in no position to sustain a lengthy strike. Within a day, the action had to be abandoned as many employees in areas unaffected by the new rosters refused to join in, and the NUR leader, Sid Weighell, understood that the union had overreached itself. Weighell, a moderate, was playing a canny game, as the first day of the strike coincided with his union's annual general meeting, and he managed to garner enough support to ensure the delegates voted to return to work.

The NUR's acceptance of new rosters led to a split with the increasingly militant ASLEF, which stood firm against flexible rostering and promptly announced its own indefinite strike, starting on 4 July. This walkout effectively closed the railway. While ostensibly ASLEF was in a battle against BR management, launching the strike was also thumbing its nose at its rival union. The leaders of the two unions, NUR's Weighell and ASLEF's Ray Buckton, loathed each other. Buckton considered Weighell to be a sell-out for refusing to take joint action, while the NUR was ever ready to sign up ASLEF drivers who were unhappy with their union's militant stance. There was a memorable *Panorama* programme at the time which featured a discussion between the two union leaders and Peter Parker, and their mutual antagonism was such that Parker had to act as peacemaker between the two on air.

The split between the two main unions was made worse because they chose different issues over which to make last-ditch stands: the NUR over driver only operation, and ASLEF over flexible rostering. The respective union leaders were at loggerheads throughout this period, which complicated matters for British Rail. Weighell, whose moderate views were out of kilter with most members of his executive – a situation which later resulted in his removal from the top job, as a result of this dispute – had slammed the actions of ASLEF over flexible rostering: 'That mob ASLEF. We agreed to negotiate and then I'm told "the eight-hour day was sacrosanct because my grandfather had worked it". It was a farce.'[16] The antagonism, however, fell short of allowing his members to cross an ASLEF picket line.

For the initial two weeks of the strike, BR was only able to run about 10 per cent of its normal service, and after negotiations proved fruitless, Parker and his Board announced that, unless a solution were found, the whole railway would be closed on 21 July and all 23,000 strikers sacked. It was a bold move which was promoted strongly by the BR press officers, who emphasized in briefings to journalists that Parker was not bluffing. The newspaper coverage was universally hostile to ASLEF – apart from the mouthpiece of the Communist party, the *Morning Star* – with even the *Guardian* siding firmly with British Rail: 'Now it is ASLEF's turn to bluster its way to the brink of disaster. It is for the union and not BR to back

off by withdrawing the strike threat. ASLEF leaders
merit ritual humiliation for not bargaining in good faith –
flexible rostering will come what may.'[17] Parker abandoned
his normal emollient stance towards the workers and
raged, in the *Evening Standard*, about the union's position,
which he called 'pigheaded, anarchic, brutal, savage,
abrupt, suicidal, selfish, stupid, foolish [and] muddled'.[18]

It was not a propitious time for a strike over an obscure
issue that few of the public would understand. The Falklands War had just ended and the soldiers returning home
from the conflict were not impressed by the lack of trains.
One troopship arrived in Southampton with a huge ban-
ner on one side which said: 'Call off the rail strike or we'll
call in an airstrike'. Under pressure from the Trades Union
Congress – the umbrella organization for the unions –
which was hugely concerned at the split between the two
rail unions, and recognized the growing public hostility,
ASLEF ordered a return to work. The union claimed
later that the defeat was down to 'the biggest and most
professional public relations exercise a nationalised industry has ever known', but in reality the weakness of its
position had become all too apparent, and by early August
half its members were working on flexible rosters.[19] The
BR board had bared its teeth and the unions had suc-
cumbed, though there was a legacy of bitterness among
the workers that in some cases was to last many years.
Moreover, this messy dispute heightened the traditional
hostility between ASLEF and the NUR, making it far
more difficult for them to present a united front in future
industrial action. There was, though, no forgiving of

scabs, as Ray Knight remembers: 'One driver who went to work during the dispute ate his sandwiches on his own in the canteen for the next 20 years as no one ever talked to him.'[20]

British Rail's victory in this dispute, according to Gordon Pettitt, 'heralded a major turning point in industrial relations'.[21] However, the 'driver only operation' issue was not resolved and festered on for more than a year over the introduction of new electric trains on the Bedford to St Pancras (BedPan) line, which was being electrified. London Underground had pioneered driver only operation on the new Victoria Line, which opened in 1968 – in fact, the trains were computer controlled and therefore the main function of the 'driver' was to operate the doors – but British Rail had been frightened to go down that path because of union opposition. However, permission to buy the new trains for the BedPan line had been granted by the government only on condition that operational savings could be made, not least because fares income, hit by the recession, was falling at the time. British Rail worked out that DOO would reduce running costs by 30 per cent and therefore was not prepared to compromise. Ironically, given the union's intransigence, Chris Green, who later went on to run Network South-East, recalls that 'a second motivating factor for introducing DOO was that recruiting sufficient numbers of guards was becoming more difficult in the South-East because higher-paid jobs with better working conditions and more sociable hours could easily be found at places such as Gatwick Airport'.[22] As a result, trains were frequently cancelled as no guard was available to staff them. To ensure safety, drivers controlled the doors and could communicate with passengers and signallers from the cab, while alarms and radios were installed in the event of driver incapacitation.

None of this satisfied the drivers' union. ASLEF blocked the arrival of the new trains, leaving them in the sidings in full view of passengers crammed into old uncomfortable stock, and refused to operate them as the dispute over safety and job protection continued well into 1983. Eventually, ASLEF was bought off with special driver-only productivity payments and the retention of guards who would carry out ticket-checking duties until natural wastage took its course, and there would be no pay cuts or compulsory redundancies. The full service on the line started in October 1983, seventeen months after the trains had been first available.

DOO was gradually brought in on suburban trains as new stock was introduced, but the concept has remained controversial, and in recent years, after privatization, there has been a series of disputes with the RMT (the successor to the NUR) over who controls the opening and closing of the doors – the driver or the guard. In an ironic twist, ASLEF has largely accepted the concept of DOO and has stayed out of these rows.

It is difficult to exaggerate the impact that a big industrial dispute in a major sector like the railway had in the 1980s. Strikes were front-page news, and every twist and turn in negotiations was covered by teams of industrial reporters whose sole job was writing about such disputes (when the *Independent*, on which I worked, was launched in 1986, it had three industrial staff – the largest specialist reporting team other than politics). The right-wing press highlighted the high pay of union officials, the extreme left-wing policies of some members and the 'wrecking' tactics they used. Politicians on both sides would routinely become involved, and the disputes would be raised frequently in Parliament. It all added to a febrile atmosphere redolent of a long-forgotten age.

Wildcat strikes and minor disputes were by no means unique to British Rail at the time as union militancy, fuelled by rampant inflation, was sweeping through the country. British industry remained rife with petty restrictive practices, which were protected by strong union activity as illustrated in sitcoms like *The Rag Trade*, a 1960s comedy set in a clothing factory with a very militant trade union. Bunking off at the end of the working week was so common that few people would ever bother to try to telephone a company after lunch on Fridays.

Chris Randall points out that this whole pattern of work at British Rail changed in the mid-1980s: 'There was a complete transformation of the culture. Not just about drinking, but the whole expectation of what working in the railway meant. There was a feeling that in safety critical work, you had to be whiter than white.'[23] He suggests that this new culture came from the top as managers in the public sector became more concerned with efficiency. But the hardline anti-union legislation brought in by Mrs Thatcher also contributed to the change in atmosphere on the shop floor. Wildcat strikes and solidarity action became more difficult, and largely illegal, weakening the hand of the unions. The flexible-rostering dispute was an early victory against the unions, but the real turning point was the 1984 miners' strike, which showed that even a strong, well-organized union could ultimately be defeated.

BR's eventual triumph in these epic industrial disputes marked a major shift in the organization, even if the victories were not as decisive as the managers would have liked. The 1980s would see BR change more fundamentally than in the previous thirty years as its structure and focus were transformed by a dynamic new leader, Robert Reid, under constant pressure from a government hostile to the railway. As part of these changes, British Rail was forced to sell off several parts of its business in what became a precursor to the full privatization of the organization a decade later.

9

Beginning the Break-Up

Despite her disdain for the railway, Margaret Thatcher was reluctant to privatize it. She realized the process would be fraught with difficulties, given the continued need for public subsidy, and she thought privatizing utilities and other state-owned companies such as the Trustee Savings Bank presented better opportunities. The decline in passenger journeys to 600 million in the economic recession of 1982, the lowest ever post-war number before the pandemic of 2020, suggested that the industry was in terminal decline. With little sign of recovery, selling such a declining industry would hardly have been an attractive proposition. However, Thatcher did press for BR's motley collection of subsidiaries to be privatized, regarding them as peripheral and beyond the normal remit of a nationalized business.

Although her government was responsible for privatizing many public enterprises, notably gas, electricity and water, selling the railway was not on the agenda in the 1980s, even though the idea had originally been mooted in Conservative party circles as early as the 1960s. The only

serious attempt was made when Thatcher's political soul-
mate Nicholas Ridley became Transport Secretary after
the Conservatives' 1983 landslide victory. After Ridley had
pushed through the privatization and deregulation of bus
services outside London, he suggested to Thatcher in
1986 that the railway should be next. He asked the Department of Transport to provide a series of options for how
the railway could be broken up and sold, and he told Mrs
Thatcher that he was keen to test the market. However,
the bus sale had gone badly, with private operators cherry-
picking popular routes and flooding them with buses,
while abandoning poorly used ones which had lost their
subsidy. This fiasco hardened the Prime Minister's opposition to rail privatization, particularly as she believed
'chuffer' trains were dear to the hearts of British people.

Therefore, when Ridley met her at Number Ten to
enlist her support for rail privatization, he was given short
shrift. She did not believe that disposing of a heavily
loss-making industry was feasible and felt – with great
prescience, as it turned out – that any sale would be far
more complicated than disposing of the utilities. According to a British Railways Board member, 'she said "railway
privatisation will be the Waterloo of this government.
Please never mention the railways to me again."'[1]

However, this did not stop her from actively promoting the sale of the various subsidiaries that British Railways
had haphazardly acquired at nationalization. Soon the
organization's hotels, ships, engineering workshops and
sundry businesses were being earmarked for disposal.
The Tories had made privatization a key element in their

1983 election manifesto and their overwhelming victory gave the policy added impetus.

Hotels were the first to go. British Railways had inherited a remarkable portfolio of hotels at nationalization, including several which had first opened their doors in the mid-nineteenth century. Given the natural relationship between travel and the need for accommodation, it could be argued that hotels and railways went together as closely as fish and chips. From modest beginnings, many of these long-established station hotels had over time been transformed into sumptuous five-star establishments. After the Second World War, however, a few had fallen into decline, partly because journey times had been cut, making it less likely that travellers would require an overnight stay. BR's subsidiary, British Transport Hotels, was one of the largest hotel chains in the country, but it was constrained by Treasury interference, which prevented investment in what was a declining but potentially very lucrative asset. In total, BTH owned twenty-nine hotels, most sited next to major railway stations, and some with their own world-class golf courses, including Gleneagles in Scotland. The Grosvenor, next to Victoria station in London, had been successfully restored in 1980 – which, as Terry Gourvish, BR's business biographer, argues, 'indicated what could be done with the right level of support'.[2] However, allowing a state-owned organization like BR to operate a business commercially ran contrary to Tory ideology. Public-sector enterprise was regarded by the Thatcher government as a form of cheating; state-owned firms should not be allowed to enjoy all the advantages of public ownership while competing with commercial rivals. To undermine BR's case for retaining its hotel business, a minor scandal attracted media attention: BTH had built up huge wine stocks, valued at more than £5 million in 1980 (a stunning £22 million in 2021 money), and even strenuous efforts to empty its cellars over the next couple of years managed to reduce that only by around £2 million.

Instead of allowing BTH to invest in its hotels to improve their profitability, the government sought buyers either for the whole group or for individual sites. A group of three Scottish hotels, including Gleneagles, was sold off first; but rather than permitting BR to try to maximize its asset through the gradual release of further properties, the government tried to force a quick sale, which resulted in the business being undervalued. BTH published a three-year plan to develop the best nineteen hotels in its portfolio in order to increase their value for the proposed sale. This was ruled out by ministers and instead, after largely unsuccessful attempts to create a series of smaller packages, the remaining twenty-three were sold in November 1982, with total proceeds of a mere £60 million. This was far less than would have been obtained had BTH been allowed to improve its stock and ride out the economic downturn of the early 1980s before selling. This set a pattern for future sales: 'expediency' was the watchword, irrespective of whether this would reduce the price, and the key was to get rid of assets come what may.

BR's ships and associated ports were next to go. They, too, were leftovers from the enterprising activity of Britain's original railway companies, which operated ferries – principally across the English Channel – and owned docks which linked in with the rail network. British Railways had carried on the tradition of operating ferries, having taken over the large fleet bequeathed by the 'Big Four' railway companies at nationalization. It ran services through its Shipping and International Division, but in 1979, prior to Margaret Thatcher's first general election victory, they were packaged and rebranded as Sealink UK Ltd. The flagship Dover to Calais route was highly profitable and Sealink's main rival, Townsend Thoresen, competed aggressively, both through a price war and by trying to run its ships faster than Sealink. The policy contributed to the *Herald of Free Enterprise* disaster in March 1987, which cost 193 lives after the Townsend Thoresen ferry left the Belgian port of Zeebrugge with its bow doors open as it was in such haste to get going in order to keep to time.

Sealink had a monopoly on the key market of people who used the ferries to connect with trains at ports, and vice versa. Although roll-on, roll-off car ferries were gradually attracting people away from this modern version of the traditional Channel packet, the service was still used sufficiently for BR's Southern Region to provide connections, with up to three fourteen-car trains laid on to meet each sailing. These would then run non-stop to London Victoria, the *Golden Arrow* or *Flèche d'Or* (on which I travelled frequently as a child and enjoyed the best high teas I ever ate) taking just six hours between London and Paris.

BR also created and ran Hoverspeed, which owned two hovercrafts capable of carrying cars across the

Channel as well as four passenger-only ones. For a time, this was a more popular – and quicker – way of getting to France than the ferries, though the ride tended to be bumpy in even mildly choppy seas, with sick bags always being provided, and the service was unreliable as it could not operate in very stormy seas. Hoverspeed was the first part of BR's shipping business to be put up for sale, and it was bought in February 1984 for a nominal sum by its own managers, who later sold it back to Sealink after it, too, was privatized.

Although the incoming Tory government had initially denied that it intended selling Sealink, the ferry business was bought by Sea Containers in July 1984 for £66 million, well short of the book value of £108 million shown in BR's accounts. The sale of BR's subsidiaries – and subsequent privatizations in the wider economy – was driven by ideology. The need to get maximum value for taxpayers – or, indeed, any consideration for passengers – was secondary. The railway, which had over many decades developed short sea routes as part of a very successful integrated transport system, lost these connections, which, in addition to the French and Belgian Channel ports, included links to both sides of the Irish border and the Isle of Wight.

Other businesses, including a laundry servicing BTH hotels, an advertising agency, Gold Star Holidays and the steam-operated Vale of Rheidol railway, were quickly disposed off in this period. Of course, only profitable businesses were put up for sale. BR had to keep its loss-making subsidiaries, causing a double whammy to its accounts, as the profits from the successful concerns had helped cover the deficits from the loss-makers.

The sale of BR's catering division, Travellers Fare, is a perfect example of the Thatcher government's determination to ensure nothing stood in the way of selling off profitable parts of the railway. Belying the image of the stale, unappetizing BR sandwich that survives today – but which was an urban myth perpetrated by stand-up comics – Travellers Fare had developed a far more appealing range of food, and had even pioneered the shrink-wrapped sandwich thanks to the intervention of Prue Leith, who became a British Railways Board member in 1977. BR also developed a series of successful brands such as Casey Jones, Upper Crust and Quicksnack, which reflected its innovative approach, as increasingly passengers chose to buy their snacks and meals at stations rather than use the on-train service. When the BR board invited offers for these catering outlets, in-house Travellers Fare was the successful bidder for more than two thirds of the near 100 sites. As a result, the government called a halt to the process and forced an outright sale, to prevent further embarrassment for its favoured private sector.

In contrast, the heavily loss-making on-board catering service provided on InterCity trains was retained. Attempts to turn this business around, through the involvement of the huge private catering company Trusthouse Forte, went disastrously wrong. In 1986, following the sale of Travellers Fare, InterCity's newly formed catering business (InterCity On Board Services, or

ICOBS) created a trendy-sounding brand, Cuisine 2000. Initially there was progress, with a much-improved range of sandwiches developed by the celebrity food writer Clement Freud (another unfortunate BR association with a child abuser). But Trusthouse Forte's now largely discredited 'cook-chill' method, which was becoming fashionable at the time, proved totally unsuitable for the extremely hot on-board kitchens, where the food deteriorated before serving. Stephen Poole, a former railwayman who worked as a manager for InterCity's catering service at the time, explained in his book *Inside British Rail* just how disastrous this proved to be, both for staff and passengers: 'The effect on the morale of the on-board chefs of having to unpack and dish up food prepared by someone else was predictably bad, while the gross inefficiencies, in terms of portion sizes, wrong deliveries and missing equipment meant the whole system slid into disrepute.'[3] It was not the much-maligned sandwiches, therefore, that should be remembered as British Rail's great catering disaster, but the melting meals on board InterCity trains. Far from being able to make the service break even, as BR had hoped, losses mounted, and Trusthouse Forte was sent packing in 1990. InterCity staff, however, were ordered to carry the can for all the failings and the losses, as, according to Poole, 'it would not have been politically acceptable at the time for staff of a state-owned industry to criticise a private company'.[4]

In fact, on-board catering services across the world are almost impossible to run profitably. They are intended as loss leaders to attract people to travel by train. As a national brand, InterCity was required to provide catering services across its business, including little-used off-peak trains which inevitably lost money as there was little demand for catering. Adding to its troubles, the arrangement with Trusthouse Forte had enabled corruption on a grand scale. One manager was dismissed for loading his car boot full of InterCity wine; another was practising the old trick of buying cheap drinks from the supermarket and selling them at InterCity's premium prices, a misdemeanour that only came to light after he died of a heart attack at work. According to Poole, 'The whole episode was extremely sordid and in all my railway experience I never came across dishonesty and incompetence at management level to the extent I did with InterCity On Board Services during the Cuisine 2000 era.'[5]

The most significant privatization by far was the sale of the railway workshops. For 140 years, BR and its forerunners had run an integrated railway, undertaking every aspect of train service provision from maintaining the fleet and the permanent way to running trains and selling tickets. Engineering amounted to about a quarter of BR's costs and there had long been dissatisfaction in government circles about the efficiency of this integrated structure. Until the 1955 Modernisation Plan, which resulted in the introduction of a wide array of diesel locomotives constructed by various engineering companies, British Rail had built all its own locomotives and carriages. Production, however, was increasingly being contracted out to private manufacturers, and BR produced its last diesel locomotive in 1987 at Doncaster. The workshops, though, which carried out maintenance – including essential work such as stripping down and rebuilding locomotives – remained entirely in-house until 1983, although their number was cut dramatically. The Modernisation Plan resulted in the number of workshops being reduced from thirty-two to twenty by the mid-1960s, with the loss of about a third of the 50,000-strong workforce. Of course, like other parts of BR, workshops had been banned by the government from tendering for private contracts, and that had hampered their productivity as they had large workforces who were idle for periods when the workload was light.

Already, in 1970, concerns about productivity had led to the restructuring of BR's massive Mechanical and Electrical Engineering Department, resulting in the creation of British Railways Engineering Ltd, or BREL as it was universally known. The privatization process began, like that of many local authority functions at the time, with what was known as 'compulsory competitive tendering'. In other words, the publicly owned body was required to seek bids for its services and products from both public and private companies in order to stimulate competition. Of course there was no guarantee that the private firms would necessarily win all the bids, but it was a way of starting the process of shifting work from the public to the private sector. In the first four years, about half of the orders for both passenger coaches and freight wagons were won by private rivals to BR, which was effectively a backdoor privatization.

Having softened up the unions through these initial

disposals, the government decided to force BR into a full-scale sale of the workshops. By 1982, several of the remaining twenty workshops were earmarked for closure, notably the massive Swindon works, which had built most of the Great Western locomotives since its creation in 1843. However, the need to restructure BR's Engineering Department and to prepare all the documentation for the sale delayed the closure programme. To package up the workshops for privatization, the British Railways Board had to split BREL into two groups – the Maintenance Group, which was to remain with BR until the privatization of the entire industry in the mid-1990s, and the New Build and Repair Group centred around the workshops at Crewe, Derby, York and Horwich.

The large Doncaster workshop was sold separately to a management buyout team, RFS Industries, while the Horwich Foundry workshop was closed and subsequently sold to Parkfield Group, which demolished the buildings and turned the site into an industrial park. The remaining workshops were then offered for sale as a group in the autumn of 1987. It was a key moment in rail history. As Gourvish puts it, 'In October 1987, the British Railways Board effectively ended 140 years of backward integration by deciding that ownership of BREL was not central to its core activities; continued ownership, it was argued, would inhibit the development of competitive sourcing.'[6] The purpose behind the sale of the workshops was, therefore, rather different to the other sell-offs as it marked the start of breaking up the core functions of the railway. While some Tory ministers may well have been aware of the significance of the sale as part of a much wider agenda, the publicly stated motive was to improve the efficiency of BR engineering. The BR board, under pressure from the Transport Secretary, Paul Channon, was keen for a quick sale, but further complex preparatory work meant a prospectus could not be produced until August 1988.

When the workshops were finally put up for sale, there was little private-sector interest. The business was not seen as an attractive proposition, despite a turnover of £300 million, because of its total dependence on British Rail for work and the consequent limited potential for growth. As a result, there were only two bids: one from a management and employee buyout team supported by Trafalgar House, a large conglomerate; the other from GEC (the General Electric Company) in partnership with Alsthom, France's principal train manufacturer. The negotiations were extremely delicate, with both bidders at times threatening to pull out. Eventually, after a tortuous process, the management-buyout team working with Trafalgar House won the day, with a bid of just £13.6 million for a business that on paper was worth £80 million. However, this valuation was affected by several complexities and the process turned out to be a very messy affair, first with an investigation from the European Commission over a £64 million loan that had been written off, and then, after the sale, with a lawsuit involving a claim against British Rail over product quality and delivery of a fleet of railcars. That claim was only settled (for £65 million) after ABB, a Swedish–Swiss engineering consortium, bought the company in 1992.

While the disposal of the workshops had the greatest impact on BR's structure and operations, by far the most lucrative privatization of BR's assets was the sale of surplus property. In 1979, 15 per cent of British Rail's 200,000 acres were reckoned to be non-operational and were transferred to a separate subsidiary, the British Rail Property Board. Although this property generated considerable income from rentals, the new emphasis on selling public assets led to an extensive and highly lucrative programme of disposals of land deemed surplus to requirements. The amounts received for land, which included former goods yards and depots in sought-after locations near stations, dwarfed the receipts from all the other disposals. In the first two years of the 1980s, the sales netted £111 million, and that rose to a staggering £319 million in the 1989/90 financial year alone. As the economy recovered, the potential for developments at existing stations grew; and after the disaster of Euston, which was demolished in 1962 amid huge protests, BR realized that working with developers to revamp stations, and using the air above them for expansion with office blocks, would provide much-needed capital as well as resulting in a greatly improved environment for passengers. In a rare concession by the government, in 1962 British Railways was granted the freedom to develop its holdings on a commercial basis. BR was slow to realize the potential value of this concession, but in the 1980s it was to prove increasingly lucrative. London's Victoria, Charing Cross and Fenchurch Street stations were all improved; and outside the capital, numerous stations, such as Hull, Aberdeen and Preston, benefitted from successful developments that boosted the local economies as well as BR's finances.

The best and most profitable of these 1980s schemes was the redevelopment of Liverpool Street station in London, which included the closure and demolition of neighbouring Broad Street. Liverpool Street, which had been expanded haphazardly since its opening in 1874, was a mess, with a crammed concourse and a zigzag of a walkway connecting the platforms. Its redevelopment provided a blueprint for the successful cooperation of the public and private sectors, and notably the design was provided by Nick Derbyshire, BR's in-house architect, which ensured that passenger needs determined much of what is widely regarded as a superb public space. As I wrote in *Cathedrals of Steam*, 'The finest historic features were retained, even if they were at times moved, and the main platform-level concourse is both a coherent whole and easily accessible from the street through a series of escalators and lifts.'[7]

Selling profitable businesses helped BR's balance sheet and provided much-needed funds for investment. But there was, of course, the loss of the revenue which had contributed to BR's operating expenses. While the gross receipts from these sales certainly helped support British Rail's investment programme, they were not a game changer. The sales during the 1980s brought in just under £1.4 billion, spread over the decade, of which all but around £200 million came from property sales. Useful, but hardly enough to plug the hole in BR's finances. Moreover, as we have seen, the proceeds invariably failed

The original Euston station building, including the famous propylaeum (known as the Doric arch), was demolished in 1962.

Glossy promotional art was produced to champion the modernity of the new airport-style building that replaced the Victorian original.

The original station was regarded as a precious part of Britain's railway heritage and its bulldozing was criticized by John Betjeman. He subsequently successfully campaigned against British Rail's attempt to demolish its near neighbour, St Pancras.

The now familiar Euston station was officially opened by the Queen in autumn 1968. It was later described in *The Times* as 'one of the nastiest concrete boxes in London'.

The modernization of British Rail involved some traditional station buildings being replaced with very basic prefabricated structures, using a system developed for local authorities known as CLASP.

New rolling stock, such as this VEP commuter train (*right*), and high-powered diesel locomotives, like this Deltic (*below*), enabled BR to offer faster and more reliable services.

With the introduction of modern trains that were far more comfortable and much cleaner thanks to the demise of steam in the 1970s, British Rail placed great emphasis on attracting people away from their cars. This was backed up by advertising which used catchy slogans that rapidly became popular with the general public.

Let the train take the strain!

The technologically pioneering Advanced Passenger Train (APT), which used a tilting mechanism to allow the train to go faster on the many bends of Britain's rail network, was introduced with great fanfare in December 1981. Unfortunately, it proved to be a failure as the technology was unreliable, and only prototypes were ever produced.

The failure of the APT paved the way for the large-scale adoption of the High Speed Train 125, which became the workhorse of its InterCity services for more than 40 years, with some still running on the network in 2022.

Take your car off the road

Relax with Motorail. The all-sightseeing, drinking, eating, talking, reading, sleeping start to your motoring holiday.

Motorail

Brochures from principal British Rail stations or Appointed Travel Agents

British Rail provided a wide variety of services beyond simple train travel, such as the very successful Motorail that enabled people to put their car on the train and travel overnight on journeys linking London with Cornwall or Scotland.

In the 1980s, BR was forced to sell off its hotels, such as this one at Gleneagles, which it had inherited from its predecessors.

The ferry and hovercraft services to the continent that BR operated under the brand Sealink included the SR.N4, the biggest hovercraft ever put into commercial service.

The sleeper services linking the capital with Scotland and Cornwall survived the rationalization of the 1980s and the privatization of the 1990s, and remain popular today.

Travel in your pyjamas

1st Class Sleeper

2nd Class Sleeper

Shaver point

Room service

Nightcap

Arrive refreshed having gained a day

Inter-City Sleepers make the going easy

This coal train, leaving empty from Fiddler's Ferry power station in Cheshire, was one of Beeching's money-saving innovations and was known as a 'merry-go-round' as the wagons could be loaded and unloaded without the train having to stop.

The InterCity brand, here shown on electric locomotives at Euston, quickly became widely known and was instrumental in attracting passengers back to rail.

Both trains and stations were rebranded in the colours of Network SouthEast, which was responsible for all commuter services operating to and from London.

The Pacer trains were introduced widely across the Provincial (later Regional) Railways network. They provided little comfort for passengers as the interior was based on a bus design, but transformed the economics of many routes by greatly reducing costs and helped avoid further closures.

THE JOURNEY FILLERS

from the 125 train buffet
≥ Travellers-Fare

Bill of Fare

Honeydew Melon	3/6
Egg Mayonnaise	2/6
Clear Vegetable Soup	2/-
Dover Sole Meuniere	17/-
Grilled Gammon Steak Hawaiian	16/-
Chicken Casserole Chasseur	16/-
Served with:	
Green Peas Creamed Spinach	
Sauté and New Potatoes	
Cold Brisket and Ham, Mixed Salads	16/-
Strawberry Sponge Flan Chantilly	3/-
Welsh Rarebit	3/-
Selected Cheeses and Biscuits	3/-
Coffee	1/9
Bread Basket of White and Hovis Rolls	
Ryvita and Butter	

This Menu is subject to alteration without notice.
Please ask for a bill and retain it

In case of difficulty please call for the Chief Steward. Failing satisfaction please write to the Field Manager, British Rail Catering (Restaurant Cars) King's Cross Station, N.1
KX/A

British Rail's catering became, quite unfairly, the butt of jokes. In fact it was something of an industry leader, introducing sandwiches in airtight packaging to preserve their freshness and taking advice from renowned experts such as Prue Leith.

A sample onboard menu offered by British Rail in the late sixties.

Quality fresh food was also cooked on the trains as part of British Rail's effort to try to attract greater numbers of business passengers.

The privatization of BR's catering services was commemorated with a special sandwich in a reference to an oft-made and misplaced criticism of BR's food offering.

The privatization of BR was much derided in the press, which picked up on the fact that it was opposed by large sections of the public.

to match, let alone exceed, the book value and therefore represented a theoretical loss. The shortfall on BREL compared with the valuation in the BR accounts may have been the most significant at £75 million, but neither of the workshops sold separately, Doncaster and Horwich, achieved even half their book value. In many cases, too, the expenses involved in the process significantly reduced the profits from the sales. This was the start of the period when the use of consultants and other contracted professionals became commonplace, a phenomenon that greatly added to the costs of seeing through these deals. For example, the sale of the modest Vale of Rheidol steam railway grossed £306,000, but the advisers, Lazard, snaffled £140,000 of it. A further £73,000 went as contributions to repairs of both the stock and the permanent way; and another £10,000 as compensation to the management buyout team, who complained of unfair treatment. Therefore, if management time in dealing with the sale were costed in, simply giving the line away would probably have been a cheaper option. While that may have been the most extreme example, there were similar stories resulting from numerous other deals.

The most important outcome of these sales was not the money they brought in, but the way they made privatization acceptable. Each disposal, in its way, was a test of how far it was possible to shift the boundary between the public and private sectors. The use of consultants, too, was insidious, and damaging to the ability of British Rail to adapt to changing circumstances. As Peter Rayner, a manager with BR for more than forty years, wrote, this

was the start of moving away from a self-sufficient organization: 'All through the 1980s, at the direct wish of a
succession of transport ministers, the railway was encouraged to employ consultants rather than step its own young
men and women up the ladder and replace them by
recruitment from below.'[8] As a result, expenditure on
consultancy quadrupled during that decade.

Fortunately, British Rail retained its graduate training
scheme, which for decades had been remarkably successful in creating a core team with the skills to run the railway.
Those who benefitted from the scheme universally speak
well of it, as it provided a grounding in all aspects of railway operations. Chris Green, who entered the scheme in
the mid-1960s, says it was a vital way of creating a team
and a collegiate ethos:

> You tried jobs around the network. It was career man-
> aged so you could be in a parcels office one month and
> then working in a ticket office the next one. The second
> Beeching report was actually positive and lots was
> happening with the end of steam, the West Coast elec-
> trification and the TGV in France, all of which suggested
> the railway indeed had a future.[9]

The advantage of having such a training scheme, which
actually had been inherited from the London & North
Eastern Railway, one of the old Big Four, was that the
graduates learnt about the railway on the ground, an
experience which developed a cohort of talented railway
managers, many of whom knew and trusted each other.
Chris Austin, who joined in 1967, explained in an

interview more than fifty years later: 'We still meet up, we still know each other.'[10] This group of skilled and talented people not only helped improve BR immeasurably in its final decade but, ironically, had the flexibility and adaptability to restructure the railway and package it up for privatization in the space of one Parliament.

First, though, BR was undergoing the most radical and successful transformation of its organization and structure under the imaginative leadership of Bob Reid. Full-scale privatization was not on the agenda in the 1980s, but in one of those strange twists of history, the reorganization of BR and, even more ironically, the development of a brilliant team of managers through its training scheme, not only created an efficient state-owned railway, but at the same time smoothed the way for privatization.

10

The Task Ahead

Of all British Railways' eight chairmen, Peter Parker would be on the podium for the top three, and likely to get the silver medal; but there is no doubt that his successor, Robert Reid (normally known as Bob, but I use Robert in order to differentiate him from his successor, who had the same name), would get the gold, particularly if the judges were BR managers. Reid, who took over in 1983, built on Parker's good work with a drive and single-mindedness that would transform British Rail and improve virtually every aspect of the organization.

Parker was unfortunate because he spent nearly all his time as chairman fighting plans for further dramatic closures, such as those set out by Serpell, as well as attempts to rein back on investment plans. Indeed, it was the fear of a drip feed of minor cuts, and his opposition to them, that led to his coining the memorable phrase, 'the crumbling edge of quality'. Parker's communication skills and inexhaustible energy had helped BR resist the most damaging of the cuts. Even though he was not a railwayman, unlike Robert Reid, he had quickly grasped the importance

of railway culture and this was to be invaluable in eventually winning the industrial dispute over flexible rostering.

Before Parker stepped down, he had a last tiger to kill,
albeit one that should have never been anything more than
a paper one. Somehow, the strange notion of converting
railways into roads for buses, and even possibly lorries, had
at various times during the history of BR attracted considerable interest within government circles. The idea had first
been put forward in the mid-1950s by an eccentric briga-
dier, Thomas Lloyd, who also believed that all the country's
railways could be replaced by precisely 3,433 buses waiting
at stations until they were full. Despite the lunacy and
impracticality of the idea, funding from the roads lobby
and the readiness of a few academics and policymakers to
promote the concept meant it remained an issue for discussion and press coverage for three decades. Lloyd and
another ex-soldier, Angus Dalgleish (only a major), formed
the Railway Conversion League, which produced a series
of densely argued pamphlets providing carefully worked-
out examples of railway lines that could be converted into
roads. These lengthy reports set out in great detail how it
would save vast amounts of money 'wasted on the railways'. They airily dismissed any doubts about the ability
of tunnels to accommodate road traffic, suggesting that
coaches, in particular, would be able to speed along
these dedicated highways. Much as today's media laps
up outlandish notions of congestion-busting and safety-
enhancing new forms of transport, such as driverless cars,
delivery by drone and hyperloops, coverage of the Conversion League was remarkably uncritical.

A failure to ask searching questions of its promoters resulted in the concept being picked up by a handful of serious and influential players. In particular, Peter Hall, a media-savvy professor of geography at Reading University, who later became a nationally respected authority on planning, expressed support for the concept. In 1975, soon after Labour had returned to government, Hall and a fellow academic were commissioned by the Department of the Environment to carry out an examination of converting six railway lines in the East of England. Their report, published in 1976, assessed the cost of transforming each of these lines, but the figures were so dubious that the department refused to publish the paper, and Hall, who later, oddly, became a fan of high-speed rail, had to seek charitable funding to pay for its publication. Richard Marsh, BR's chairman at the time, was amusingly dismissive:

> This was a fatuous idea. The buses would need to run very close together at high speeds to provide capacity equal to that of a train. After they had been running for a few months, they would be so close together they could be linked and then all one would have to do would be to remove the drivers apart from the front one and hey presto, at vast public expense, Reading University would have reinvented the train.[1]

Even then the idea refused to die. When Mrs Thatcher swept to power in 1979, the madcap scheme found support from one of her favourite advisers, Alfred Sherman. He was an important figure in the Tory party at the time

since he, along with Sir Keith Joseph, had founded the
influential right-wing think tank the Centre for Policy
Studies, which produced a series of reports that informed
many of the most radical policies in the Thatcher years.
At the height of his influence, in September 1980, Sherman wrote a paper advocating widespread replacement
of rail tracks with roads and set out the details in a lengthy
memo to Thatcher. He called rail 'an anachronism', which
was 'run simply to keep Sidney Weighel [*sic* – he meant
Weighell, the leader of the NUR] ... happy', and suggested that 'if we convert rail to road, we can have the
best road system in the world, and the best system of
public transport (first-class bus-coaches with WCs,
springing etc) as well as utility ones with much lower petrol costs'.[2] Sherman also saw conversion as a way of
pushing through privatization, since the new roads would
be tolled and financially self-sufficient.

Sherman instigated a research project by his old colleagues at the Centre for Policy Studies to look at the
potential of converting a series of lines and to examine
another of his ideas, the construction of 'ringways' for
motor traffic above railway lines in London. Instead of
ignoring this continued line of attack on the very concept
of railways, which again was attracting considerable publicity, Parker decided to take the bull by the horns. He met
Sherman, along with Thatcher's chief economic adviser,
Professor (later Sir) Alan Walters, for lunch and explained
that he would set up a study to give serious consideration
to the idea. It was a courageous move as it implied the
concept was potentially viable; but by commissioning

Coopers & Lybrand (now PricewaterhouseCoopers) Parker was confident that a serious examination of the principles would show they were unworkable. And so it proved.

The report, published in 1984 after Parker had left BR, made it clear that the idea did not stack up. Not only would the tunnels be too small and therefore dangerous, but also the fact that roads need far more sophisticated and consequently expensive drainage than a railway convinced ministers to ditch the idea. The report concluded:

> In general, a two-track railway is too narrow to support anything other than a single carriageway road. It proved just possible to fit a route for coaches (but not private cars) into the route approaching Marylebone through the tunnel under St John's Wood, for example, but it involved coaches passing each other in the tunnel with no safety barriers to separate them, at high closing speeds with close headways.[3]

It was astonishing that it had taken the combined might of Coopers & Lybrand and British Rail, as well as three decades of debate, to come to such a patently obvious conclusion.

The longevity of the clearly impractical idea of concreting over railways showed the level of opposition that railway managers were up against and which at times restricted their ability to invest and innovate. While it is easy to dismiss the Railway Conversion League as simply a bunch of obsessive British eccentrics, the fact that serious intellectuals like Hall and Sherman actively supported the concept gave it unwarranted credibility and prolonged a discussion which was never worth having in the first place. (Even after the demise of the League, its adherents and disciples would turn up at many meetings on rail topics which I chaired at party conferences and other events in the 2010s to press their case; but fortunately, later, I recognized them and learnt to avoid calling on them to speak when it was time for questions.)

The other line of attack had been to push for another series of radical cutbacks, as outlined in the Serpell report published in 1983. Although the report was rejected, BR remained under pressure to modernize, and by the time of its publication change was already underway, since Parker had created the preconditions for reform by tackling industrial relations issues. Killing off the Serpell report had given BR some room to manoeuvre, but Parker recognized his time was up, as he had been a Labour appointment who would never be trusted by the Tories. Parker had hired Robert Reid as chief executive, a new post within BR, which effectively ensured he would succeed him. Parker, an outsider in the industry, accepted that to enable thorough reform of BR there needed to be a career railwayman, someone steeped in railway history, but sufficiently courageous to fight against traditions that hampered progress. Robert Reid was very much a railwayman, but he was not quite as imbued with the industry's culture as many of his fellow railway managers. Parker realized that only an insider, and a very skilled one at that, could make the necessary changes. Throughout Reid's career, he had challenged both established practices and his colleagues. As Peter Trewin, who was the last secretary of the British Railways Board, says: 'Parker had started to turn the supertanker around, but it needed someone else to finish the job.'[4]

It was soon after the publication of the Serpell report and its rapid binning that Robert Reid succeeded Peter Parker, in September 1983. The British Railways Board had found a man capable of pushing through the radical reforms needed and Reid, as chief executive, had already begun the process. There is universal agreement among BR managers of that generation, several of whom were interviewed for this book, that Reid's leadership was the key to the complete change in the culture of BR which made its final decade such a success. John Nelson, who worked as Reid's personal assistant and later headed Network SouthEast, is not a man prone to hyperbole, but his praise of Reid is typical: 'I and practically all my contemporaries agree that he was probably the greatest railwayman of modern times.' Reid did not see himself as an engineer or an operator. Instead, according to Nelson, 'his guiding principle at every stage in his career was serving and developing the market. He viewed the railway through a commercial prism.'[5] This was unusual for such a senior railway manager, as commercial staff were often at the bottom of the hierarchy, which was dominated by engineers and operators.

Unlike Parker, Reid was not loved by those around him, nor was he clubbable. Born in Kent, he spent some of his childhood in India, where his father was governor of Assam and later of Bengal. Reid served as an officer in the Royal Tank Regiment in the Second World War and spent three years as a prisoner of war in Italy before escaping. According to Trewin, 'He was shy, and found social contact difficult. He built a tight band of people around him, particular younger ones, who shared his view about the direction the industry needed to take.'[6] Reid was under no illusion that there would be opposition to his reform agenda at BR, particularly from the barons – the regional managers, usually known as general managers, who wanted to retain the old hierarchical structure that gave them almost total control over their fiefdoms. Reid had a fierce temper and was not averse to confronting people in front of their peers at meetings, where the person who had been allocated the seat opposite him was likely to be the target of sharp questioning. Nelson saw the tactic used many times: 'Although he would land punches directly onto the immediate object of his assault (in this case me), his messages were really meant to be picked up by every[one] else in the room. It was an effective method and one he used remorselessly in propagating his message of change.'[7]

Reid was, above all, a leader. As his daughter told Nelson, 'He wasn't really a deputy sort of person.'[8] That seems to be very apt since in my conversations with Reid's former colleagues they invariably described him as frightening or intimidating, and not someone who would easily take orders. A newspaper profile neatly summed up his austere image: 'Bob Reid looks like an underfed but unusually cheerful Scottish divine [churchman].' Skipping over the word cheerful, Reid replied that his 'spare,

rugged, starved appearance' was down to his Presbyter-
ian background. 'It didn't stop sin, just stopped you
enjoying it.'[9]

The railway Reid took over had, as we have seen,
changed radically in recent times, but it still retained many
aspects that were more suited to the early rather than the
late twentieth century. In particular, there was the power
of BR's general managers, who remained a law unto
themselves. They were, by and large, a conservative force,
who sought to maintain the traditions of their territories,
which essentially were based on the boundaries of the
Big Four companies which had run the railway between
1923 and 1948. This silo mentality manifested itself in
many ways, and despite the various attempts to rein in the
barons' power, they still had so much clout that the Board
struggled to impose unified strategies across the organization. Reid himself had seen it first-hand during his rise
to the top, as John Nelson recalls: 'As Board Member for
Marketing, he had been at the epicentre of the management matrix in which the General Managers of BR's six
regions exercised substantial influence, to the extent
that if they chose, they could frustrate centrally-driven
initiatives.'[10]

The Western Region in particular was resistant to
cooperation and to change, not least because its history
and traditions stretched back unbroken to Brunel's Great
Western Railway, founded in 1833. For example, if the
manager of the Western Region wanted a particular type
of engine to run its express services, then he got it, irrespective of the fact that there would be enormous savings

of scale if the regions all combined their purchases and limited them to a small number of standard locomotives. As we have seen, that was one of the reasons why, after the 1955 Modernisation Plan was published, such a vast number of different types of diesel were developed.

This fierce defence of regional autonomy also explains why, after the formation of British Railways, basic safety systems to prevent accidents had been installed in only some of the regions. Stephen Poole, who had a thirty-year career with British Rail, relates how the Western Region refused to install the modern Automatic Warning System developed by BR, which alerts drivers when passing a signal at danger. Instead, the region retained its own bespoke, archaic equipment, which had been developed in Edwardian times as the first such safety system on the network. It was not until 1975 that the Western finally introduced the new equipment, but, as Poole says in his book *Inside British Rail*, 'by how long and at what cost the national implementation of this vital safety equipment was delayed by the Western's early intransigence is a matter of debate'.[11]

Less seriously – but often to passengers' detriment nonetheless – Poole recounts how regions fought each other to ensure they had enough locomotives to run their services. They would hoard locomotives rather than sharing them equitably, which led to cancellations for lack of traction and daft games being played:

We guarded our own regional locomotive fleets jealously, even though most machines could in fact travel anywhere on the railway. A favourite trick when traction was short was to send a type of locomotive on an inter-Regional working that could not be driven by the receiving Region's crews. In that way the traction always came back home and the other Region had to find power for the next leg of the working.[12]

For Reid's reforms to be successful, therefore, he had to overcome the power of the barons. Chris Green, who at various times ran BR's Network SouthEast, InterCity and ScotRail businesses, was convinced that Reid was right to address the failing regional structure: 'Although it was good that at the regional level we had a lot of freedom to do things, on the negative side it meant that if there was an old engineer in charge who, for instance, did not believe that continuous welded rail was better, he could block it for ten years.'[13] (In fact, as we have seen, once continuous welded rail has been installed it is far safer and cheaper to maintain than the older jointed track, which was laid in short sections attached and bolted together by fishplates.*) Green's comments illustrate the point that every system has its strengths and weaknesses, but breaking up the traditional regional structure and injecting a measure of central coordination was, on balance, long overdue. Reid was right to push this forward, but the

---

* Continuous welded rail is the reason that trains no longer make the 'tagadaga tagadaga' sound beloved of generations of rail fans, as the beat was caused by the train's wheels passing over the connection between sections of rail.

strength of the 'baronies' explains why it took him several years to complete the job, as we shall see.

However, it was not just BR's regional structure that was a barrier. The various 'functional' departments, such as operations and engineering, often failed to coordinate their activities and work schedules, existing instead as a series of silos in each region led by managers who perceived other departments as the enemy. The lack of integration ran deep, as John Nelson illustrates:

> There was no common management at any meaningful level of the industry between the various disciplines – not only was there none between the commercial and operational sides of the railway, nor was there any commonality between the engineering and the operational, and even within engineering, it was divided by function: civils, signalling, electrification, mechanical and so on were all separate organisations.[14]

While the general managers in the regions were called the barons, the heads of these various functional units were known as the bishops. And the barons and bishops rarely worked in concert. Although, as Nelson explains, these managers did sometimes sit around the same table at various levels in the hierarchy – divisional, regional and board – the powers being vertical. In other words, decisions went up through the hierarchy but not across: 'As a result, there was no possibility for managers of different disciplines to work together to insist on an outcome.'[15] While there were a lot of good people who wanted the best for the railway, they were hampered by this inflexibility. When more adventurous managers attempted to work across boundaries, the initial focus was always on the benefits for the region or for the particular function as, in essence, it was a production-led railway where neither efficiency nor the needs of passengers were the priority.

The hierarchy over which the general managers of British Rail presided was not only rigid but also a reflection of values that were fast disappearing in wider society. Visitors to the BR headquarters at 222 Marylebone Road (now returned to its former use as a hotel, the luxurious Landmark) were shocked at finding scenes that were more like pre-war Britain than the nation that was changing rapidly under Thatcher. There were separate toilets for different levels of staff and three restaurants – with the top one, for use by the higher grades who were known as 'officers', enjoying table service from waitresses in what they called their 'mess'. Indeed, many of those who ate there were ex-army people who proudly displayed their rank on the door of their offices, even though Stephen Poole and others who worked for BR at the time suspected that many of the ranks were merely honorific.

This elitism was not merely a headquarters phenomenon. Poole recalls working at Waterloo in the early 1980s, where 'the Officers' Mess was through a grand door next to the Victory Arch, while the rest of us had a grotty canteen overlooking the platform that was used for [diesel-powered] Exeter departures and so was full of diesel fumes'.[16] He relates how, even when the facilities were finally merged into a staff restaurant for all grades, the 'officers' were discreetly given vouchers for meals at the Charing Cross Hotel. Staff, however, when travelling around the network were entitled to reductions at station buffets for tea and sandwiches, but oddly not coffee, which at the time was perceived as a foreigners' beverage.

It was not only the catering that was segregated. The regional managers and a few other senior colleagues were provided with cars and chauffeurs right up to the 1980s so they did not have to use the trains that they were being paid to provide. Every general manager also had his own private saloon carriage, which could be hitched to loco-hauled trains, reminiscent of the way the aristocracy attached their travelling coaches to a flat wagon in the early days of the railway. Ostensibly the saloon cars, which were well-furnished and had basic catering facilities, were used for inspections, but in reality their most common purpose was as a way of entertaining impressionable VIP guests (for example, the general manager of the Western regularly used his coach to take National Coal Board directors to see the rugby at Cardiff Arms Park). These saloons were still in use in the early 1980s when Reid took over, but opportunities to ride in them were limited, not out of concern that they could be perceived as elitist, but because most trains were now in fixed formations which prevented an extra coach being attached to the back. If managers did want to slum it on the railway, all of them had free lifetime passes for first-class travel, which were provided in wallets of different materials according to grade – leather, silver or gold. These 'priv' passes also included very large discounts on foreign rail travel for them and their families.

The first attempt to change BR's archaic regional structure was the Field organization, an internal report produced in 1974 which recommended that the six regions be replaced with eight territories as a way of shaking up the organization. Despite considerable work being carried out to implement the plan, which included offices for the new territories being built in places such as Basingstoke and Guildford, the scheme met with steadfast resistance within BR and was finally shelved by Reid.

It was, however, only a postponement of the inevitable. Unlike Parker, Reid, who claimed to have no particular political views, had some protection in high places, which enabled him to think of the longer term rather than having to firefight daily battles. He was friends with Nicholas Ridley, the Transport Secretary appointed by Thatcher after the June 1983 general election, with whom he went fishing and shooting, and he was also on first-name terms with Denis Thatcher, the Prime Minister's husband, who was a quiet *éminence grise*. According to Peter Trewin, 'Reid was given a three-year target to reduce the deficit by 25 per cent and Ridley's side of the deal was to ensure that he wasn't interfered with politically.'[17] In the event, Reid exceeded that target. This secret accord between Reid and Ridley certainly helped to create a more stable atmosphere within BR and it allowed Reid to lay the groundwork for his revolution without having constantly to look over his shoulder at the financial situation.

Reid had always felt the Field initiative was neither sufficiently radical nor robust enough for the type of reorganization he wanted to implement. But he realized that moving too fast would risk paralysis, so he devised a more coherent structure which initially would overlay the regions rather than replacing them, which remained the eventual aim. Reid devised the concept of 'sectorization', a rather dry and confusing term for what was, however, a fundamental change in the way BR operated, which affected every level of the organization. Essentially, 'sectorization' meant the creation of a series of five businesses which reflected the purpose of the railway rather than its geography. It is unclear when the term was first used and Reid himself admitted that it had been 'rolling around for years' before he took up the concept and developed it in detail.[18] Of the five sectors, three – InterCity, London & South East and Provincial – were for passenger services, while the other two – freight and parcels – were for goods. The two goods sectors and InterCity were designated as the 'commercial railway', which was expected to pay its way, while the other two were recognized as loss-making and therefore part of the 'social' railway eligible for subsidy.

The plan, which had been in preparation throughout 1981, was launched at the beginning of 1982, when Reid was still chief executive but generally seen as Parker's successor. The announcement was very much presented as a fait accompli as it included the appointment of five people to head the sectors, though initially they had only a skeleton staff and had to scout round 222 Marylebone Road looking for available space. The idea, according to the BR board, was:

> [to] introduce a cutting edge in the battle to control costs and inject business criteria into a much wider range of decisions affecting rolling stock, infrastructure and administration. Business plans will line up with business responsibilities and there will be a much better understanding of where the railway business as a whole is making, and where it is losing, money.[19]

In effect, sectorization was, at last, a move away from the production-led railway – where all the emphasis was on how to keep the trains on the track and operating to the schedule – and on to a focus on the commercial aspects, with each sector being run as a business with separate accounts and therefore the ability to determine profits and losses on activities. Gordon Pettitt sums it up well: 'It was a fundamental change in the direction of the railway towards being business-led and putting passengers first.'[20]

The initial task for the sector managers was to start running each one as a business. In other words, they would have control over both revenue and costs, with the ability to make commercial decisions based on their judgement of the financial outcome. Previously, this had not been possible, which meant that potentially exciting marketing initiatives were often dismissed on the grounds that they would be expensive, even though overall they might generate far more revenue than they cost. The difficulty with establishing these businesses was that there were, initially at least, three interlocking power bases in

the industry: sectors, regions, and functions such as engineering and operations. Reid's long-term strategy was to
give sectors the overall control of the other two; but having seen the failure of past efforts, he had to tread carefully
and move more slowly than he might have liked.

Not surprisingly, the general managers in the regions –
the barons – were furious at the loss of their power and
fought their corner, but to no avail. As a last-gasp effort
to save themselves, they put forward an alternative structure retaining the regions at the heart of the railway but
with more detailed accounting methods. They saw the
creation of sectors as irrelevant to the future of British
Rail. As Nelson puts it: 'The general managers, literally,
had territorial control and behaved like gods in their own
fiefdoms. They could not see why this change was needed.'[21]

Reid recognized that, to overcome this resistance, change
had to be gradual but also radical. Initially, the whole process was something of a stab in the dark. As George Muir,
who has written a biography of Reid, puts it:

> In truth, it was not at all clear how sectorization would
> work out in practice. The process was therefore
> approached one step at a time, something which the
> social scientist, Charles Lindblom, has called 'a strategy
> of disjointed incrementalism', the reaching of a radical
> position by a series of moves which would have been
> impossible to achieve in one single move.[22]

The doomed Serpell report proved to be the last attempt
to close major parts of the railway and the atmosphere
within government post-Serpell was, according to Terry

Gourvish, 'much more positive than the critics of 1983 could possibly have imagined'.[23] However, there was still one last battle over a proposed major closure: the scenic 73-mile-long Settle–Carlisle railway, one of the last main lines built in Britain. It had survived Beeching, largely because it was a diversionary route for services to and from Scotland when either of the East or West Coast lines was closed. In effect, it was a little-used third connection between England and Scotland and therefore was deemed surplus to requirements. The trigger for the closure proposal was the condition of the elegant Ribblehead viaduct, with its twenty-four arches stretching 100 feet above the surrounding countryside, the most notable feature on a line that had been built with great difficulty and loss of life in the 1870s. BR claimed the viaduct alone would cost £5 million to repair (it later increased the estimate to £15 million) and said a further £4 million would be needed for other parts of the route. As battle lines were drawn, engineers commissioned by campaigners to keep the line open disputed BR's original repair bill for the viaduct. The proposal to shut the line was contained in BR's corporate plan published after the 1983 election and can be seen as the last gasp of the Beeching closure programme.

BR was on the defensive from the start, promising that the closure would not take place until 1988 at the earliest, which gave opponents plenty of time to organize. Moreover, as a reflection of the fact that there were different factions within BR over the future of the line, a very commercially minded and innovative railway manager,

Ron Cotton, was appointed to run the local train service while it awaited its seemingly inevitable fate. This showed that while there were senior BR managers, including Reid, who very much wanted to see the line closed, perhaps as a prelude to other cuts of 'uneconomic' routes, there were others who were prepared to defend every mile of track.

Cotton had earned a reputation as a brilliant marketing man when, as divisional passenger manager at Liverpool, he had devised the saver ticket, which gave passengers a very cheap return journey, a key innovation that has survived to this day, albeit in a slightly different form. Cotton was a big, tall man with a smart demeanour, who exuded an air of authority, and he immediately inspired the campaigners against closure. Even though shutting the line remained the official policy, he sought to work out ways of improving the service. He was not the sort of railwayman who was going to simply run down the service to ensure that the line could be closed with a minimum of fuss. On the contrary, he set about attracting more passengers through a series of clever marketing initiatives.

He reopened several small stations that had been closed in 1970, which primarily served the large number of hikers who visited the area. He also encouraged charter-train operators to use the scenic line for steam excursions. Within three years, annual passenger numbers on the line increased from 93,000 to just under 500,000, boosting the campaign to save the line which was attracting widespread support both locally and nationally. The campaign became a cause célèbre with much favourable press coverage, but despite various plans to obtain private finance for the line being put forward both by ministers and local activists, BR still pursued its closure policy. In May 1988, campaigners were disappointed to hear the transport minister David Mitchell announce that the government 'was minded to consent to BR's closure proposal'.[24] It was, though, the final desperate attempt to push through the unpopular policy. Renewed campaigning, a public hearing and a critical report by the local Transport Users' Consultative Committee eventually forced a U-turn in April 1989. It turned out that the Ribblehead viaduct could be repaired far more cheaply and that the closure would cause hardship to local people. Even among Tory ministers, it was a divisive issue. Bizarrely, at the same time as the junior transport minister Michael Portillo was announcing that the line was saved, his boss, Paul Channon, was complaining it was a waste of money, as he did not believe that 'hardship in itself' justified its retention.[25] Portillo, on the other hand, understood that there was an almost religious devotion to the line, and on BBC Radio Leeds he mentioned how the Settle–Carlisle line was 'different from most railway lines: it's historic, it's scenic, it has great tourism interests'. Little did Portillo know that a new career as a presenter of railway documentaries, awaited – though that was still some way off.

There is no doubt that this saga was prolonged by the strength of the forces within both government and BR who were desperate to close the Settle–Carlisle route. Lined up against them, however, were powerful defenders of the line, backed by a staggering 22,150 objectors who had responded to the consultation procedure. In his book on the campaign, James Towler, one of the leaders of the resistance to closure, set out his thoughts on their victory:

> At the end of the day, those fighting to save the line owed much to Sir Robert [Reid] and his senior managers. It was British Rail's arrogance, its inclination for being 'economical with its interpretation of statistics' and its penchant for scoring 'own goals' which continually undermined its credibility, not least with regard to the cost of repairing the Ribblehead Viaduct.[26]

As the authors of *Holding the Line* emphasize, this was the final nail in the coffin for any major rail closures: 'The message for the board and BR senior managers was clear: further significant closures were not likely to be worth the management time and effort.'[27] Since lobby groups had strengthened and were able to launch a major campaign to fight cuts, the tide had turned and consequently there have been no further significant closures. Indeed, government concern about the strength of feeling among the public over rail cuts ensured that the legislation for privatization passed in 1993 made the closure procedures so onerous that they have only been used for very minor stretches of redundant track.

Apart from this vain attempt to close this now very successful line, BR's 1983 corporate plan was mostly optimistic and positive, as Ridley had removed some of the immediate financial pressure on BR, thanks to the agreement with Reid envisaging a 25 per cent cut in subsidy within three years. Reid was effectively given a free hand to implement major reform without ministers constantly double marking his efforts and, in a key change, was allowed to attempt to cut subsidy not only by making cuts but also, crucially, by boosting revenue. This was a plan to build a better railway and not simply one that cost less. Reid set out his agenda in an article in *Railnews*, the BR staff newspaper:

> We have to step up the pace of change . . . we have to sharpen our marketing skills, develop our response to the needs of the customer and realize that if we want to sell a product it has to be a good one . . . We do not do enough as individuals to make our customers welcome.

He was also merciless about the organization's past failings: 'British Rail used to be not so much a management but a vast administrative machine. Profit was not a dirty word; it was a word that didn't exist.'[28]

He turned the organization on its head. Commercial people who used to be minor functionaries within the regions became at his command the managers of the entire business. The traditional production-led railway became a business-led, commercially minded organization. Even though Reid was a shy man, his success was based on his ability to assess people, not simply as a judge of character but also because he was remarkably good at selecting exactly the right people for particular jobs. In this way he was able to build coherent teams which were then allowed to get on with the job. He was able to place people who would make things happen, but in their own way, and who would accept responsibility for success or failure. There was a steeliness about him. He admitted that he did not have a consensual style of running the industry. He knew what he wanted and made sure that he would get it.

Right from the start, sectorization showed several early signs of demonstrable improvements which, most importantly, were noticed by the press and even the wider public. The fact that the sector managers in their decision-making were able to take into account all of the financial implications on their businesses, rather than being forced only to consider costs, enabled them to take a far more strategic and long-term approach. An early example was the effort by John Welsby, who had been appointed head of Provincial Railways, to find more economic ways of running train services while also attracting more passengers. Provincial Railways was the dumping ground of lines that did not fit into the InterCity or London & South East (later renamed Network SouthEast) sectors, as its original name – 'Other Provincial Services' – suggested. It was the unfashionable part of the railway, operating suburban trains in regional cities and longer distance services on the lines connecting them.

Before sectorization, this ragbag of services had been run by twenty divisional passenger managers, each with their own agenda. Their regional bosses largely left them to get on with day-to-day running of the railway with little interference. This was the heart of the social railway, carrying just 13 per cent of passengers but absorbing much of the subsidy required to keep the railway going. Revenue from ticket sales accounted for just a quarter of the costs, with the rest coming from the Department of Transport.

Like his fellow sector directors, Welsby had been hand-picked by Reid. He was bright, dynamic and not old-school railway. In fact, he was not even a railwayman, but had been seconded from the Department of Transport; Reid wanted someone who had extensive experience of government since Provincial was the most political of the sectors, as it was so dependent on subsidy and covered large swathes of the country. That reliance on continued government support meant it was also the part of the network under most pressure to keep cutting costs.

There was no shortage of challenges. Many of the stations were dismal and neglected, the trains were old and unreliable hand-me-downs from other parts of the network, and the singling – reducing a two-track railway to one to save on maintenance costs – of many little-used lines cut capacity and made timetabling far harder. Provincial services were the lowest priority for decision-making from the regions, which still controlled many aspects of running the railway, on matters such as maintenance, renewals and timetabling. It was also a dumping ground for costs. To ensure InterCity met its profit targets, the costs of running and maintaining assets it shared with Provincial, such as stations, were invariably allocated to Provincial, which skewed the true economic picture. Provincial was seen as a backwater, and experienced railway managers tried to avoid getting posted there. Ironically, that proved a benefit, as younger people, many from BR's graduate training scheme, took on key jobs and challenged their old-school bosses. Many rose to higher things, notably Welsby himself, who became the last chairman of British Rail before it was broken up, and several of his managers went on to run the train operating companies created by the privatization.

Mark Causebrook, who later headed the privatized Central Trains and Thameslink, was typical of the new generation. He remembered an 'explosion of talent and freedom' eager for change as Welsby confronted traditional ways of working, many of which were old-fashioned practices rooted in the steam era, such as train crews being required to sign on for work at out-of-the-way depots that had once housed steam engines but were now largely redundant. 'We challenged the regions and the functions on crewing, depot manning, the proposed singling of double track. Some regional general managers and the barons [or bishops] who ran the functions couldn't handle being challenged by these young whippersnappers.'[29]

When Welsby arrived as the head of Provincial Railways in 1982, he had just four staff, three from the passenger department and a secretary. He instinctively realized that he could not throw all the balls in the air at once and that managing the sensibilities of other managers was crucial:

> I decided to leave service provision largely alone in the initial stage; it would have involved major rows with general managers who would have gone out of their way to make sure I screwed up . . . Acceptance was more difficult for me because I did not have a railway background; worse, I was a Department [of Transport] man.[30]

Welsby quickly worked out how to save money while maintaining the existing level of service. The key was to acquire rolling stock suitable to the service being offered. Traditionally, Provincial Railways had been the last repository of old stock no longer needed by InterCity, which was often not fit for purpose. His search for a new type of train was in itself groundbreaking. The divisional managers who previously were in charge of these local services never had the clout to purchase rolling stock as it was beyond their pay grade. Rolling stock was a centralized function and they merely accepted what was given to them.

The need now was urgent. The early diesel multiple units had provided a great service in replacing loco-hauled trains, as the resulting efficiency had saved many branch lines from closure. However, they were now up to thirty years old and required replacing, and there were still many lines where they had not yet replaced loco-hauled trains. Welsby realized that if diesel multiple units were used throughout the network, quicker turnarounds and more efficient use of trains would mean that the stock of around 4,000 vehicles could be cut to 2,500 within a decade and, hey presto, all the required cost savings would be achieved. Moreover, the trains would provide a better service, which would attract more passengers.

Welsby wanted a light vehicle, powered by diesel units under the carriages, and simple enough to be maintained in local depots. The answer proved to be a bus on train tracks. British Rail had already commissioned prototypes of what became known as Pacers, which used existing

269

bus bodies designed by Leyland on a bogie developed for freight vehicles. Because the small freight and parcels depots at little-used stations had been closed, Provincial was no longer required to provide guards' vans. They were much missed by cyclists, who found far greater restrictions in their efforts to travel round the network, with bicycles banned on many routes. Disabled people who, while often feeling humiliated at being dumped in with the sacks of post and sundry parcels, now also found it more difficult to travel on many rural routes as the Pacers were accessed by difficult stairs and a bus-type door that left little room for manoeuvre. However, dispensing with guards' vans saved huge amounts of money.

Work on the Pacer prototypes started in 1977, but by the time Welsby moved to Provincial Railways only a few of them were in operation. A bus body fitted on a chassis and supported by just four wheels meant these light-weight, cheap trains were suitable for rural areas and low-volume commuter services. They were certainly not pretty, or particularly comfortable, as they gave a very bumpy ride on poor track. Moreover, the seats seemed to have come second-hand from redundant double-deckers. They were noisy, too, as they had a clunky gearbox that less adept drivers struggled with, which only added to the passengers' impression that they had mistakenly boarded a bus misrouted in error on to the railway. And, like on a bus, they could even see out of the front. Mostly the Pacers were in two-car units, often replacing single cars, and consequently increasing capacity. In the summer of 1981, the prototype Pacers were demonstrated to the Passenger

Transport Executives, created, as mentioned before, by Barbara Castle to run the train and bus services in regional conurbations such as Merseyside, South Yorkshire and Tyne & Wear. The West Yorkshire representatives were so impressed that they immediately ordered a batch of twenty, thereby confirming that this type of train would be the basis of the Provincial Railways fleet. The trains began operating in West Yorkshire in 1983, and after a few teething problems they provided a largely trouble-free if basic service. British Rail consequently ordered a further fifty Pacers the following year, and these were used on routes throughout the country, including Cornwall where, bizarrely, they became known as 'Skippers'.

In all, 165 Pacer trains (totalling 340 carriages, as there were a few three-car units) in four different versions were built by British Railways Engineering Ltd with Leyland and later by Scottish-based Hunslet-Barclay. The economies were so great that, at a stroke, the introduction of Pacers ensured that these rural lines were no longer under threat of closure.

Although they were a great improvement on the old loco-hauled ancient carriages they replaced, the Pacers were the butt of much criticism, probably because nothing was done to disguise the fact that they were as cheap as they looked. They were originally built as a stopgap intended to have a maximum lifespan of twenty years, in the expectation that they would be replaced when budgets allowed, but in fact some survived in service until 2021, and even then were scrapped only because of new disability regulations.

Welsby also introduced a rather more sophisticated vehicle, the Sprinter, which originally was produced in two versions, one designed by BR's own in-house unit and the other by Metro-Cammell. Two further versions were produced later, built by Leyland and Metro-Cammell respectively, and this fleet became the mainstay of the longer routes operated by Provincial Railways. The Sprinter name was used as the basis for a PR campaign, which showed that Parker's legacy of an emphasis on positive publicity had been retained after his departure. In January 1986, the first of the Sprinters took a group of civic dignitaries and press across the Midlands, where at several stations athletes on the train ran a series of 100 metre races along the platforms to publicize the fact that services on the routes with the new trains would have greatly improved timetables. The local Midland Provincial manager, Bob Goundry, explained how the combination of these two types of train, the Pacers and the Sprinters, transformed the service and, crucially, the image of Provincial Railways:

> The first Pacers showed it was possible to replace the diesel multiple unit fleet with fewer vehicles that were cheaper to maintain and could run on less expensive track. As the technology advanced from Pacers to Sprinters and later to Super Sprinters with a maximum speed of 90 mph, it became possible to develop new patterns of services, particularly on cross-country routes, which revolutionized this neglected area of travel, producing very significant revenue increases while making cost reductions.[31]

Indeed, BR accounts showed that savings from using these modern diesel multiple units more than halved the maintenance costs for Provincial.

Provincial was seen as being most at risk from competition from the car and therefore likely to continue to decline. However, Welsby and his cohort of young managers reversed that trend and passenger numbers started growing, both justifying the new investment and transforming the image of the sector. The number of passenger miles annually rose from a nadir of 2.9 billion in 1982 to 3.6 billion in the 1988/9 financial year, an increase of just under a quarter.

It was not only Provincial Railways which benefitted from the new structure of BR; the other two passenger sectors, InterCity and London & South East, would soon show improvements. It was the latter, led by Chris Green, the most innovative rail manager of his generation, which would undergo the most radical transformation – starting with a name change.

I I

BR

Chris Green, the Oxford graduate whose parents had tried to dissuade him from joining such a backward-looking industry as the railway in the 1960s, rose quickly through the ranks after completing his graduate management traineeship, where he cut his teeth on the electrification of the West Coast Main Line. His first big job was as chief operating manager for Scotland, where he arrived in 1982, just as sectorization was taking effect.

Green, a naturally dynamic figure, saw himself as a marketing man intent on selling the railway to the public, a rather radical thought for BR at the time. He was incredibly thorough and meticulous, media savvy, and always willing to publicize the railway's achievements under his leadership. His vision accorded well with Robert Reid's ideas, and he would go on to innovate in his subsequent leading roles at Network SouthEast and InterCity. As soon as he arrived in Scotland, Green reorganized the timetable so that High Speed Train services arriving at Edinburgh connected with trains to the rest of Scotland, with easy to remember regular services on every route.

An obvious improvement, but one that clearly had not been thought out before.

Quickly promoted to deputy general manager and later general manager, he was intent on changing the public image of railways north of the border. 'We were pretty much a music hall joke at the time as the service was so poor,' he recalls.[1] He set up a brainstorming session to find a new name for the service, as he thought 'British Rail, Scottish Region' was not only cumbersome but did not sufficiently recognize the specific nature of the country's railway. 'A small group of us met and reached unanimous agreement on a new name. It needed to reflect the railways and the country. The Scots wanted to be able to call it "our railway", so "ScotRail" was the obvious answer.'[2] The launch of the name, together with a logo that incorporated St Andrew's Cross, in September 1983 was slightly overshadowed by Green jokily announcing that there would be a 'charm school' for train conductors, a remark that was widely picked up in the local press. Nevertheless, the launch was successful and led to favourable press coverage, and it may even have contributed to the upsurge in Scottish nationalism. 'It helped enormously with staff loyalty and therefore better customer service. Suddenly, ScotRail was top of the headlines as a patriotic name that made Scots feel they had acquired their own railway . . . and the name entered the language almost overnight.'[3] Green is particularly proud that no expensive design agency was involved in the search for the new name or the rebranding, and its success is demonstrated by the fact that the name ScotRail survived privatization as the subsequent private operators never dared to try to change it.

Throughout his time at ScotRail, Green was very conscious of competition from the recently deregulated coach businesses. Companies such as Stagecoach and FirstGroup, both of which had Scottish origins, were expanding rapidly and running frequent services between major towns and cities:

> We reckoned it was fight or flee, and we decided to fight. The Scottish Office were more intent on improving roads and bridges, so we realized we needed modern trains, new locos, faster journey times and we slashed fares, with the sort of special offer the coach companies were making: some £1 fares Glasgow to Inverness; and an overnight train to London for a fiver, though you had to sit up.[4]

The result was that ScotRail managed to resist the competition, increasing travel on its long-distance trains by 25 per cent in 1986, the first year after bus and coach deregulation.

Green was given a lot of freedom by BR, both because its headquarters was 400 miles away in London, but also thanks to his skill at manipulating ScotRail's budget:

> The big signalling schemes were coming in much cheaper than expected, and we spent the spare cash before anyone found out. There was underspending in other areas and Reid hated sending money back to the Treasury at the end of the financial year, so while we thought we

would get caned for overspending, he was in fact grateful privately.[5]

Green used some of the spare cash to paint all the stations and fit them with white tiles to make them brighter and establish a coherent image for the business.

Inevitably, his efforts were noticed by Reid, who offered him the top job in another sector, the London & South East commuter network. The railway around London, such a vital part of its infrastructure, was in a rundown state at the start of the sectorization process. Reid was under pressure from the Transport Secretary, Nicholas Ridley, who was angry about the condition of the network and was pressing for improvements. Complaints about delays, cancellations and the poor state of both trains and stations were a constant backdrop to attempts by managers to produce a reliable service in the face of underinvestment and a railway system that, unlike London Transport, was fragmented. As the authors of the history of what became known as Network SouthEast report, 'This was a dysfunctional period when the Government felt it was paying huge subsidies without any obvious benefit while the [British Railways] Board felt it was unclear what sort of railway the government wanted and the Treasury had no confidence in the railway's investment cases.'[6]

Peter Parker had begun the process of improvement with the launch of a 'Commuters' Charter' in 1979, in an effort to introduce performance targets and accountability. Bizarrely, the government's response was to launch an inquiry by the Monopolies and Mergers Commission (now the Competition and Markets Authority) into whether BR's rail services in London and the South-East provided value for the £400 million public subsidy they received. Rather helpfully, the Commission's report, published in October 1980, recommended that there should be a manager in charge of London and the South-East, which forced Parker, and his successor Robert Reid, to flesh out the ideas for sectorization and specifically to ensure a unified approach across the London commuter market. The British Railways Board had originally considered splitting London's suburban services in two, divided by the Thames, but following the Commission's report, it decided to push ahead with the creation of just one unified sector, which proved to be the correct solution. But even after the Board committed itself to this unified approach at the end of 1981, there were attempts, encouraged by ministers, to allow the private sector to enter the London commuter rail market. One idea, prompted by the Treasury, was to hand over the lucrative London Victoria to Gatwick Airport service to a new private company; a second proposal, initiated by a local entrepreneur, was to bring in a private company to run services out of Fenchurch Street on the London, Tilbury & Southend line. Although nothing came of either initiative, mainly due to an economic downturn, BR realized it had to reform or face greater private-sector involvement.

Carving out a clear London & South East sector from the old regional structure was complicated because almost all the London terminus stations had both long-distance and commuter services running out of them. Working

out which should be under the control of the London &
South East or the InterCity sector was not immediately
apparent. The London & South East sector's first head,
David Kirby, had the problem of trying to establish the
ground rules for splitting up these disparate services with
a minimum of disruption. Establishing a profit-and-loss
balance sheet and allocating the costs between the commuter and main-line services was no easy task. It led to
anomalies, such as Network SouthEast eventually assum-
ing responsibility for nearly all rail services south of the
Thames, including routes to places as far afield as Wey-
mouth and Bournemouth in Dorset. North of the river it
ran to King's Lynn in Norfolk and even to Worcester,
more than 130 miles from London; however, the newly
created non-stop London–Gatwick service and trains to
Ipswich and Norwich were not included in the London &
South East sector. Indeed, InterCity ran Paddington services to Reading and Exeter while Network SouthEast
also operated trains to those two destinations from Waterloo. These anomalies were an inevitable consequence of
reorganizing a network as huge as British Rail, which had
been created by Victorian private companies competing
against each other and which, as a result, often ran services from different London stations to the same
destination.

Chris Green cited the North London line, which runs
round the centre of the capital north of the Thames, as
an example of why the creation of Network SouthEast
made it easier to improve commuter services: 'The North
London line had been run by the Eastern Region but

went through the Western and the Southern as well. Bringing the service under one management was an obvious solution.'[7]

The establishment of Network SouthEast also ensured that commuter services were no longer the poor relation, as Green recalled:

> Much of the infrastructure for the commuter services was in a less good condition than for long-distance services. For example, the main lines out of Paddington, King's Cross and Euston had modern 125 mph continuously welded track for the fast lines, but 75 mph jointed track for the slow ones used by the commuter trains.[8]

The first significant initiative for Network SouthEast was the creation of the Capitalcard, which could be used on both London Underground and British Rail services, an innovation that the BR board had long sought. The Department of Transport had resisted this obvious innovation because Underground fares were cheaper – the result of the 'Fares Fair' system introduced by Ken Livingstone when he was leader of the Greater London Council (GLC) – and standardization might result in a reduction in BR income. The need to create a series of zones in circles around central London was a necessary part of the new system, and inevitably there were complaints by people who felt their local station was in the wrong one. Nevertheless, there was widespread public support for the new scheme and it became the basis of the Travelcard that survives to this day. The key advantages of the Capitalcard were that it could be incorporated into season tickets and included bus travel. As a result, far from costing the combined transport system money, the introduction of an all-London card made travel so much easier that passenger numbers soared, more than covering the loss through the reduction in some fares.

Green arrived at London & South East at the beginning of 1986 and set about applying the programme he had successfully introduced in Scotland. A new name for the sector, Network SouthEast, was proposed by J. Walter Thompson, the large advertising company called in to advise on the relaunch. There were many other suggestions, such as LondonRail, SouthRail, Coast & Country, and some attempts that sounded more science fiction than railway, such as LASER (London And South East Railway) and Star Track, but fortunately these were rejected. There was no obvious equivalent to ScotRail, but while the name Network SouthEast was not particularly exciting it was self-explanatory, and it turned out to be crucial in establishing a coherent image for the diverse train services in and around the capital. Green arrived at a good time since, as well as the introduction of the Capitalcard, the government had given approval to a scheme devised by Ken Livingstone's GLC to reopen the half-mile-long Snow Hill tunnel which connected north and south London through the City. It was a link that unaccountably had been closed for passenger traffic in the First World War, and then even goods traffic stopped running through it in the 1960s, despite its obvious potential to enable cross-London services. The tunnel reopened in 1988, which enabled the operation of a vast array of

services linking suburban and even long-distance destinations, such as Peterborough, Brighton and Cambridge,
on both sides of the river.

The Capitalcard and the growing London economy
had given a new life to rail services in the capital, helping
to reverse the decline of passenger numbers and creating
something of a boom on London's vast suburban network. Consequently, the subsidy for these rail services
began to be reduced, allowing the British Railways Board
to consider further investment initiatives. Unfortunately,
the abolition of the Greater London Council in 1986, a
reckless act resulting from the anger of Mrs Thatcher at
its left-wing stance – exemplified by anti-Tory posters
placed on the roof of County Hall across the river from
Parliament – left London, uniquely of any such major
city, without a system of local unified governance. This
lack of a body representing London stymied plans for
further electrification and for several proposed expan-
sions of services within the capital. Instead, the focus for
Network SouthEast's investment plans shifted to rail
schemes outside the capital, where local authorities were
often willing to contribute part of the cost.

The challenge facing Green, as he later explained in a
book he co-authored on the history of Network South-
East, was in 'wiping away 20 years of grime and making
rail the smart, modern way to travel in the South East'.[9]
The key was to improve off-peak income to provide more
investment and create a virtuous circle. Already, the
annual subsidy had been cut by a quarter to £300 million
and would continue to decline for the rest of the decade.

The success of Network SouthEast was dependent on cooperation with the old regions. Here Green and his team were fortunate that by far the largest chunk of Network SouthEast was in the Southern Region, which was headed by Gordon Pettit, who was a strong supporter of sectorization and would go on to run Provincial Railways. Pettitt, a very experienced manager much in the Reid mould, worked very closely with Green to push through investment schemes and support the various initiatives being launched.

Green, a Londoner who knew the capital well, used his first few months at London & South East to commute from various parts of the network, seeing first-hand its rundown condition. He addressed the problem with a comprehensive approach which considered every aspect of the railway service. However, he insisted that there would be a period of silence with no launches or PR announcements for the first three months: 'In that time, we would get the performance up so that we were not promoting a lousy railway, but instead we would have something to show. We cleaned up all the trains, recruited missing staff as there was a 10 per cent vacancy rate which affected performance, and went for quality.'[10]

Branding was crucial. Once the Network SouthEast name had been chosen, it had to be sold to the public, together with a colour scheme and an overall image, much like the one developed by British Rail twenty years before. At the heart of the design was the name, together with a rhombus symbol of red, blue and grey or white diagonals, which was reproduced everywhere on stations and trains, and even on the 9,000 station lamp posts which were painted in the first month.

It was the most obvious and simplest innovations which made the biggest difference. In the past, since marketing was undertaken by the regions and they only promoted their own routes, there was no map showing all the available train services in the London area. There was nothing to encourage people to connect between destinations reached from different main-line stations. Therefore the production of the first Network SouthEast map was seen as revolutionary, even if it seemed patently clear that it should have been done years before, especially given that London Underground had produced its famous schematized and colourful version designed by Harry Beck as far back as the 1930s. It is testimony to its importance that the Network SouthEast map survived privatization in the 1990s, which separated out the various routes into different franchises, with the simple addition of the names of the new private operators.

A Network SouthEast manifesto was produced and 850,000 copies in full colour were handed out to staff and commuters over the space of a couple of days. It set out how the railway was going to be improved, with specific dated commitments, and it helped to ensure that such publicly made promises were realized. As Green stresses, 'Putting out a manifesto and making it public ensured we – and therefore the Board or ministers – could not back down on the commitments.'[11] The manifesto's fundamental message was that Network SouthEast was on the up, and change was underpinned by quality.

All these innovations were carried out quickly, ahead of a major launch on 10 June 1986. Green prepared the way with 'Operation Pride' four months beforehand. He leaked a story about a major makeover for London's embattled commuters to the *Sunday Times* and was quite open about the fact that his own commuting experience in his first months in the job had been dire. Green negotiated a truce with the *Evening Standard* to try to stem the flow of negative stories:

> I went to see the editor who said to me, 'You do realize that we sell newspapers on the basis of bad news in the railways?' And I responded that all I am asking for is a few months during which we can tell your readers what we are doing; and for three years they were very supportive, until the end of the 1980s, when there was a series of strikes.[12]

A locomotive was renamed *Evening Standard*, which attracted favourable publicity, and the paper published the quality standards that were promised in 'Operation Pride' (this was long before 'Pride' events were associated with the gay community). An extra 1,700 staff were recruited, who ranged from cleaners to booking clerks, and according to the history of Network SouthEast, 'the public evidence of change was to be cleaner trains and stations – backed by an accelerated painting programme for 250 stations each year. Letters from MPs gradually changed from grumbling about performance to campaigning for their stations to be modernised first', with, of course, an opening ceremony which they could attend.[13] The staff were not forgotten. Their often Dickensian accommodation in mess rooms was upgraded and they were briefed comprehensively before the changes were announced. To create a sense of unity, all staff were issued with name badges and ties, and many ticket office staff were provided with uniforms for the first time.

The launch venue was Waterloo, where all train services were operated by Network SouthEast, and the station had been given a makeover in Network SouthEast colours. It was effectively a test bed for the rebranding of stations: 'The replacement of black tarmac with white terrazzo was to become an NSE trademark. The modernised shops, barrier lines, advertising and indicators were complete in their new NSE branding.'[14] Several guests reported that it felt as if they had arrived in an airport, something BR managers took as a compliment. To give substance to the launch, the Network SouthEast card was unveiled, offering a third off the cost of all off-peak journeys and available for purchase for £10 by all adults, and therefore extending the possibility of cheaper travel beyond the young and the old, who already had their own railcards. In fact, in an effort to convince people to fill the vast number of empty seats outside the peak times, Network SouthEast went further, by allowing up to three people to hold its Network card jointly and obtain the same discount whether they were travelling together or not, and up to four children could travel for a flat fare of just £1.

The widespread availability of the discounts was groundbreaking and a reflection of the freedom BR had at the time to make commercial decisions without seeking permission from government ministers. Traditionally, the Treasury has been suspicious of discounted rail fares, and even today it continues to block the introduction of a national railcard offering a discount, like the BahnCard in Germany. It is notable that, while the Network card survived after privatization, it doubled in cost and its use was limited to longer journeys.

Green believes the launch was a key moment in the history of the Network SouthEast project. He and his team were committed to raising quality standards at the same time as reducing subsidy. Delivering on both was essential, and increasing passenger numbers in the off peak, when trains were running with average loadings of just 25 per cent, was the key. He set out five commitments: to improve income, quality, stations, trains and infrastructure. He saw empowerment of Network SouthEast's six local subsectors as the way to deliver these changes quickly. Power was devolved to managers in the subsectors who were able to make substantial operational and marketing decisions. Green felt that with 900 stations under his charge, dividing them into groups of 150 enabled changes to happen far faster.

Indeed, Network SouthEast ventured into the world of marketing in a far more comprehensive way than British Rail had ever done. As well as the Network card, the marketing director, Tony Skeggs, launched 'a summer of fun' in 1987, which involved the distribution of three million brochures to households in the region listing ideas for school-holiday rail trips, and a further 1.5 million to incoming tourists highlighting activities that could be undertaken by train. The campaign was supported by extensive TV and radio advertising. Again, as with the InterCity campaigns, the advertising was innovative and memorable.

There was never any attempt by Network SouthEast to promote its peak services; instead, it commissioned a series of adverts to attract leisure travellers to the cheaper trains available after 9.30 a.m. These initially focused on the One Day Travelcard, but later featured 'Edgar the Swan', who could 'swan' about London by evolving into a crazy supercar which became a joined-up bus, Tube and train that was shown running on the railway tracks. For another campaign, Waterloo station was closed on a Sunday morning in 1988 so that an army of 'commuters' could tap dance across the concourse, making the point that a hush fell over the station after the 9.30 a.m. rush was over, and this proved to be the most memorable commercial. The comedian Tony Hancock also featured in a later advertisement, rather oddly waiting for a train that he missed because he went to the loo.

After the damaging strikes of 1989, Skeggs wanted to relaunch Network SouthEast and he was approached by Adrian Boyd, an entrepreneur, to sponsor a flower show at Hampton Court to rival the famous Chelsea show. The event, in 1990, which was opened by Princess Anne, attracted half a million visitors, many of whom arrived on the six trains per hour run specially by Network South-East from Waterloo, including occasional *Tudor Rose* specials, a premium service featuring gardening celebrities, drinks and canapés.

The selling of Network SouthEast was so successful that it resulted in almost total awareness of the brand, with a survey of the London public showing that 90 per cent of respondents in the capital knew of the name. Today, all this might seem like basic marketing, but it illustrates that the campaign was being created and run by a publicly owned organization which was criticized both at the time and subsequently for being unadventurous and conservative. Indeed, one of the often-expressed reasons for supporting rail privatization was the unimaginative and old-fashioned nature of British Rail.

Of course, there were downsides. Not all the stations presented a pleasant aspect for travellers; many were not staffed at night, posing a security risk, and a series of strikes at the end of the 1980s over working practices and driver only operation damaged the Network SouthEast brand. The junior minister for transport David Mitchell was very engaged with the progress at Network South-East and, quite remarkably, paid out of his own pocket the prizes for the so-called Mitchell Cup, which went to the route that had made the biggest improvement in the past six months. Because, cleverly, the award was based on 'improvement' rather than performance, 'the Mitchell Cup proved especially motivating to staff on the "Cinderella" routes where the biggest changes were needed – and they rose to the occasion'. As a result, 'rundown inner London routes suddenly experienced the pleasant surprise of finding the Minister on their station to congratulate them on their improvements in front of a gaggle of press cameras'.[15]

Network SouthEast was an undoubted success. Its income increased from £680 million to £1 billion between 1982 and the end of the decade, when the series of strikes stymied any further growth. Of course, the booming London economy, stimulated by the so-called Big Bang – the deregulation of the City in October 1986 – underpinned this rise, but the increase of a quarter in off-peak travel, at virtually no cost, was a major factor. Not only did the annual subsidy fall by more than a third, but investment also rose by nearly three quarters, turning Chris Green's hoped-for virtuous circle of self-financing improvements into reality.

There were, however, a series of accidents which overshadowed the short history of Network SouthEast. The first, a major disaster just south of Clapham Junction in December 1988, was the worst by far. Overall, British Railways' safety record had improved considerably since its creation forty years previously. Traditionally, the approach to safety had been, to put it very crudely, to crash and learn. In other words, detailed investigations of the causes of accidents led to safety improvements, but there were still areas where either the lessons had not been learnt or the railway had been too slow to implement change. However, there had not been an accident with more than thirteen deaths since a derailment caused by a broken rail at Hither Green in south-east London in 1967, in which forty-nine people died. Significantly, the rate of fatal accidents had declined markedly in this period, too: whereas train accidents in the 1950s and 1960s were occurring several times per year, by the 1970s they were a rarity, and there were very few in the 1980s. This reduction was down to the introduction of numerous safety measures, and also to the greater crash resistance of new rolling stock, which helped reduce the death toll.

For staff, too, the improvements were impressive. In 1949, the year after British Railways was created, 209 railway workers had been killed on duty, but this had fallen to 105 in 1965 – still a huge number, and demonstrating the danger, in those days before hi-vis, of certain tasks which meant working next to live track, such as shunting in noisy yards and checking the rails on the permanent way. Therefore some of this reduction was the result of changed methods of working, such as shutting lines down to carry out repairs and the mechanization of checking trackwork, while technological developments, such as the ending of steam and the consolidation of signal boxes, improved the safety of the working environment. Within the next decade, numbers of workers killed annually were down to around thirty to forty, but it was not until the 1990s that the casualty rate was reduced to single figures every year. In the twenty-first century, in most years there have been no deaths.

Despite the improvement for both passengers and workers, there were gaps in British Rail safety procedures which were exposed by the Clapham crash and two subsequent accidents on the London suburban network, which traditionally has been the site of many of the worst disasters because of the high levels of heavily loaded trains on lines where the interval between services can be as short as a minute. The Clapham disaster was to be a dreadful eye-opener for many rail managers, given that it was caused by very basic errors, and it would lead to a major reform of BR's safety culture. It came as a shock to BR and the travelling public because it could so easily have been prevented.

During the morning rush hour of 12 December, the 0718 from Basingstoke to London Waterloo, a crowded twelve-car train with 900 people on board, was approaching Clapham Junction when the driver saw the signal ahead of him change from green to red. He stopped his train at the next signal, but just after he phoned the signal box, the following service from Bournemouth, which was also carrying a full load of passengers, smashed into the back at high speed, and a third train, fortunately empty, travelling in the other direction, hit the wreckage. There were thirty-five deaths and nearly 500 injuries in what remains the worst rail accident in the UK since 1967.

The immediate cause was a loose wire in a cabinet housing signalling equipment. New wiring had been installed, but the old wiring had been left in place without being properly isolated and it had shorted, causing a green aspect on the signal to be shown when it should have been red. An independent inquiry chaired by Anthony Hidden QC found that Brian Hemingway, the signalling technician responsible, had worked for ninety days consecutively without a break and had never been warned that there were fundamental errors in his normal working practice. Not only had there been no independent inspection of his work, no one had informed him that his method of simply cutting off unused wires and tucking them behind others, rather than isolating them with tape, was inherently unsafe. Hemingway was not alone in using these fundamentally flawed working methods, which were rife across the network. The inquiry revealed that there were twenty other instances of untaped wires being tucked into corners in similar signal cabinets near the scene of the accident. Consequently, while Hemingway's actions were the primary cause of the disaster, Hidden named eleven of his superiors who were responsible for this systemic failing.

BR immediately accepted responsibility for the disaster. Both Robert Reid and Gordon Pettitt rushed to the scene and spoke to the media to express their regrets and accept liability. Reid was badly affected personally. On the day that the Hidden inquiry was published, nearly a year after the disaster, he confided to a friend that he felt responsible: 'It was as much my fault as anyone else's. I put pressure on people. Perhaps I overdo it. You can't just point the finger at this guy, because I'm involved; I took the decisions which led to him being under pressure.'[16]

In fact, among all the changes brought about by sectorization, safety improvements had been, if not quite forgotten, insufficiently addressed. While, as mentioned above, there had been a long period of improved safety after the war, progress had stalled. In contrast to the 1960s and early 1970s, when the rate of accidents – a better measure than fatalities – had fallen by half, the rate of improvement had slowed by the time Reid became chairman of BR in 1983. Although, as we have seen, the number of track workers killed on the railway had been falling for years, not least because increasingly work was done when lines were closed, there were still sixteen deaths in 1987 and there was an air of complacency and inevitability. This was epitomized by a statement made by David Rayner, the joint managing director (Railways), shortly before the Clapham disaster. Responding to the figures for track-worker fatalities, he told *Railnews*: 'We have very adequate rules and safety practices but, in the end, everything boils down to individuals observing them sensibly, to the letter, for their own safety and for that of their colleagues. It's as simple as that.'[17] Except it was not as simple as that. The culture within which people work is equally, if not more, important. As the Clapham accident showed, it was a matter of supervision and management, a point that Hidden made very clearly in his report:

It is not enough to talk in terms of 'absolute safety' and of 'zero accidents'. There must also be proper organisation and management to ensure that actions live up to words.

Sadly, although the sincerity of the beliefs of those in BR at the time of the Clapham Junction accident who uttered such words cannot for a moment be doubted, there was a distressing lack of organisation and management on the part of some whose duty it was to put those words into practice. The result was that the true position in relation to safety lagged frighteningly far behind the idealism of the words.

The report demanded that 'The concept of absolute safety must be a gospel spread across the entire workforce and be paramount in the minds of management.'[18]

Not surprisingly, given the strength of Hidden's words in his report, his inquiry led to a raft of changes in BR working practices, most notably in the way that the installation of signalling equipment was planned, wired and tested. While these measures improved the safety of signalling work, which was taking place across the network as outdated mechanical systems were being replaced with modern electronic ones, there was a downside for the public as work tended to be concentrated in longer periods, necessitating more closures and diversions.

Overall, after the Hidden report, BR increased its spending on safety by around £150 million annually over the five-year period until the beginning of the privatization process in 1994. This included the fitting of data and voice recorders – 'black boxes' – to many trains, notably on suburban Network SouthEast services. Hidden also recommended the installation of a new radio system allowing permanent communication between driver and signal workers – 'ship to shore' or, officially, Cab Secure Radio – but the full implementation of all these programmes was constrained and delayed by government financial restrictions on BR. Nevertheless, this increased emphasis on safety after Clapham bore fruit, with the rate of accidents falling at a rate much faster than before the disaster.

There were two other fatal accidents on Network SouthEast's routes in the subsequent three years, which highlighted how safety improvements had previously been somewhat neglected. A collision caused by a driver passing a red signal at Purley near Croydon in March 1989 resulted in five fatalities, while two people were killed when a train crashed into the buffer stops in Cannon Street station two years later. These were both driver errors which would have been avoided had there been a more effective system to prevent trains from passing signals at danger. As we saw in Chapter 10, a basic device, the Automatic Warning System, had long been available, but it had not been universally introduced until the 1970s, and a more secure system, the Train Protection and Warning System, which would actively stop trains from passing red lights, was introduced across the railway network only after the government mandated it following the post-privatization disasters at Southall in 1997 and Ladbroke Grove in 1999.

Despite all the improvements and all the enthusiasm generated by the creation of Network SouthEast, there remained still parts of the suburban network which had not seen much investment and where complaints were still frequent. After Clapham and a period of industrial disputes, the truce with the *Evening Standard* came to an end and the paper was always on the lookout for the latest 'misery line'. For a while, the unwanted title was bestowed on the commuter line out of Fenchurch Street to South-end, on the Essex coast. Even Reid admitted that the service had 'fallen to a wholly unacceptable level' and that passengers were right to complain of 'delays, cancella-tions, filthy and freezing carriages of indeterminate age and dangerous to women at night'.[19] Hamstrung by renewed restrictions on British Rail's investment plans and by the need to spend more on safety, some lines in the early 1990s were neglected and promised improvements did not materialize. There would, however, be further organizational changes which were designed to make BR more efficient and better able to generate more funds for investment, as we will see in the next chapter.

The third passenger sector to be included in the restructuring of British Rail was InterCity, which had already been in existence for fifteen years when the process was begun, albeit only as a marketing brand. InterCity had been effective at rationalizing British Rail's long-distance service in that period, resulting in a major financial turnaround; up to the economic downturn of the early 1980s, it had delivered a profit for six years, though this was more of an accounting device than a true reflection of the situation on the ground. This would change in 1982, when InterCity became a standalone business.

Robert Reid was very keen to ensure that InterCity returned quickly to profitability and ensured the scales were weighted in its favour. As a result, all the profitable lines were included as part of its remit, including the East and West Coast Main Lines, express services out of Paddington and St Pancras, and the main Cross Country services linking regional centres without going through the capital.

Cyril Bleasdale, who was the first director of the Inter-City sector, initially had to battle to carve out the extent of his empire and ensure it did not include routes that were performing badly. A couple of years after InterCity was hived off, therefore, in 1984, the services to Norwich out of Liverpool Street and, rather oddly, the non-stop airport shuttle between Victoria and Gatwick, would be added to it; but other routes, such as the trans-Pennine services, Waterloo to Bournemouth and Edinburgh to Glasgow, were rejected on the basis that they were unlikely to contribute to its profitability. Moreover, as mentioned before, various costs which should have been shared between Provincial Railways and InterCity were allocated to the former in order not to burden the latter. This was a rather naked attempt by BR to create a highly profitable sector to show the government that it could run a business that earned a decent return on capital. It was a rebuke, too, to the findings of the Serpell committee which had confidently asserted that InterCity was not capable of delivering a profit.

Returning InterCity to profitability was not just a matter of waiting for the nation's economic situation to improve. This was a period when the number of households owning cars was increasing rapidly, with only a short hiccup during the recession of the early 1980s, and the motorway programme serving nearly all major towns and cities was near completion. This gave deregulated coach companies an opportunity to speed up their services and offer lower fares because of reduced costs. Domestic aviation, which was also being deregulated and consequently attracting new entrants to the market, was another source of competition.

To counter the threat of the airlines, InterCity launched

an 'Executive Service' in 1983, with an eight-point marketing initiative aimed at business travellers, who were used to their every need being looked after on planes in business and first class. Moreover, first class was a useful earner for British Rail. Although accounting for only 12 per cent of InterCity revenue at the time, the profitability was high, and it was important for the image of the railway that affluent travellers used the service. They would spread the message to their peers that taking the train was a perfectly respectable way to travel. In order to try to retain this premium market, and to see off airline competition, the Executive Service included a number of perks, such as free parking spaces at stations, tea and coffee served in china cups, and complimentary newspapers. In those days before mobile telephones, payphones were introduced in the lobbies at the end of carriages (when I used them, they were both rather expensive and had somewhat dodgy connections; but then one still hears people in 2021 shouting, 'I am on the train . . . Sorry, I did not catch that. Can you hear me?').

While these various initiatives resulted in an improved service, they did not quite do the trick. In particular, according to Tanya Jackson, author of *British Rail: The Nation's Railway*, 'One aspect that drew criticism was the on-train catering, which was at the time in the hands of Travellers Fare. Quality was too dependent on which crew was on duty, and sometimes there was no catering at all.'[20] British Railways had rather turned away from a focus on premium services in the egalitarian 1960s, but now decided it was a useful source of revenue to help fund the whole network, just as airlines massively overcharge their business- and first-class passengers to subsidize those in the back of the plane.

Therefore there was another relaunch, in 1985, with the Pullman brand at the heart of it. It was pretty much the same offering, though with the 'Great English Breakfast' provided on several early trains without the need to pay a supplement, and additional care taken to ensure the right sort of personnel were providing the service. The coaches were given names – *John Lennon*, for example, was allocated to the Liverpool route – and the concept proved so successful that within a few years more than fifty daily trains offered a Pullman at-seat service. Some of these Pullman services were also given names, such as *The Master Cutler* serving Sheffield and *The Golden Hind* which went to Plymouth – a popular move which helped boost sales of first-class tickets.

Reid had been anxious to expand InterCity's stock of its popular Mark 3 coaches used on the High Speed Trains – he had hoped to purchase 180 more to provide an extra coach to seven-car trains – but the government allowed BR to obtain only another sixty, all of which were deployed on the West Coast and the Great Western.

There was better news, however, about electrification. In July 1984, Nicholas Ridley announced that the government had approved a scheme to electrify the East Coast Main Line, which, despite the operation of the huge Deltic diesels, had become something of a poor cousin to the electrified West Coast. In fact, the final section of the West Coast Main Line electrification, between the junction to

Liverpool and Glasgow, had not been completed until 1974 – and even then, the go-ahead was only given by the Labour government in 1970 as an incentive to the Scottish public just before a crucial by-election in Ayrshire.

The East Coast electrification had long been mooted, and equally the subject of hesitation by the politicians, but it was finally given the go-ahead by Nicholas Ridley on the basis that it would provide improved productivity and reduced costs as well as a ten-minute reduction in the journey time between Edinburgh and London. Clearly, Reid's friendship with Ridley had borne fruit, as the Transport Secretary managed to sell the scheme to the Cabinet. Former Network SouthEast managing director John Nelson recalls that this was a remarkable coup for BR's chairman. 'Reid secured the electrification of the East Coast Main Line against all opposition, really. The government did not want it, the civil servants did not want it, but Reid persuaded them to do it. That was a huge achievement.'[21]

The East Coast, too, had been electrified from King's Cross to Hitchin in Hertfordshire for suburban services; but after this was completed in 1978, the plan to put up the wires for a further 300 miles all the way to Edinburgh stalled because of government doubts over whether the investment offered value for money. After Ridley finally agreed, work started in 1985. The Great Eastern Main Line, which was electrified from London only as far as Colchester, was also converted in this period. A two-year project to extend electrification all the way to Norwich saw electric services start in May 1987.

The final cost of the East Coast project, which included new rolling stock, was £344 million at 1983 prices, a very small increase on the original budget of £332 million. The work was carried out in phases, reaching Leeds in 1988, York a year later and finally Edinburgh in 1991, with services starting just eight weeks later than scheduled. This was an impressive achievement, given electrification required some 30,000 masts to be erected and a dozen power feeder stations to be built, while 100 bridges had to be raised to provide clearance for the overhead line equipment. As happens with many new electric trains, they caused interference with the signalling system which consequently had to be extensively modified. A few corners were cut, such as a lack of robustness in the masts which resulted in all too frequent wire collapses at times of high winds; but managing to keep within the budget for such a complex scheme was an impressive feat. Indeed, it contrasted sharply with the next major main-line electrification, the Great Western in the mid-2010s, which was carried out after the break-up of the railway and whose costs soared out of control, ending up three times greater than the original estimate.

Procuring a new set of electric trains for the East Coast had the added positive side effect of releasing some much-needed High Speed Train sets for other lines. The British Railways Board gave approval to develop what became known as the InterCity 225 electric locomotive. Based on the work carried out for the design of the Advanced Passenger Train in the 1970s, it was the most powerful locomotive on the network at the time. It could

run at 140 mph (225 kph), and actually reached 162 mph
in a test run in September 1989. Another trial run between
London and Edinburgh took just under three and a half
hours; but operating such non-stop trains was, in practice, difficult, because of the shortage of capacity on the
tracks. Unfortunately, the Class 91, as it was known, was
never able to reach more than 125 mph in regular service
because, again, as with the Advanced Passenger Train,
BR made the mistake of specifying a speed that could
not be achieved on its tracks without a total change of the
signalling system. Sadly, therefore, the thirty-one train
sets which were produced never lived up to their '225'
billing.

In line with new procurement procedures, the manu-
facture of the locomotive and its coaches – a new Mark 4
design – was put out to tender rather than being carried
out in BR's own workshops. This was a departure from
past practice and resulted in what the history of InterCity
describes as 'a new and clearly effective style of *business-led*
project management'. Its success was the result of having
'a clear project with measurable objectives; a dedicated
yet accountable project team and a number of disciplined
and simple systems of control'.[22] There were the usual
and inevitable teething problems, which took a couple of
years to sort out, but there was an immediate positive
effect on passengers as soon as the full electrified service
was introduced in 1991. Passenger numbers increased
during the first year, though the subsequent recession led
to a reduction.

Given its designation as a part of the 'commercial

railway', InterCity had to make a profit. When the sector was created at the bottom of the economic slump of the early 1980s, the once-profitable services were losing £100 million a year on revenue of around £400 million. Following the arrangement mentioned above between Ridley and Reid, subsidy for InterCity was supposed to end in April 1988.

Under pressure from the British Railways Board, Bleasdale immediately set about trying to improve the economics of the business by allocating the spare sets of trains to key routes. Having been given commercial freedom, he was able to deploy the trains to lines where they would earn the most revenue. The Midland Main Line – the services to the East Midlands and Sheffield from St Pancras – was particularly poorly performing as it was operated with slow, ageing rolling stock. Bleasdale decided to transfer a few HST sets to the line, improving journey times and offering a more comfortable experience for passengers. This is precisely the sort of decision that would have been impossible under the old structure of regional management. Armed with the figures which came out of the new accounting system – over which he had control – Bleasdale was able to show there was immediate benefit. Passenger revenue went up by a third in the first four weeks because now commercial considerations were supreme. This showed that the sector directors, who were still trying to establish themselves, had clout.

Costs also needed to be addressed. Some savings were immediately clear, such as making better use of HSTs to replace loco-hauled stock. Five task forces were set up to work on plans for each of InterCity's subsectors, covering West Coast, East Coast, Great Western, Midland and Cross Country, and their aim was to reduce costs by 10 per cent on each of these lines. This was achieved thanks to improvements to the maintenance of both the fleet and the infrastructure, again made easier by the fact that all of this was under the control of the unified management of the sector. On the West Coast, there were huge savings as a result of adding driving-van trailers to the trains, which meant they could be driven from either end, obviating the need for the locomotive to be changed at terminus stations. New, more powerful locomotives were also introduced, from late 1987, replacing the first generation of electric engines introduced in the 1960s.

With costs reducing, and passenger income rising by 10 per cent, BR's annual report for 1988/9 proudly announced that 'in its first year as a fully commercial business, InterCity turned an operating loss of £86m into a profit of £57m'. It was not just cost-cutting measures, such as the better use of rolling stock, and the economic upturn that delivered this turnaround. There was, too, a bit of cheating, because (as mentioned previously) not only had profitable routes been added to InterCity's portfolio, but various loss-making destinations, such as Barrow-in-Furness and Cleethorpes, were no longer served. Dumping costs like this on to Provincial Railways ensured InterCity's move into the black, and profits increased in the next few years, until the recession of the early 1990s.

There was another factor. Fares rose above the rate of

inflation every year throughout the period of sectorization, and BR tended to put prices up more on routes that were overcrowded in order to reduce pressure to invest in them. This infamously became known as 'choking off' demand, which made sense in narrow economic terms for BR but was nonsensical for an organization and, indeed, a government intent on pursuing policies that were supportive of the environment and of enabling those without cars to travel cheaply.

The turnaround in British Rail's fortunes did not go unnoticed. While inevitably there were still negative stories in the press, there was, for the first time, some remarkably favourable coverage, exemplified by this editorial in the *Observer* in September 1985:

> Since 1980 Britain has actually developed the most cost-effective railway network in Western Europe, far more so than France, Italy or West Germany. As many as 27 per cent of the industry's workers have gone over the past five years and a further net saving of 15,000 staff is expected by 1987, with cuts in the managerial grades in particular. At the same time, we have not seen any dramatic axing of branch lines, and the fears of a Beeching-style closure operation following the Serpell report of January 1983 have proved groundless ... In the past, Mrs Thatcher may have felt BR was a bottomless pit of wasteful public expenditure. Now, in the language of Chancellor Nigel Lawson, it is beginning to look like a good investment.

This was praise indeed, and there was similar coverage

in other newspapers. Of course, there were critical articles, too, but sectorization had begun to turn around the
public image of the railway. However, while sectorization
was beginning to bed in, it was still only a half measure
and there were further changes to make. The continued
existence side by side of the regions and the sectors could
only be temporary, as Reid knew. It took nearly a decade
before he embarked on the final reorganization which
would herald British Rail's best years, just before the
ultimate assault from government.

I2

The Pinnacle

Just like 'sectorization', the term 'organizing for quality' is banal business speak, but it signified another important step change in the history of British Rail. 'OfQ', as it became widely known, created the most efficient and commercially driven structure in BR's fifty-year history. Sadly, however, it was brought to a premature end by the most radical privatization ever attempted on a railway network anywhere in the developed world.

By the late 1980s, sectorization had clearly demonstrated its viability. InterCity was profitable again – though, as we have seen, with a bit of creative accountancy – and Network SouthEast was breaking even, thanks in part to a booming economy following the Big Bang in the City. That was a remarkable achievement for a suburban railway, whose main function was carrying people in and out of the centre of London during the rush hour. Overall, BR was thriving, with train miles up by almost a fifth from 1985 to 1988, while costs per passenger dropped by nearly a third.

However, Robert Reid's reorganization plan was not

yet complete. The ultimate objective had always been to replace the regions with sectors that would be genuine standalone businesses. The term 'organizing for quality' was coined by Ivor Warburton, then the general manager of the London Midland Region, who saw it as reflecting the BR board's desire to put quality and customer focus at the heart of its operation. Underpinning OfQ was the creation of three passenger and three freight sectors (a late addition was Rail Express Systems, which carried mail) which would encompass the whole British Rail business. Therefore a series of subsectors – five each for InterCity and Provincial, and nine for Network SouthEast – would be established as profit centres and, effectively, subsidiaries of the main sectors.

In 1990, Bob Reid, a former chief executive of the oil giant Shell, who had worked there for thirty-five years, succeeded his namesake as BR chairman. He had been selected as a safe pair of hands but quickly became a thorn in the government's side, objecting to many of the more extreme ideas being put forward for selling off the railway.

Bob Reid proved to be a good choice for the railway. Unlike many executives brought in from other industries, he understood the peculiarities of railway culture right from the start, as John Nelson recalls:

> He did not come merely with the self-confidence of someone who had been successful in his own previous sphere; neither did he present himself as someone who knew all the answers. He displayed no arrogance and

was someone who listened . . . [and] was open, honest and straightforward in the post-Clapham period. With BR moving in an increasingly business focused direction, Reid II was the ideal successor to his namesake.[1]

Bob Reid endorsed the basic concept of OfQ, even though there were objections within BR, mostly – inevitably – from the regional managers, who would lose their traditional role within the new structure. There were concerns that splitting engineers into groups accountable to the different sectors would increase bureaucracy and cost. One group of senior staff even produced a 34-page dossier arguing against the change, but the new structure was generally welcomed by most senior BR managers. Despite some protests by the train drivers' union ASLEF, OfQ was adopted remarkably quickly despite its radical nature.

The transformation started with the East Coast Main Line and was completed by late 1992, by which time the re-elected Tory government had announced plans to privatize the railway. BR managers knew OfQ was unlikely to survive, although there were hopes that its best elements would be retained (which proved forlorn, as we will see in the concluding chapter).

OfQ delivered radical change. InterCity, for example, went from a business with just 350 mostly operational staff to one employing 35,000 people after the engineering functions were transferred into the sector. For the first time since the demise of the Big Four railways in 1947, cost and revenue would be the responsibility of a manager able to make decisions that would affect the financial situation. This had never happened previously in BR's history.

John Nelson, who succeeded Chris Green as head of Network SouthEast, says this was a wake-up call for engineers:

> Until then, the main identification of the track workers, supervisors and management was with civil engineering, not with a business. After OfQ, they were more likely to identify with the business, as they could see the contribution they were making to the success of the business in a way that was not really possible before, and I think that brought tremendous benefits.[2]

Achieving change through all the layers of BR management was never an easy task, but as one of the managers pushing through the new structure put it, the single biggest task was 'to create the belief in middle management that it was going to happen', especially since numerous previous attempts at reorganization had foundered on the rocks of internal resistance.[3]

Inevitably, the new structure wasn't perfect. The high cost of maintaining infrastructure meant that simple jobs like painting station waiting rooms were often pushed down the list of priorities in order to protect the bottom line, even though peeling paint was not a good advertisement for the railway. Concerns over the break-up of engineering teams were well founded but not insoluble, provided there was flexibility in the system to ensure that teams from one sector could be drafted in to help another one when there was a big project or unexpected demand. As Terry Gourvish explains, while there was added complexity because big engineering teams were split up, which resulted in some internal trading rules when people or equipment were used by different sectors, 'the process required goodwill as well as strictly commercial transactions'.[4] Much of that goodwill, however, would be lost when the railway was privatized, resulting in added costs and a myriad contracts. There was, too, a cost to creating the OfQ structure, estimated at between £50 million and £70 million, much of which was spent on redundancies. Nevertheless, while there has never been a perfect way to run a railway, BR came close to achieving it with OfQ. John Edmonds, the manager who had seen through the transformation, called it, correctly, 'the biggest change in organisation ever undertaken on Britain's Railways'.[5] Gourvish adds that the process was very much in line with business thinking at the time:

> From a broader perspective, the changes were very much in tune with the business gurus' preaching of the virtues of 'flexibility', leaner management and a focus on 'core competences'. They also reflected an interest in learning some of the secrets of Japan's 'economic miracle', including her enthusiasm for *keiretsu* (loose but effective conglomerate holding companies), the obsession with quality, first advanced by [the noted management consultant guru] Edwards Deming, and the *kaizen* (continuous process) approach to management-led improvement.[6]

In other words, British Rail was at the forefront of contemporary modern management thinking.

In terms of staffing, one of the biggest effects of OfQ was to reduce the number of staff working at headquarters to just 640 from 17,000, most of whom were redeployed to the sectors, although there were a few redundancies. Overall staffing numbers were initially little changed, though by 1994, before the start of the privatization process, they had been reduced to 109,000, a drop of 13 per cent since the reorganization.

Nelson points out that this was the first time British Rail had a truly integrated structure. Although BR always had control of all aspects of the railway, the way it was structured into regions and functions meant that the separate hierarchies did not interact except at the very top. As Nelson puts it: 'Prior to 1982, the term "silo management" could almost have been coined with the railways in mind.'[7]

It had taken nearly half a century, but BR had at last got it right, almost by accident. BR had been pushed into reorganizing by a government that wanted to separate out the commercial and social railways, quite possibly with the eventual aim of selling off the former. But while the motivation for the change might have come from government, the result was a far more logical way of running a railway. Even loss-making parts of the business benefitted from the concentration on their particular task at hand, and this made it easier to motivate people to find solutions rather than just avoiding responsibility. This resulted in a genuinely integrated railway that was focused on passengers. Nelson describes it well:

The way track and signalling systems were configured to accommodate the trains and the way timetables developed to meet specific needs were far, far more likely to provide the best outcomes if the key managers responsible for delivering them were seated round the same table, accountable not just to a single chief executive but to one another in a tightly managed, well-motivated team.[8]

It was the end of the silo system. In this new structure, engineers, who tended to override other managers by expressing concerns about safety or emphasizing the necessity of a particular project, were now forced to take account of the wider implications of their decisions. It made them more likely to come up with innovative solutions to specific issues, rather than merely arguing that 'things are always done like this'.

It would be a big mistake to characterize this reorganization as dull and technocratic and as having little impact on the quality of passenger services. Quite the opposite. It affected every aspect of the running of the railway and the improvements to passenger services were noticeable. There was, in effect, a rolling programme of changes across much of the network, which the sector managers could implement far more easily than under the old structure.

One of Green's legacies on Network SouthEast was the concept of 'total route modernization'. This involved an integrated investment plan incorporating refurbishment of the track, signalling and stations, as well as the introduction of new rolling stock, in effect creating a new railway. This was carried out on the Chiltern line out of Marylebone and resulted in a significant boost in passenger numbers. Green had hoped that the neglected services out of Fenchurch Street would be next, but unfortunately this was delayed by lack of money and killed off by privatization.

It was thanks to Green, too, that Network SouthEast received a huge wave of new rolling stock. Although there had been a steady stream of new trains following the start of the sectorization process, there were still far too many of the old 'slam-door' type. In Europe, only Portugal and Greece still had these trains in suburban service, and BR was desperate to phase them out, but persuading the government to fund a replacement programme was no easy task.

Green had been pressing for modern trains to replace slam-door stock and BR started developing what became the Networker in 1988. A very detailed business case examining all the options, including double-decker trains (impractical because of the extra time involved in getting passengers on and off the trains, and because of the small size of the loading gauge) and longer coaches (also ruled out because of the cost of straightening curved platforms), won over the Transport Secretary, Cecil Parkinson. He took the idea to Mrs Thatcher at a weekend meeting at Chequers, and in August 1989 he was able to announce the contracts, worth a total of £690 million, which included the cost of building a depot at Slade Green in south London. The order for nearly 150 four-car units was split between two manufacturers: BREL, which became part of ABB, a Swedish–Swiss consortium, in 1992; and Metro-Cammell, which later became part of Alstom, the French company that produced the TGV. Having two suppliers of basically the same train caused numerous difficulties; for example, their spare parts tended to be different, adding to the cost and complexity of maintenance. The trains started operating in early 1992 and quickly proved popular, despite a few, fortunately very rare, incidents of units suddenly decoupling, and the lack of air conditioning.

Chris Green took over as managing director of Inter-City at the beginning of 1992 and was keen to increase brand loyalty with improvements to the catering service, the creation of customer welcome teams and the hiring of a dedicated sales force – all of which were designed to match the airlines' quality of service.

By 1990, InterCity had become an established brand, rated as one of Britain's top 150 businesses. It pushed its luxury products – Premium and Pullman – hard, but had to be careful not to appear elitist and alienate leisure travellers who filled off-peak services, albeit at a heavy discount. To attract them, InterCity introduced cheap advance fare tickets (called Apex) across its network and backed this up with extensive advertising based on a slogan developed by the huge advertising agency Saatchi & Saatchi: 'Welcome to a city – Welcome to InterCity.'

The implementation of OfQ enabled InterCity to maintain its profitability even in the recession that followed Black Wednesday on 16 September 1992, the day when Britain was forced to exit the European Exchange

Rate Mechanism to prevent the collapse of the pound. In 1992/3, profits increased to £65 million, and the following year reached £100 million, thanks both to growth and to what Green called 'a grinding attention to attacking costs'.

There was also progress at the loss-making Provincial Railways. Gordon Pettitt, who had been head of the Southern Region, took over from John Welsby in May 1990, but only after insisting on key changes:

> Before accepting the job, there were two things that had to change. My first target was the name 'Provincial', which seemed a totally misleading name for just under half the national network and dismissive of Scotland, Wales and much of England . . . The second was headquarters. While all sectors had been located in London, it seemed wholly inappropriate for Provincial.[9]

The name change to Regional Railways was simply slipped through, without even asking the BR board, when Pettitt presented his plans for OfQ. And he soon found much cheaper and more appropriate offices in Birmingham.

Pettitt faced several immediate challenges. Pacers, which were the backbone of many services, were unreliable, with gearbox failures and jamming brakes. Performance was so bad, with sometimes up to half of the trains out of action, that the Passenger Transport Executives, which paid British Rail to provide the service, were starting to withhold payments. Pettitt identified several persistent problems, which required modification to the doors, the gearboxes and the brakes, and reliability improved enormously, with the Pacers surviving until 2021. The ones in use in Cornwall, however – the 'Skippers' – were moved elsewhere in the 1990s because the tight bends and steep inclines on the branch lines where they were mostly used caused excessive wear, which made them uneconomic.

Pettitt was also conscious of competition from the car, now that the motorway network had been completed. The renaming of the organization reflected the way that services were focused. The new Sprinter trains that were now entering service could operate far faster than the loco-hauled stock they were replacing, and consequently they were better able to compete with cars on medium-distance regional journeys.

Following OfQ, Regional Railways became a large organization with 30,000 employees, and the subsectors, now known as profit centres, were crucial to its success. As with the other sectors, Regional Railways became a fully integrated railway, and its profit-centre managers had considerable powers over both generating new traffic and reducing costs. Pettitt stipulated that as much as possible of all aspects of the railway – marketing, planning and operation – was to be carried out by the profit centres: 'I tried to devolve the maximum I could. In the end we even split up the PSO [Public Service Obligation, the subsidy to loss-making lines] – though we couldn't be accurate to the last penny.'[10] The profit centres were allowed to take on extra staff to improve customer service, even though this was an additional cost, as long as they met their overall annual budget set by the sector. All

this gave the profit-centre managers a sense of ownership, rather than a feeling that they were subject to the
whims of the BR board.

Soon after his arrival at Regional Railways, Pettitt issued
a 'Prospectus for Quality' showing the aspiration for better reliability and punctuality, as well as a reduction in
infrastructure costs. He believed that travellers would
stick to their cars unless offered equally high standards of
comfort and amenity, such as adjustable seats, carpets and
catering. It was not until April 1991 that Regional Railways became a fully fledged independent sector within
BR with its own board and a new identity, based on Provincial's blue stripe.

During his two years in charge, Pettitt showed what a
dynamic state-run organization could do with a loss-
making service. But this period also demonstrated the
fundamental problem of having the government breath-
ing down the railway's neck and controlling the purse
strings at inappropriate moments. It was easier giving a
sense of purpose to InterCity, which was inherently
profitable – especially given its finances had been skewed
in its favour – and to Network SouthEast, which was not
only a flagship organization serving a high-profile market
but was also breaking even. Regional Railways, that ragbag of passenger services, the remnants of the network
that remained after the two other organizations had
cherry-picked their routes, was a more difficult sector to
motivate.

John Welsby had already begun to transform the disparate group of services which made up Regional Railways

into an effective railway and Pettitt accelerated that process. When, however, the government responded to a downturn in the economy by freezing all new rail investment in 1991, Regional Railways was hit particularly hard, as it had a programme to spend £300 million on rolling stock and other improvements over the next three years. It was the downside of being in the state sector, particularly with a government that never saw the railway as a business but instead viewed it as a burden on the state finances which had to be controlled through cost-cutting, and disciplined when the wider economy was in crisis. It was not BR's independence that was the problem – it was the lack of it.

Pettitt believes the freezing of investment was a missed opportunity to establish a different type of relationship between BR and the government. He wanted the government to clearly explain the purpose of Regional Railways:

> In all the time I have worked in the railway, no one has ever said what is it for? No government has ever done that. When I was at Regional Railways, it was beginning to show major reductions in cost but also a big increase in passenger numbers. None of this achievement was being recognized, but rather, the government set the general objective of 'get the cost down, and then down again by another £20 million or so'. That was not sustainable or sensible.[11]

In response to the government's failure to define what his railway was for, Pettitt – who has a very unsentimental attitude towards the railway, characterized by his questioning of the need for little-used lines and services – took a big risk. He commissioned a review from Paul King, the planning and marketing director he had brought in from the shoe industry, to take a hard look at the network and work out the profitability of each service and the social benefits generated by them. In addition, King was asked to assess how costs could be reduced in order to improve the financial situation. It was a potentially explosive intervention since it risked restarting the whole debate about closures. The findings were indeed dramatic, but not surprising. Of the 5,618 miles in the Regional Railways network, revenue from the fare box on more than 1,000 did not even meet the cost of crewing, fuelling and cleaning the trains, let along making a contribution to longer-term costs such as the rolling stock, track maintenance, signalling and station staff.

There was a conundrum. In predominantly urban areas, where the local roads were growing ever more congested, increasing motorization made it far more advantageous to travel by train. On the other hand, rising car ownership was bad for the railway in rural areas as it reduced the number of people likely to use services. Therefore the implication was that Regional Railways should concentrate on inter-urban services, and on those likely to contribute to a reduction in road congestion, rather than spending a lot of money, as Pettitt puts it, on services 'trundling round Lincolnshire'. Rural and other loss-makers absorbed a disproportionate amount of government grant and this would become worse as car ownership rose. The harsh truth was that railways in lightly populated areas are not a sensible method of transport once car ownership becomes prevalent. This was not exactly news, but the review did expose this harsh truth.

Pettitt and King even devised a formula to assess whether an investment scheme was viable, based on factors such as revenue per vehicle, vehicle utilization and loadings (how many people were on each train). As a result of the review, Regional Railways melded together various short inter-urban services to offer long-distance routes across Great Britain that offered connections between several major urban centres not well served (or served at all) by InterCity, such as Brighton–Great Malvern, Milford Haven–Penzance and Cardiff–Portsmouth. Similarly, services to the two airports which were newly connected to the rail network, Manchester and Stansted, were also operated from towns and cities across the country. An upgraded version of the Sprinter, which became available from 1989, helped to improve the speed of these connections.

Fundamentally, Pettitt and King were seeking clarity by providing evidence to the government and then asking what it wanted to do. After all the ways of reducing costs were exhausted and all measures to improve revenue examined, the key question was, according to King, 'What do you want to buy because this is what it costs and why are you buying it?'[12] The government, already beginning to think about privatization, never came back with an answer and the break-up of the railway into twenty-five franchises, explained in the next chapter, meant that such strategic and coherent thinking was lost. Pettitt still regrets this failure: 'This type of thinking could have been used to define the shape and nature of the franchises, but the review and the thinking behind it was simply kicked into the long grass.'[13]

This missed opportunity did, at least, show that the government had no interest in closing little-used lines. Indeed, the trend was in the other direction. One measure of the way that British Rail and indeed government had changed during the 1980s was that closures were no longer on the agenda – with the exception of the battle over the Settle–Carlisle line – but reopenings definitely were. Stations long abandoned and sections of route cut off by Beeching were being brought back into the network. The impetus often came from local people who were fed up with not having a connection to the network and who were able to make the case that there would be demand for a restored service. The creation of the Passenger Transport Executives stimulated the more rail-oriented local councils into supporting reopenings, particularly of stations, and there was further encouragement in 1981 in the form of new legislation – the Speller amendment to the 1962 Transport Act – which allowed British Rail to be more adventurous around reopenings. The new law enabled BR to try out services on new routes and then withdraw them if there was insufficient demand, without going through the lengthy and cumbersome closure procedure. Research by Leeds University at the time showed that the number of passengers needed to justify a new station or reopening was far lower than had been previously thought and this encouraged local groups to come forward with schemes.

This stimulated something of a golden age of reopenings and expansion. Whereas there had been a trickle of new station openings in the 1970s, with three or four every year, it turned into something of a flood in the mid-1980s, promoted strongly by the Railway Development Society (now Railfuture), which emerged as a strong pro-rail pressure group. Between 1985 and 1994, there were 157, an average of fifteen per year, with the peak period being the two years from the start of 1986, when fifty stations were added to the network. Most of these additions fitted the pattern supported by Pettitt, as they tended to be in urban areas where patronage was immediately quite high, rather than on the branch lines culled by Beeching. Several lines and links were reopened, too, notably in areas that had been affected by mine closures, such as the Robin Hood line in Nottinghamshire and Aberdare–Abercynon in South Wales. Scotland, too, saw some prominent reopenings, and it was noticeable that when local or regional government was given a say in transport issues, there was often strong support for rail schemes.

As if to show the sometimes contradictory forces within BR, the 1980s were the final years of a period when it embarked on its notorious 'closure by stealth' policy for lines it was keen to shut. The tactic was to gradually reduce the train service to such an extent that it was no longer of much use, and then to announce that, since no one was using it, the line might as well be closed. In fact, as the focus turned towards expansion and reopenings, these tactics were largely abandoned except, as mentioned previously, over the failed attempt to close the Settle–Carlisle route.

It is always tendentious and risky to speak of golden ages, but the last decade or so of British Rail was undoubtedly its finest period and an example of a successful state enterprise. There is certainly no doubting that, while British Rail rather drifted in the 1970s and struggled under the pressure of increased competition, high inflation and reduced investment, there were happier times thereafter. All the indicators moved in the right direction during the 1980s, with good levels of investment, increased passenger numbers – though freight declined – much-needed new rolling stock and improved passenger satisfaction. The 1994 timetable, the last produced by BR, was reckoned to be the best ever. The press, too, was kinder to British Rail than it had been in the past, though there were still negative articles based largely on past failings.

One legacy of BR was a group of superb managers, most of whom were graduates of the organization's management training scheme. Too numerous to mention, though many have been quoted in earlier chapters, they were a dedicated group of men (and an all too small number of women) who first restructured the organization to make it far more effective and efficient, and then enabled it to be privatized while maintaining its operations. Their talents flourished through sectorization and, later, OfQ. Terry Gourvish, who is not uncritical of BR, highlights the achievements of a few of these managers:

[Robert] Reid revolutionised the way in which middle management handled costs and revenues, [John] Prideaux took InterCity into profit, and [John] Edmonds transformed British Rail's Cinderella business, Provincial. Chris Green created the important brands ScotRail and Network SouthEast; [and] in the face of gloom and under-funding, he introduced marketing innovations and encouraged a greater sense of pride in service provision.

As Gourvish also notes, many of these managers went on to work in the higher echelons of the privatized railway for many years: 'If the intention of privatisation was to inject some *new* managers into train operating, there has been precious little evidence of it.'[14] Remarkably, according to Roger Ford, technology editor of *Modern Railways*, after a quarter of century of privatisation, 'in 2021, 60 per cent of train operating companies and 60 per cent of Network Rail's route directors were former BR managers', which demonstrates the all-round railway skills that this group was able to obtain within the BR system.[15]

Another demonstration of BR's entrepreneurial and commercial spirit can be seen in its overall manpower, with the 640,000 people employed by the newly created organization in 1948 reduced to just 109,000 when it was preparing to be privatized – representing the loss of 10,000 staff every year throughout its history. The cosy culture of a 'job for life' and restrictive practices that prevented technological development had been ended by BR. There was a negative aspect to this, as there was a loss of the sense of loyalty and dedication that character-ized the railway when it was nationalized, but in many cases this was merely a front for an inefficient culture.

There were technical successes, too. Although the Advanced Passenger Train was a failure, its development helped to provide the basis for future successful tilting trains, and the High Speed Train which was developed in its stead was an undoubted success, as demonstrated by its longevity. British Rail, too, led the world in signalling technology, such as solid state interlocking (software that prevents the conflicting movement of trains), electronic control centres, the use of fibre optics and portable ticket-ing machines.

Of course there were downsides, notably government pressure on BR to introduce above-inflation fare increases, the constant worry that the good relationship with minis-ters during much of the 1980s would sour, the continued decline of freight – though this did relieve some over-crowded routes so that more passenger trains could operate – and a negative culture within some parts of the organization, such as petty thieving of fares income, and a tendency for people to 'knock off' early unless properly supervised, although this was not unique to the railway and in any case improved during the 1980s. Industrial relations also got better during BR's tenure, but still remained a source of conflict and inefficiency right to the end. Much of the investment had been made possible by the sale of property, which was not an inexhaustible source, and there was a nagging concern among managers that the government would suddenly reduce support for the railway because funding was only guaranteed on a year-to-year basis. Not only was this fear realized with the recession of 1991, which hit the industry hard and led, as we have seen, to an investment embargo, but it contributed to many people within the organization favouring privatization on the basis that it would end this dependence on government whim. To some extent, this has been borne out. Railtrack, and then Network Rail, were required to draw up five-year investment plans; this spending, once agreed through a complex mechanism involving the Rail Regulator (later the Office of Road and Rail), was largely guaranteed. This provided the industry with a new level of certainty, but the argument that it was necessary to privatize the railway to achieve this does not hold water. It would be perfectly possible for a government to guarantee future levels of spending on the railway, as it does for many other aspects of state expenditure. As John Nelson puts it: 'BR was almost a role model of how to run a state-owned railway on a shoestring.'[16]

There is a strong case for saying that BR did not deserve the fate that it suffered. Breaking it up for a fire sale in a hurried and unplanned way ended up costing billions of taxpayers' money and did nothing to improve the passenger experience. In one of the odd aspects of the rapid privatization, BR was required to provide more than £2 million in grants to sixty-seven management-buyout teams among its staff, seventeen of which were successful in their bids. Perhaps the greatest testimony to BR's success was that it was able to destroy itself so efficiently when asked to do so by the Tory government elected in 1992.

13

Epilogue

The privatization of the railway and its quarter of a century long aftermath ought, of course, to be the subject of another book.[1] This one is about British Railways and how its reputation has been traduced by those who sought to break it up, even though it had become a model of how a successful state-owned organization could be run. However, it is important just to outline the bare bones of the privatization process and highlight its flaws.

The most damning aspect of the change was that the highly competent, articulate and successful group of managers whose efforts have been covered in depth in earlier chapters were simply ignored by the politicians and their advisers. As Chris Green told me in an interview in 2001: 'We had meetings with the Department of Transport but they had already taken a view that they wanted BR to be privatised as 100 companies. They ignored BR. The unique feature of rail privatization is that the nature of the organization was not decided by experts but by consultants and politicians.' He added that one of the government's key aims of the privatization was 'to break union power, though they could not say that publicly'.

BR's success in turning itself around through sectorization attracted widespread attention on the other side of the Channel. An analysis of government support for railways across the Continent found that BR's subsidy was a mere 0.16 per cent of gross national product, compared with the Continental average of 0.52 per cent, more than three times as much. The editors of the authoritative *Oxford Companion to British Railway History*, published in 1997, noted that the cost reductions and the efforts to maximize fare revenue 'led to BR, on statistical comparisons with almost all European railways, showing the highest productivity and also the lowest level of funding by government'. They added, rather cruelly, 'that did not affect public perception of shortcomings in service quality in some areas', which, interestingly, suggested that a bit of extra government support to improve the railway would not have gone amiss.[2] In fact, investment levels were comparatively high in relation to other railways in Europe, but most of this money was being spent on the improvements required to accommodate the traffic using the Channel Tunnel, which had been under construction since 1988. BR had just announced its 1994 timetable, which was termed 'the best ever' by two consultants in their book on rail privatization.[3]

But all this was to no avail. Whatever BR did, and however good its performance, it was doomed. The die was cast with the result of the 1992 general election, won surprisingly by John Major's Tories with a very vaguely worded commitment to rail privatization in the manifesto. The justification for privatization was difficult to discern, and four years of discussion and at times acrimonious debate within the Tory party had left the government with a policy but with no clear way of implementing it. As already mentioned in Chapter 9, there had been various schemes dreamt up by Tory politicians over the years, but largely they had either been rejected or forgotten. Mrs Thatcher had, as we saw, firmly put Nicholas Ridley in his place when he came to her with the idea, but subsequently she vacillated over the issue. Her instinctive dislike for the public sector clashed with her political antennae, which had detected that the railway was much dearer to the hearts of the British people than boring old gas or electricity, the subject of recent sales. Ridley's successor but one, Paul Channon, persuaded her to allow him to set out five possible options for the sale of the railway at the Conservative party conference in September 1988, but when he was replaced by Cecil Parkinson, she grew cold on the idea and tried to prevent the new Transport Secretary mentioning it at the 1989 conference. But the lady who famously claimed she was 'not for turning' wavered, and at the following year's conference, held two months before her resignation, Parkinson announced that the government was now 'determined to privatise British Rail' and went on to emphasize the approach by saying, 'The question now is not about whether we should privatise it, but how and when.'[4]

A working group of ministers and officials from the Department of Transport was set up to establish how this could be achieved, but its work was distracted not only by Thatcher's replacement by John Major in the autumn of 1990 but also by the departure of Parkinson and the appointment of Malcolm Rifkind. There was fierce disagreement between the Treasury and the Department of Transport over whether there should be a vertically integrated model, where track and operations were kept together, or – as the Treasury favoured – a track authority model, which allowed different operators to run on tracks owned by a separate company. At one point, the Treasury was intent on creating an auction to sell each individual train path to the highest bidder – £x million for the 0800 from Kings Cross to Leeds, £y million for the 0900 – a madcap idea which was at the extreme end of free-market thinking and foundered on the rocks of reality when it was pointed out that train services are highly interdependent and people wanted the freedom to take any train, not just those of a particular operator. Various models were put forward for selling off the railway: retaining the sectors, reverting to the Big Four that existed pre-war, offering the whole of BR as a single entity, or separating the infrastructure from the operations in the track authority model.

These various options were still being discussed when the 1992 general election was called. There was no plan, and no worked-out method of carrying out the policy. Even the Tories themselves had expected to lose the election, and consequently they were particularly ill-prepared to deliver on what was a very complex and largely unpopular policy. Post-election, there were tales of young Tory party whippersnappers charging round Whitehall in search of ideas on how to sell off the railway that they could take to ministers.

All this led to a situation where, having won the election, no one knew quite how to privatize the railway. It was left to the new Transport Secretary, John MacGregor (no other department had suffered from such a busy revolving door as Transport), to produce a White Paper in great haste within a couple of months of the Tories' May 1992 victory.

Given the unresolved debates about the new structure for the privatized railway – notably the differences between the Treasury and the Department of Transport – as well as the lack of a strong political figure to push through the process, the eventual format was developed on the hoof. And crucially, in the absence of a strong voice in the Department of Transport, the Treasury won the main argument by pushing the track authority model, arguing that this was the only way to enable on-rail competition. As Jon Shaw notes in his introduction to a book on rail privatization:

> The decision to adopt the track authority model should not be regarded as the result of a detailed policy analysis. Despite the protracted evolution of rail privatisation policy and the existence of numerous models advanced by academics, think-tanks and civil servants, there is a strong possibility that MacGregor did not have the time

to choose the track authority model on the strength of a lengthy and thorough evaluation of which would be the most effective or successful means of rail privatisation.[5]

Indeed, there is a lot of evidence that the process was rushed and never properly evaluated. Since Labour was likely to win the next general election, and was opposed to the sale, it was felt that the railway would have to be off-loaded within the space of one Parliament, meaning that the White Paper setting out the plan had to be prepared in great haste. The decision to choose the track authority model was justified by ministers on the basis that it was a requirement of a new European Union Directive to split member states' railways in this way in order to facilitate on-rail competition. This point was consistently pressed by the Treasury's special adviser on rail privatization, Sir Christopher Foster, and ultimately MacGregor seems to have been forced into accepting the separation, even though the directive only specified the need to ensure that there was separate accounting between the operators and the track authority, rather than the much greater division that was eventually created. It was utterly disingenuous of various Eurosceptics in the Tory party to argue strongly that an obscure and widely ignored directive had to be obeyed to the letter, but this irony was rather lost in the rush to push through the legislation. In reality, the track authority model was pushed through not because of some spurious claim that European laws had to be obeyed, but because the Treasury was dead set in its desire to liberalize the railway market and create on-rail competition.

Within a few weeks of the election, a short White Paper was produced by the government setting out its privatization plans, MacGregor having argued there was no time to produce the usual Green Paper consultation document first. It was remarkably sparse and incredibly vague, lacking much of the requisite detail for such an important and complicated policy. My description at the time remains accurate:

> It was a thin, badly drafted and inadequate document which outlined, in very broad terms, the way the industry would be privatized. It set out, for the first time, the concept of franchising – inviting different operators to bid for the right to run a set of services for a fixed period – but with just 100 short paragraphs, it begged more questions than it answered.[6]

Many of its suggestions were never applied. It suggested a likely thirty-five to forty franchises when, in fact, there were eventually twenty-five. It stressed that network benefits – the ability to buy a ticket that could be used throughout the railway – would be preserved when, in fact, operators later sold tickets just for their own services. It made no mention of selling off the track authority, which became Railtrack, but in fact this ended up being the only part of the railway that was placed on the stock market. The notion of disposing of the stations through a stations authority was quietly dropped. And, oddly, two regulators rather than one were established.

In a rational world, the sectors would have been retained and privatized as units, or perhaps a regional structure, like that of the Big Four between the wars, would have been recreated. But privatization was not about rational decision, as Terry Gourvish points out: 'The transfer of ownership seemed to have become an end in itself rather than the means to an end.'[7] Breaking up the sectors was particularly counter-productive given the strength and widespread recognition of the InterCity brand. There were last-ditch attempts by BR managers to persuade the government to ensure that the separate businesses which made up the brand would retain the InterCity name after privatization, but these efforts were to no avail. Network SouthEast, too, disappeared – although, as mentioned before, at least its map survived. And oddly, the name InterCity survived, too, but only on the numerous railways abroad which had adopted it for their long-distance services.

Although there was never a coherent explanation given by ministers, the various reasons set out for the privatization at the time were a mix of:

- The high cost of the railway to the taxpayer and the need to reduce subsidy
- The decrepit state of the network
- Taking government out of the running of the railway
- Encouragement of private enterprise and flair
- The creation of competition
- Improving efficiency

There is only space here to highlight a few of the most egregious aspects of privatization. The fragmentation and sale damaged the rail industry and led to a series of disasters – initially, in terms of safety, and then, over a much longer term, financially. In my book *On the Wrong Line*, published in 2005, I explained how the cause of the four major train accidents during the early days of privatization – Southall in 1997, Ladbroke Grove in 1999, Hatfield in 2000 and Potters Bar in 2002 – could be traced to the way that the industry had been broken up and sold off with insufficient regard to the safety implications.

While the safety risks have been addressed through a series of improvements, the financial implications remain to this day. Right from the start of the privatization process, the amount of subsidy increased substantially because of the inefficiencies built into the complex structure created by the sell-off. The various interfaces between the series of companies that were created inevitably led to the need for complicated contracts which in turn required legal support and a byzantine procedure to allocate the causes of delays, which, according to one of the numerous inquiries into the working of the industry, required 400 delay-attribution clerks.

In terms of the aims cited above, none were achieved. Far from reducing the burden on the taxpayer, privatization actually increased it. The initial cost of fragmenting and then selling the railway was estimated conservatively at £600 million, and many of its assets – notably the rolling stock – were sold very cheaply due to the rush to get the railway into the private sector. And, longer term, BR's grant – the Public Service Obligation – of just under £500 million in 1989/90 (which was £655 million in

1997/8 prices) more than doubled to £1,425 million in the first fully privatized year of 1997/8. This pattern continued throughout the whole period of privatization. Rather than costs gradually reducing, as the government hoped, they kept on increasing, so that the railway subsidy hovered around £4 billion annually after privatization, and Network Rail's accumulation of £55 billion in debt to the government effectively added another £2 billion to the yearly subsidy since it will never be paid off.

While the condition of the network undoubtedly improved, this was paid for by government money, as grant to Railtrack and later Network Rail, and therefore these enhancements cannot be ascribed to privatization. The notion that government can ever escape responsibility for the railway was quickly disabused by the series of accidents mentioned above. It was ministers who had to stand up in Parliament and explain what happened, as well as having to implement measures to mitigate future disasters. Moreover, since the dream of a subsidy-free railway proved ever elusive – and, as mentioned numerous times in this book, is a Holy Grail that will never be found – government remained as the guarantor of rail services as well as the determinant of how they are provided. The private sector's role throughout was one of providing services and, at times, some investment; but the government was always in control.

The franchisees which took on the running of the railway have had a patchy record. While some provided good services with a focus on customer care, others performed miserably and several had their contracts terminated.

Overall, they were not required to invest, since their contracts were, for the most part, too short to justify large-scale expenditure and, therefore, their focus tended to be short term. Oddly, because the franchises were short and the role of the private sector was limited, there was very little opportunity for the private sector to demonstrate its 'flair'. As this book shows, there was, in fact, no shortage of commercial nous in BR when it was allowed the freedom to express it.

The competition issue is the most scandalous failure as the concept was flawed from the outset. As more perceptive politicians and commentators swiftly noted, the idea of franchising out chunks of the network was incompatible with open access – the notion that the railway should be opened up to on-rail competition – since there was the risk that profitable services would be cherry-picked by the franchisee's competitors. Astonishingly, MacGregor himself realized this very early on, as Jon Shaw notes: 'MacGregor argued that he knew on-rail competition would not work but delayed announcing this for tactical reasons.'[8] In other words, rather shockingly, the politician pushing through the new structure for the railway was aware right from the start that the main premise for choosing it was invalid. In the event, the Rail Regulator resolved the problem by essentially banning competition, except on a few underprovided routes, such as London–Hull.

The attempt to undermine union power was another consummate failure. By splitting the network into twenty-five franchises, the government inadvertently stimulated competition between the various operators for labour, notably drivers, whose wages soared as they played off the franchisees against each other. However, in other respects, there was more contracting out of functions such as cleaning services, which made it more difficult for unions to organize workers.

A quarter of a century of trying to work within this deeply flawed structure did not create a system as good as the one that existed when the industry was sold off. It proved impossible to iron out the inherent flaws and now, as I write, the government has finally admitted that the whole structure is dysfunctional and has embarked on a root-and-branch reform.

As I was finishing this book in the summer of 2021, the government at last published a long-awaited review of the industry. The process which had started in 2018 under the chairmanship of Keith Williams, a John Lewis executive and former British Airways chairman, had been much delayed both by arguments within government and by the Covid-19 pandemic. Taking the form of a government White Paper, *Great British Railways* set out plans for the future of the railway.

The government is proposing to create a new 'guiding mind' for the industry – which is to be called Great British Railways, since it would be too embarrassing to simply reuse the British Railways name. However, despite the implication, and the use of the old BR double arrow design as the new organization's logo, Humpty Dumpty is not being put back together again. Given that whole chunks of BR, such as the rolling stock and the engineering companies, have been sold off, this is not a recreation of the BR described in this book. Moreover, the operations will still be provided by the private sector, although on a much more restricted contract basis, with revenue going to Great British Railways rather than, as with the franchising system, to the private operators. One cannot, however, fail to notice that this is a retreat from full-on privatization and a return to the past, not least because the double arrow is going to be used on all trains and stations. Rather helpfully, the Paper accepts much of the criticism of the structure created by the 1993 Railways Act and instances many of the failures caused by privatization. These criticisms reflect much of what I have written in the past quarter of a century, which I could summarize but are probably best expressed as a lengthy *mea culpa* from the Tory government. These quotes are all taken from the White Paper and illustrate neatly that the aims of privatization cited above have not been achieved.[9]

So what happened to 'the creation of competition'?

Breaking British Rail into dozens of pieces was meant to foster competition between them and, together with the involvement of the private sector, was supposed to bring greater efficiency and innovation. Little of this has happened. Instead, the fragmentation of the network has made it more confusing for passengers, and more difficult and expensive to perform the essentially collaborative task of running trains on time ... A lack of innovation and incentive to modernise is partly responsible for this. (p. 13)

... Even before the pandemic, it was clear that this system was no longer viable. Such competition as there was had diminished, and UK companies were increasingly reluctant to even bid for franchises. (p. 18)

And to 'the high cost of the railway to the taxpayer and the need to reduce subsidy'?

The model put in place at privatisation has not done enough to deliver a more cost-efficient sector and many costs have consistently risen faster than inflation, with taxpayers and customers having to foot the bill. (p. 13)

And to 'taking government out of the running of the railway'?

The sector's structures do not work: people working in the rail industry are disempowered, and central government should not be so closely involved in operational decisions. Complex and adversarial relationships between operators, suppliers, Network Rail and government do not meet the needs of passengers, freight customers or taxpayers. (p. 14)

And to 'encouragement of private enterprise and flair'?

No leader or organisation at local, regional or national levels has responsibility and accountability for making the whole system work. Today's system does not always encourage the different parts of the sector to work together, nor reward them for doing the right thing or incentivise them to act in the overall interest, rather than a narrow agenda. Instead, co-ordination is governed by a costly, inflexible spider's web of often adversarial relationships, penalties and disconnected incentives. Network Rail and the train companies employ, for instance, almost 400 full-time staff, known as 'train delay attributors', to argue with each other about whose fault a delay is. (p. 15)

And to 'improving efficiency'?

Around 40 per cent of delays are disputed, representing significant sums of money, and as a result are debated over through an extensive escalation process, 199-page principles and rules document and an adjudication process overseen by an independently-chaired panel. Previous adjudications include, among other things, who was responsible for a train being so crowded that a passenger fainted, causing delays while they were taken off; and whether a pheasant is a small bird (in which case, according to the principles at the time, the train operator was to blame for a delay caused by hitting one) or a large bird (Network Rail's problem). (p. 15)

In relation to the timetable chaos of May 2018, which resulted in the launch of the inquiry, the White Paper said:

Services across the north and south east of England were disrupted for many weeks after the late delivery of infrastructure improvements by Network Rail, miscalculations by both it and operators in preparing timetable changes, and a failure of accountability and oversight throughout the process, led to a collapse in the national timetable. (p. 18)

As for the decrepit state of the network, this was largely remedied by vast quantities of extra government cash and allowing Railtrack and its successor, Network Rail, to pay for improvements by building up debt to the staggering amount of £55 billion by 2021. And as for the unstated reason of destroying the rail trade unions, as mentioned above, the wages of train drivers have soared after privatization as the privatized train operating companies have competed against each other.

The White Paper, therefore, set out a catalogue of the mistakes that had been made in breaking up British Rail. The amusing aspect of this is the way that the tone of the White Paper suggests it was a party other than the Tories which created the privatized structure and kept on propping it up in various ways over the intervening quarter of a century. And the preferred solution is: 'A simpler, more integrated structure [which] will cut duplication, increase Great British Railways' purchasing power and economies of scale, and make it easier and cheaper to plan maintenance, renewals and upgrades' (p. 8). One could hardly make it up.

One of the oddities of this story is that there is a small part of the United Kingdom's rail network that was left out of the 1993 Railway Act and allowed to continue without being privatized or fragmented. The rail network in Northern Ireland was considered too small to bother separating out or privatizing, and the political situation in the province too delicate to upset with such a radical move. Therefore, in the post-BR era, Northern Ireland Railways has continued to operate as a vertically integrated railway under state ownership. It has invested in new trains and upgraded its infrastructure, and it achieved its highest ever passenger numbers of fifteen million in the year 2018/19, before the pandemic. Despite the fact that the United Kingdom was in the European Union, there was no pressure on the railway in Northern Ireland to separate out its functions and the British government left it very much to its own devices, even paying for the recent high level of investment.

Railways pose a series of unique problems in terms of corporate structure. They are geographically spread, have huge sunk assets, require continuous investment, government subsidy and excellent safety standards, and employ thousands of people. Over the near two centuries of the existence of railways, most have been run in an integrated way through a single organization. There is no mystery as to why. A railway system is a network in which all parts are connected. Carving out different aspects, such as signalling, engineering, operations and safety management, makes no sense, since none is a business in itself. They are all interdependent and therefore need to be run together. Strangely, it has taken politicians more than a quarter of a century to learn that lesson.

Acknowledgements

I was given tremendous help in writing this book by a wide variety of former BR managers and workers who shared their recollections. They provided much detailed information and countless stories about an organization which may have been flawed but which they all believed should never have been broken up and fragmented in the way it was.

Therefore I would like to thank, in no particular order, Ivor Warburton, John Nelson, Chris Austin, Gordon Pettitt, Rupert Brennan Brown, Mark Walker, Charles Belcher, Chris Randall, Peter Trewin, Ray Knight and several who wish to remain anonymous. Terry Gourvish also gave me of his time.

Chris Randall also did a fabulous and thorough job editing my manuscript, and Roger Ford and Michael Williams gave it the once-over, pointing out crucial mistakes.

I am grateful to them all but, of course, all errors are mine. Thanks are also due to my agent, Toby Mundy, in batting so well for my interests and to the publishing director at Penguin, Rowland White, for his forbearance at the inevitable delay and his unfailing support for the project. My wife, Deborah Maby, was as ever incredibly helpful in supporting me and keeping me sane, especially as much of this book was written during the second lock-down in the winter of 2020/21.

If you would like to comment on the book or have information you would like to share, email me at Christian.wolmar@gmail.com, or visit my website: www.christianwolmar.co.uk. My Twitter handle is @ christianwolmar.

Timeline of Major Events

1923 Creation of 'Big Four' railway companies as a result of the passage of the 1921 Railways Act

1947 Passage of Transport Act creating the British Transport Commission and the Railway Executive

1948 (1 January) British Railways takes over the operation of the railway from the Big Four

1953 Passage of Transport Act abolishing the Railway Executive

1955 Modernisation Plan launched with introduction of many diesel locomotives
Last year in which British Railways makes an operating profit

1959 Ernest Marples becomes transport minister

1960 *Evening Star*, the last BR steam locomotive, enters service, but has a working life of only five years
Blue Pullman trains introduced

1962 Transport Act abolishes British Transport Commission and creates British Railways Board with Richard Beeching as its first chairman

1963 Publication of Beeching's *Reshaping of British Railways* report, leading to closure of around 6,000 route miles and 4,000 passenger stations and halts, and eventually leaving around 11,000 route miles

and 2,400 stations by the time the closure programme was halted in the 1970s

1968 (4 August) Last steam engine withdrawn from service on the standard gauge railway

Barbara Castle's Transport Act sets out separation
of funding for commercial and social lines

1974 Transport Act creates the Passenger Service Obligation to support loss-making services

1976 Peter Parker becomes British Railways Board
chairman

First High Speed Trains enter service

1982 British Rail is reorganized into three passenger and
two freight sectors

1983 Serpell report, with most extreme version suggesting that the railway should be cut to a mere 1,630
route miles

Robert Reid becomes BR chairman

1991 OfQ ('organizing for quality') introduced, which
replaces regions with sectors

1993 Passage of Railways Act to break up and privatize
the railway

1996 (4 February) First privatized train service runs
between Twickenham and Waterloo

1997 (1 April) Final British Rail service arrives at Fort
William

A Note on the Ministry

The government department dealing with transport has gone through several names during the period covered in this book and therefore readers may be confused. The official contemporary names were:

1946–1970	Ministry of Transport
1970–1976	Department of the Environment
1976–1997	Department of Transport
1997–2001	Department for the Environment, Transport and the Regions
2001–2002	Department for Transport, Local Government and the Regions
2002–present	Department for Transport

The trading name for British Railways was changed to British Rail in 1965, but the organization always retained the longer version for official purposes and the board remained the British Railways Board.

References

Introduction

1 Cited by Reuters, 19 May 2021.

1. The Sparks Effect

1 Interview with author.
2 Michael R. Bonavia, *British Rail: The First 25 Years* (David & Charles, 1981), p. 101.
3 Ibid., p. 82.
4 Interview with author.
5 John Betjeman, *London's Historic Railway Stations* (John Murray, 1972), p. 135; Alan A. Jackson, *London's Termini* (Pan Books, 1972; first published 1969 by David & Charles), p. 29.
6 Interview with author.
7 British Railways Board, *Your New Railway: London Midland Electrification* (1966), p. 7.
8 Ibid., pp. 8–9.
9 Ibid., p. 9.
10 Interview with author.

11 O. S. Nock, *Britain's New Railway: Electrification of the London–Midland Main Lines from Euston to Birmingham, Stoke-on-Trent, Crewe, Liverpool and Manchester* (Ian Allan, 1966), p. 209.

2. The Inheritance

1 T. R. Gourvish, *British Railways, 1948–73: A Business History* (Cambridge University Press, 1986), p. 16.
2 Ibid., p. 67.
3 Ibid., p. 27.
4 Ibid., p. 5.
5 Ibid., pp. 12–13.
6 David Henshaw, *The Great Railway Conspiracy: The Fall and Rise of Britain's Railways since the 1950s* (Leading Edge, 1994), p. 54.
7 Ibid., p. 59.
8 Michael R. Bonavia, *British Rail: The First 25 Years* (David & Charles, 1981), p. 54.
9 Ibid., p. 52.
10 Tanya Jackson, *British Rail: The Nation's Railway* (The History Press, 2013), p. 95.
11 Interview with author, quoted in Christian Wolmar, *Fire and Steam: A New History of the Railways in Britain* (Atlantic Books, 2007), p. 271.
12 Wolmar, *Fire and Steam*, p. 271.
13 David Meara, *Anglo-Scottish Sleepers* (Amberley Publishing, 2018), p. 39.
14 All quotes in ibid.
15 Email to David Meara.
16 Jackson, *British Rail*, p. 90.

17 Quoted in Mike Phillips and Trevor Phillips, *Windrush: The Irresistible Rise of Multi-Racial Britain* (HarperCollins, 1998), p. 87.

18 Simon Bradley, *The Railways: Nation, Network and People* (Profile Books, 2015), p. 212.

19 Interview with author.

20 Bradley, *The Railways*, p. 227.

21 David St John Thomas and Simon Rocksborough Smith, *Summer Saturdays in the West* (David & Charles, 1973), p. 33.

22 Ibid., p. 77.

23 Henshaw, *The Great Railway Conspiracy*, p. 59.

3. New for Old

1 Michael R. Bonavia, *British Rail: The First 25 Years* (David & Charles, 1981), p. 90.

2 David Henshaw, *The Great Railway Conspiracy: The Fall and Rise of Britain's Railways since the 1950s* (Leading Edge, 1994), p. 228.

3 British Transport Commission, *Modernisation and Re-equipment of British Railways* (1955), p. 6.

4 T. R. Gourvish, *British Railways, 1948–73: A Business History* (Cambridge University Press, 1986), p. 67.

5 Quoted in Derek H. Aldcroft, *British Railways in Transition: The Economic Problems of Britain's Railways since 1914* (Macmillan 1968), p. 153.

6 Quoted in Gourvish, *British Railways, 1948–73*, p. 256.

7 Gourvish, *British Railways, 1948–73* p. 256.

8 Ibid., p. 304.

9   G. F. Fiennes, *I Tried to Run a Railway* (Ian Allan, 1967), p. 78.

10 Charles Loft, *Last Trains: Dr Beeching and the Death of Rural England* (Biteback Publishing, 2013), p. 95.

11 *Report from the Select Committee on Nationalised Industries: British Railways*, H.C. 254 (1960), para. 164.

12 Fiennes, *I Tried to Run a Railway*, p. 77.

13 Henshaw, *The Great Railway Conspiracy*, p. 47.

4. Beeching's Double Act

1   *The World's Carriers*, April 1960.

2   Charles Loft, *Last Trains: Dr Beeching and the Death of Rural England* (Biteback Publishing, 2013), p. 154.

3   Chris Austin and Richard Faulkner, *Holding the Line: How Britain's Railways Were Saved*, 2nd edn (Goodall, 2018), p. 52.

4   Hansard, House of Commons Debates, 3 February 1955, vol. 536, col. 1328.

5   Michael R. Bonavia, *British Rail: The First 25 Years* (David & Charles, 1981), p. 113.

6   Quoted in Austin and Faulkner, *Holding the Line*, p. 52.

7   Ibid., p. 53.

8   Ministry of Transport, *Reorganisation of the Nationalised Transport Undertakings* (1960), Cmnd 1248, p. 4.

9   Quoted in Austin and Faulkner, *Holding the Line*, p. 54.

10 Anthony Sampson, *Anatomy of Britain Today* (Hodder & Stoughton, 1965), p. 582.

11 G. F. Fiennes, *I Tried to Run a Railway* (Ian Allan, 1967), p. 76.

12 *The Times*, 16 March 1961.

13 T. R. Gourvish, *British Railways, 1948–73: A Business History* (Cambridge University Press, 1986), p. 324.

14 David Henshaw, *The Great Railway Conspiracy: The Fall and Rise of Britain's Railways since the 1950s* (Leading Edge, 1994), p. 146.

15 The report was reproduced as a facsimile by HMSO in 2013.

16 Austin and Faulkner, *Holding the Line*, p. 110.

17 Interview with Beeching by Hunter Davies in *A Walk Along the Tracks* (Weidenfeld & Nicolson, 1982), p. 14.

18 Austin and Faulkner, *Holding the Line*, p. 67.

19 Henshaw, *The Great Railway Conspiracy*, p. 232.

20 All those references: R. H. N. Hardy, *Beeching: Champion of the Railway?* (Ian Allan, 1989), p. 12.

21 Interview with Beeching by Davies in *A Walk Along the Tracks*, p. 14.

22 Quoted in Austin and Faulkner, *Holding the Line*, p. 75.

23 Quoted in ibid., p. 61.

24 Cabinet minute, quoted in Austin and Faulkner, *Holding the Line*, p. 82.

25 Austin and Faulkner, *Holding the Line*, p. 82.

26 Henshaw, *The Great Railway Conspiracy*, p. 118.

27 Ibid., p. 232.

5. Establishing an Identity

1 David Lawrence, *British Rail Designed, 1948–97* (Crécy, 2016), p. 108.

2 Andrew Haig, 'BR: A House Style', unpublished thesis (1967), in author's library.

3 The Beauty of Transport website: https://thebeautyoftrans-port.com/2015/03/18/the-full-xp-british-railways-corporate-identity-1964-1986-part-1/.

4 Lawrence, *British Rail Designed*, p. 174.

5 The Beauty of Transport website: https://thebeautyoftransport.com/2015/05/13/on-line-typeface-rail-alphabet-typeface-uk/.

6 The Beauty of Transport website: https://thebeautyoftrans-port.com/2015/03/18/the-full-xp-british-railways-corporate-identity-1964-1986-part-1/.

7 Tanya Jackson, *British Rail: The Nation's Railway* (The History Press, 2013), p. 97.

8 Lawrence, *British Rail Designed*, p. 172.

9 Ibid., p. 171.

10 Ibid., p. 168.

11 Ibid., p. 171.

12 John Betjeman, *London's Historic Railway Stations* (John Murray, 1972), p. 8.

13 Lawrence, *British Rail Designed*, p. 82.

14 'New Stations for the Southern', *Modern Railways*, December 1967, p. 643.

15 Lawrence, *British Rail Designed*, p. 85.

16 Simon Jenkins, *Britain's 100 Best Railway Stations* (Viking, 2017), p. 25.

17 G. Freeman Allen, *British Railways after Beeching* (Ian Allan, 1966), p. 92.

18 Simon Bradley, *The Railways: Nation, Network and People* (Profile Books, 2015), p. 529.

19 Ibid.

6. War on Rail

1 Charles Loft, *Last Trains: Dr Beeching and the Death of Rural Britain* (Biteback Publishing, 2013), p. 246.

2 Both quotes in Barbara Castle, *The Castle Diaries, 1964–1976* (Papermac, 1990), p. 42.

3 *Drive*, spring 1967.

4 *Drive*, spring 1968.

5 Both quotes in Barbara Castle, *Fighting All the Way* (Pan Books, 1994), p. 387.

6 Interview with author.

7 Loft, *Last Trains*, p. 259.

8 *The Times*, letters, 11 June 1973.

9 Richard Marsh, *Off the Rails: An Autobiography* (Weidenfeld & Nicolson, 1978), p. 166.

10 Ibid.

11 Loft, *Last Trains*, p. 260.

12 Both quotes in Marsh, *Off the Rails*, p. 167.

13 Chris Austin and Richard Faulkner, *Holding the Line: How Britain's Railways Were Saved*, 2nd edn (Goodall, 2018), p. 130.

14 Quoted in ibid., p. 141.

15 Ibid.

16 Quoted in Austin and Faulkner, *Holding the Line*, p. 141.

17 British Railways Board, *Opportunity for Change: Comments by the British Railways Board on the Government Consultation Document* (July 1976).

18 Labour Party National Executive Committee Research Paper, RE 725 (July 1976), p 3.

19 Austin and Faulkner, *Holding the Line*, p. 147.

20 https://www.railwaysarchive.co.uk/documents/HMG_ TransportPolicy1977.pdf, annex.

21 Ibid., p. 21.

22 Peter Parker, *For Starters: The Business of Life* (Jonathan Cape, 1989), p. 200.

23 *Guardian*, 21 January 1983.

24 All these quotes in Chris Austin and Richard Faulkner, *Disconnected!: Broken Links in Britain's Rail Policy* (Oxford Publishing Company, 2015), p. 21.

25 Parker, *For Starters*, p. 275.

26 Letter of 7 February 1983 to Mrs Thatcher, in Sir Alfred Sherman's papers, Royal Holloway College, University of London, AR MT/M/7/3.

27 Austin and Faulkner, *Disconnected!*, p. 15.

28 *New Statesman*, 24 September 1976.

7. *The Changing Shape of the Train*

1 G. Freeman Allen, *British Railways after Beeching* (Ian Allan, 1966), p. 162.

2 Ibid., p. 165.

3 Peter Parker, *For Starters: The Business of Life* (Jonathan Cape, 1989), p. 267.

4 Stephen Potter, *On the Right Lines? The Limits of Technological Innovation* (Frances Pinter Publishers, 1987), p. 46.

5 Ibid., p. 57.

6 Ibid., p. 59.

7 *Guardian*, 8 December 1981.

8 *Daily Mail*, 8 December 1981.

9 Parker, *For Starters*, p. 272.

10 Ibid., p. 273.

11 Roger Ford in Chris Green and Mike Vincent, *The InterCity Story, 1964–2012* (Oxford Publishing Company, 2013), p. 18.

12 Quoted in Potter, *On the Right Lines?*, p. 102.

13 Ford in Green and Vincent, *The InterCity Story*, p. 20.

14 Ibid., p. 22.

15 Ibid., p. 23.

8. All Change

1 Peter Parker, *For Starters: The Business of Life* (Jonathan Cape, 1989), p. 263.

2 Ibid., p. 263

3 British Railways Board, *European Railways Performance Comparisons* (1980).

4 Parker, *For Starters*, p. 269.

5 Interview with author.

6 Ibid.

7 All quotes interview with author.

8 Philip S. Bagwell, *The Railwaymen: The History of the National Union of Railwaymen*, Volume 2: *The Beeching Era and After* (George Allen & Unwin, 1982), p. 51.

9 Ibid., p. 73.

10 Ibid., p. 63.

11 Ibid., p. 52.

12 Ibid., p. 157.

13 Ibid., p. 82.

14 All quotes interview with author.

15 All quotes interview with author.

16 *Evening Standard*, 1 July 1982.

17 *Guardian*, 30 June 1982.

18 *Evening Standard*, 1 July 1982.

19 Quoted in Chris Austin and Richard Faulkner, *Holding the Line: How Britain's Railways Were Saved*, 2nd edn (Goodall, 2018), p. 177.

20 Interview with author.

21 Ibid.

22 Ibid.

23 Ibid.

9. Beginning the Break-Up

1 Quoted in Christian Wolmar, *On the Wrong Line: How Ideology and Incompetence Wrecked Britain's Railways* (Aurum, 2005), p. 50.

2 Terry Gourvish, *British Rail, 1974–97: From Integration to Privatisation* (Oxford University Press, 2002), p. 237.

3 Stephen Poole, *Inside British Rail: Challenges and Progress on the Nationalised Railway, 1970s–90s* (The History Press, 2018), p. 102.

4 Ibid.

5 Ibid.

6 Gourvish, *British Rail, 1974–97*, p. 245.

7 Christian Wolmar, *Cathedrals of Steam: How London's Great Stations Were Built – and How They Transformed the City* (Atlantic Books, 2020), p. 293.

8 Peter Rayner, *On and Off the Rails: The Anecdotal Reminiscences of More than 40 Years at Work with British Railways* (Novelangle, 1997), p. 117.

9 Interview with author.

10 Ibid.

10. The Task Ahead

1 Richard Marsh, *Off the Rails: An Autobiography* (Weidenfeld & Nicolson, 1978), p. 169.

2 From Sherman's papers, quoted in Chris Austin and Richard Faulkner, *Holding the Line: How Britain's Railways Were Saved*, 2nd edn (Goodall, 2018), p. 196.

3 Quoted in ibid., p. 201.

4 Interview with author.

5 John Nelson, *Losing Track: An Insider's Story of Britain's Railway Transformation from British Rail to the Present Day, 1968 to 2019* (New Generation Publishing, 2019), p. 63.

6 Interview with author.

7 Nelson, *Losing Track*, p. 68.

8 Ibid., p. 65.

9 *Daily Telegraph*, 19 August 1985, profile by Graham Turner.

10 Nelson, *Losing Track*, p. 65.

11 Stephen Poole, *Inside British Rail: Challenges and Progress on the Nationalised Railways, 1970s–90s* (The History Press, 2018), p. 19.

12 Ibid.

13 Interview with author.

14 Ibid.

15 Ibid.

16 Poole, *Inside British Rail*, p. 95.

17 Interview with author.

18 Quoted in Nelson, *Losing Track*, p. 71.

19 British Railways Board Management Brief, 10 December 1981.

20 Interview with author.

21 Ibid.

22 Taken from an early draft of George Muir, *Bob Reid's Railway Revolution: Sir Robert Reid, How He Transformed Britain's Railways to be the Best in Europe* (Unicorn Publishing, 2021).

23 Terry Gourvish, *British Rail, 1974–97: From Integration to Privatisation* (Oxford University Press, 2002), p. 202.

24 Hansard, House of Commons Debates, 16 May 1988, vol. 133, col. 681–8.

25 Quoted in James Towler, *The Battle for the Settle and Carlisle* (Platform 5, 1990), p. 296.

26 Towler, *The Battle for the Settle and Carlisle*, p. 296.

27 Austin and Faulkner, *Holding the Line*, p. 234.

28 *Railnews*, October 1988.

29 Quoted in Gordon Pettitt and Nicholas Comfort, *The Regional Railways Story, Sectorisation to Privatisation: Three Decades of Revival* (Oxford Publishing Company, 2015), p. 10.

30 Quoted in ibid., p. 11.

31 Quoted in ibid., p. 27.

11. BR

1 Interview with author.

2 Ibid.

REFERENCES

3 Quoted in Gordon Pettitt and Nicholas Comfort, *The Regional Railways Story, Sectorisation to Privatisation: Three Decades of Revival* (Oxford Publishing Company, 2015), p. 21.

4 Interview with author.

5 Ibid.

6 Chris Green and Mike Vincent, *The Network SouthEast Story, 1982–2014* (Oxford Publishing Company, 2014), p. 11.

7 Interview with author.

8 Ibid.

9 Green and Vincent, *The Network SouthEast Story*, p. 19.

10 Interview with author.

11 Ibid.

12 Ibid.

13 Green and Vincent, *The Network SouthEast Story*, p. 33.

14 Ibid.

15 Ibid., p. 55.

16 Taken from an early draft of George Muir, *Bob Reid's Railway Revolution: Sir Robert Reid, How He Transformed Britain's Railways to be the Best in Europe* (Unicorn Publishing, 2021).

17 *Railnews*, September 1988.

18 Anthony Hidden QC, *Investigation into the Clapham Junction Railway Accident* (HMSO, 1989), pp. 117 and 163.

19 Taken from an early draft of Muir, *Bob Reid's Railway Revolution*.

20 Tanya Jackson, *British Rail: The Nation's Railway* (The History Press, 2013), p. 179.

21 Taken from an early draft of Muir, *Bob Reid's Railway Revolution*.

22 Both quotes in Chris Green and Mike Vincent, *The InterCity Story* (Oxford Publishing Company, 2014), pp. 83–4.

12. The Pinnacle

1 John Nelson, *Losing Track: An Insider's Story of Britain's Railway Transformation from British Rail to the Present Day, 1968 to 2019* (New Generation Publishing, 2019), p. 93.
2 Interview with author.
3 Richard Goldson, quoted in Nelson, *Losing Track*, p. 97.
4 Terry Gourvish, *British Rail, 1974–97: From Integration to Privatisation* (Oxford University Press, 2002), p. 383.
5 Quoted in ibid.
6 Gourvish, *British Rail, 1974–97*, p. 383.
7 Nelson, *Losing Track*, p. 98.
8 Ibid., p. 99.
9 Interview with author.
10 Quoted in Gordon Pettitt and Nicholas Comfort, *The Regional Railways Story, Sectorisation to Privatisation: Three Decades of Revival* (Oxford Publishing Company, 2015), p. 40.
11 Interview with author.
12 Quoted in Pettitt and Comfort, *The Regional Railways Story*, p. 46.
13 Interview with author.
14 Gourvish, *British Rail, 1974–97*, p. 445.
15 Interview with author.
16 Ibid.

13. Epilogue

1 My book *Broken Rails: How Privatisation Wrecked Britain's Railways* (Aurum, 2001), which was later revised as *On the Wrong*

Line: How Ideology and Incompetence Wrecked Britain's Railways (Aurum, 2005), covers the privatization process and its immediate impact.

2 Jack Simmons and Gordon Biddle (eds.), *The Oxford Companion to British Railway History: From 1603 to the 1990s* (Oxford University Press, 1997), p. 57.

3 Nigel G. Harris and Ernest Godward, *The Privatisation of British Rail* (The Railway Consultancy Press, 1997), p. 55.

4 http://news.bbc.co.uk/1/hi/uk_politics/982037.stm.

5 Jon Shaw, 'Designing a Method for Rail Privatisation', in Roger Freeman and Jon Shaw (eds.), *All Change: British Railway Privatisation* (McGraw-Hill, 2000), p. 22.

6 Wolmar, *On the Wrong Line*, p. 59.

7 Terry Gourvish, *British Rail, 1974–97: From Integration to Privatisation* (Oxford University Press, 2002), p. 385.

8 Shaw, 'Designing a Method for Rail Privatisation', p. 23.

9 Department for Transport, *Great British Railways* (2021), CP 423.

A Selective Bibliography

This is very much a selected list of those books that I have found most useful or instructive; it is not an attempt to be comprehensive, given the vastness of the railway literature out there.

For a general history of Britain's railway, my own book *Fire and Steam: A New History of the Railways in Britain* (Atlantic Books, 2007) and Simon Bradley's *The Railways: Nation, Network and People* (Profile Books, 2015) are the most recent.

In respect of comprehensive histories of BR, the fullest is the two-volume business history by Terry Gourvish, *British Railways, 1948–73: A Business History* (Cambridge University Press, 1986) and *British Rail, 1974–97: From Integration to Privatisation* (Oxford University Press, 2002), which provides fantastic detail on the creation, operation and demise of the organization. Tanya Jackson's *British Rail: The Nation's Railway* (The History Press, 2013) is a useful if somewhat oddly structured account. Michael R. Bonavia's early history of BR, *British Rail: The First 25 Years* (David & Charles, 1981), is a short account of that period by an insider, while the title of G. Freeman Allen's comprehensive *British Railways after Beeching* (Ian Allan, 1966) is rather misleading since it covers only the immediate aftermath of the Beeching era. The best account of the build-up to the Beeching era, and how there was no clear strategy behind the closures, is David Henshaw's *The Great Railway Conspiracy: The Fall and Rise of Britain's Railways since the 1950s* (Leading Edge, 1994).

The Beeching report and its aftermath have stimulated a vast literature. Charles Loft's *Last Trains: Dr Beeching and the Death of Rural England* (Biteback Publishing, 2013) is an assessment of the impact of the report, while R. H. N. Hardy's *Beeching: Champion of the Railway?* (Ian Allan, 1989) is a rare book supportive of BR's first chairman. The thoroughness of BR's design frameworks is lovingly well set out in David Lawrence's *British Rail Designed, 1948–97* (Crécy, 2016). A fierce critique of the early days of the organization, *The Train that Ran Away: A Business History of British Railways, 1948–1968* (Ian Allan, 1973), was written by Stewart Joy, a former chief economist of the organization.

There are numerous books on BR written by former protagonists in the organization, although very few have been published recently. One good exception is *Losing Track: An Insider's Story of Britain's Railway Transformation from British Rail to the Present Day, 1968 to 2019* (New Generation Publishing, 2019) by John Nelson, who held several senior jobs in the final days of BR. A rather eccentric account of the period is *On and Off the Rails: The Anecdotal Reminiscences of More than 40 Years at Work with British Railways* (Novelangle, 1997) by Peter Rayner; while the most famous, which cost the author his job on the railway because it was unauthorized, is *I Tried to Run a Railway* (Ian Allan, 1967) by G. F. Fiennes. Two former chairmen of

BR wrote autobiographies which lent heavily on their time on the railway: Richard Marsh, who had also been a transport minister for a time, wrote *Off the Rails: An Auto-biography* (Weidenfeld & Nicolson, 1978); while Peter Parker, an engagingly witty writer, penned *For Starters: The Business of Life* (Jonathan Cape, 1989). A recently published biography of the first Sir Robert Reid has been written by George Muir, *Bob Reid's Railway Revolution: Sir Robert Reid, How He Transformed Britain's Railways to be the Best in Europe* (Unicorn Publishing, 2021). One incisive account from the coalface of railway management is Stephen Poole's *Inside British Rail: Challenges and Progress on the Nationalised Railway, 1970s–90s* (The History Press, 2018), which provides some hair-raising stories of the daily operation of the railway.

Oddly, many politicians who have been in the transport ministry for part of their careers often devote little attention to that period. One good exception is Barbara Castle in *The Castle Diaries, 1964–1976* (Papermac, 1990), which covers her work at a crucial time in the ministry in the late 1960s.

Chris Austin and Richard Faulkner have produced two very well-researched and detailed accounts of how the railway has faced opposition within government and how the damaging programme of closures was undertaken with little understanding of their impact: *Holding the Line: How Britain's Railways Were Saved* (2nd edn, Goodall, 2018) and *Disconnected!: Broken Links in Britain's Rail Policy* (Oxford Publishing Company, 2015). A great account of a successful protest movement against closure, *The Battle for the Settle and Carlisle* (Platform 5, 1990*)*, was written by James Towler, one of the leaders of the campaign.

There are comprehensive volumes on each of the three passenger business sectors established in the final fifteen years of the organization: *The InterCity Story, 1964–2012* (Oxford Publishing Company, 2013), by Chris Green and Mike Vincent, and their *The Network SouthEast Story, 1982–2014* (Oxford Publishing Company, 2014); and *The Regional Railways Story, Sectorisation to Privatisation: Three Decades of Revival* (Oxford Publishing Company, 2015) by Gordon Pettitt and Nicholas Comfort.

On rail privatization, my book *On the Wrong Line: How Ideology and Incompetence Wrecked Britain's Railways* (Aurum, 2005) is an account of the background to the sale and its highly damaging effect on both the safety and the finances of the rail industry. Nigel G. Harris and Ernest Godward's *The Privatisation of British Rail* (The Railway Consultancy Press, 1997) provides a very good straightforward explanation of the break-up and fragmentation of the railway.

Picture credits

Brian Harris / Alamy Stock Photo: p.15, bottom
Central Press/Hulton Archive/Getty Images: p.4, middle
Clive Jones / Alamy Stock Photo: p.1, middle
Collection David Lawrence: pp.2, bottom left & right; 7, bottom right;
    11, top, middle & bottom left
Crown Copyright: pp.2, top; 6, top, middle & bottom left; 7, all pic-
    tures; 9, middle; 13, top left
Daily Mirror/Mirrorpix/Mirrorpix via Getty Images: p.4, bottom
David Farrell/Getty Images: p.9, bottom left
David Ford: p.10, middle
Evening Standard/Hulton Archive/Getty Images: pp.8, middle left;
    11, bottom right
Finnbarr Webster / Alamy Stock Photo: p.10, bottom right
Fox Photos/Getty Images: page 8, middle right
Fox Photos/Hulton Archive/Getty Images: p.8, bottom left
Graham Clarke / Deltic Preservation Society: p.10, bottom
Image Scotland / Alamy Stock Photo: p.13, top right
John Wiltshire: p.1, bottom
Keystone Press / Alamy Stock Photo: p.8, top left
NW Spinks: p.4, top
PA Images / Alamy Stock Photo: p.16, left
Paul Bigland: p.14, all pictures
Popperfoto via Getty Images: p.8, top right
Private Eye Magazine: p.16, right
Public Domain: pp.9, top; 10, top; 12, top
Rolls Press/Popperfoto via Getty Images/Getty Images: p.13, middle

Index

ABB 236, 317
Aberdare-Abercynon line 325
Aberdeen 237
accidents 33–4, 291–2, 294–5,
    296–7
  after privatization 339, 340
  Clapham Junction rail crash
    291, 292–6
  and Mark 1 carriages 45–6
  see also safety
Advanced Passenger Train (APT)
    165–78, 303, 304, 328
advertising *see* marketing
air brakes 67
Allen, Geoffrey Freeman 126, 161
Alsthom 236, 317
Anglo-Scottish Car Carrier
    Service 38–40
Anne, Princess 289
Advisory, Conciliation and
    Arbitration Service (ACAS)
    217
Ascot 47
Ashford-Hastings route 137–8
ASLEF (Amalgamated Society
    of Locomotive Engineers
    and Firemen) 197–8, 214

and APT 169
driver only operation 222
flexible rostering 218, 219–20
and NUR 218–19
OfQ 311
strikes 218–21
Atlantic Coast Express 52
Austin, Chris
  Beeching report 86, 88–9, 98
  on bias towards affluent rail
    passengers 145
  on closures 156
  graduate training scheme
    240–41
  Settle–Carlisle line 264
  singling 137–8
  Stedeford report 79–80
Australia 185
Automobile Association (AA)
    131–2
aviation xiii, 14, 18, 106, 175,
    185, 299
Avocet line 134
Azuma 186

Bagwell, Philip 200, 203–4, 205,
    206, 207–8, 209

Baldwin, Peter 148
Balfour Beatty 8
Barney, Gerry 109
barons 64–5, 126, 161, 250, 251,
    254, 260, 268
Beatles 100
BedPan line 216, 221
Beeching, Dr Richard xi, 9, 62,
    82–4, 92, 94, 105–6, 128
    appointment 73, 75–6, 82, 84–5
    corporate identity 107, 109
    departure 99–100
    *The Development of the Major
        Railway Trunk Routes*
        (second report) 95–8, 99,
        101, 133, 240
    electrification 94–5
    industrial relations 199–200
    Reshaping of British Railways
        (first report) 84, 85–95,
        100, 101, 162
    on Stedeford committee
        79, 81–2
Betjeman, John 11, 116
BICC (British Insulated
    Callender's Cables) 8
bicycles 48–9, 114
Birmingham New Street
    station 10
bishops 25
black boxes 296
Bleasdale, Cyril 298–9, 305
Bletchley flyover 66
Blue Paper 143–4, 156
Blue Pullmans 159–62, 180
Bonavia, Michael

British Transport Commission
    meetings 57–8
    and electrification 7–8, 9
    liveries 32
    steam locomotive policy 30–31
    and Stedeford committee 80
Boyd, Adrian 289
Bradley, Simon 44, 47–8, 127
braking systems 168, 180
Branchline Commission 69–71
BREL (British Railways
    Engineering Ltd) 190, 234,
    235, 239
    HSTs 183
    Networker 316–17
    Pacers 271
British Rail 101, 111, 353
    see also British Railways
British Rail Property Board 237
British Railways (BR) xv,
    xvii, 353
    beginning the break-up
        225–39
    Blue Paper 143–4, 156
    Chief Mechanical and
        Electrical Engineering
        Department 167, 177, 234
    common carrier obligation
        24, 65
    corporate identity 31–3,
        106–115, 127
    Field organization 257, 258
    functional departments 254–5
    funding xiii, 128, 135–6, 139,
        190, 191, 264–5, 266–7, 321,
        328–9, 332

headquarters 21, 255
Modernisation Plan 5, 6,
    9, 17, 59–73, 75, 84–5,
    100, 108, 120, 128,
    233, 234
myths ix–x
name change 111
nationalization 17–26, 53–4
organizing for quality 309–310,
    311–15, 326
pre-privatization golden age
    326–9
privatization x–xiv, xv, xvii,
    309, 323–4, 329, 331–42
Pullmans 35–6
regions 25, 27–8, 64–5, 126,
    251–5, 257, 260
sectorization 241, 258–60,
    266–73, 279, 307–8, 309
Serpell report 150, 151–5,
    193, 248
Shipping and International
    Division 229
Stedeford committee 79–81
see also InterCity; Network
    SouthEast; Provincial
    Railways; ScotRail
British Railways Board 79, 82,
    353
APT 177–8
Design Panel 107
electrification 7
HST 177–8
InterCity 162
and orange paper 147
sectorization 259

A Strategy for High Speed 177–8
workshop privatization 236
British Railways Engineering Ltd
    see BREL
British Railways Research and
    Development Division 166
British Transport Commission
    (BTC) 19–21, 56, 57
abolition 79, 83
closures 71–2
Design Panel 107
electrification 6, 7
insignia 32
Modernisation Plan 67–9
and Pullman 36
steam locomotive policy 27, 29
British Transport Hotels (BTH)
    227–8, 230
Broad Street line 141
Broxbourne station 118
Brunel, Isambard Kingdom 169,
    181, 251
Buckton, Ray 218–19
bus services 190–91, 226
bustitution 96, 146, 149
Butler, R. A. 62

Cab Secure Radio 296
Callaghan, Jim 149–50
Calvert, Margaret 110
Campbell, Ian 171
camping coaches 50–51
Cannon Street station rail
    crash 297
Capitalcard 281–2, 283
Captials Limited 35

car ownership 56, 78, 131–2,
    187, 299, 322–3
Carlisle 67
Casey Jones 231
Castle, Barbara 128, 129–34, 135,
    136, 156, 195–6, 271
catering
    cafeterias and tea trolleys 37
    HST 180
    InterCity 300, 301
    privatization 231–3
    sandwiches ix, x, xvii
Causebrook, Mark 268
Centre for Policy Studies 246
Channel Tunnel 332
Channon, Paul 236, 263, 333
Charing Cross station 237
Chiltern line 316
City Link 192–3
Clapham Junction rail crash
    291, 292–6
CLASP (Consortium of Local
    Authorities Special
    Programme) 116–17
Clean Air Act 1956 33
clock-face timetabling 163
closures
    1970s 139–42
    1980s 324–6
    Beeching 81–2, 83, 85–94,
        95–101, 105–6, 138
    Blue Paper 143–4, 156
    by stealth 72, 325–6
    Castle 132, 133–4
    cost-benefit analysis 156–7
    in privatization legislation 264

reopenings 324–5
Serpell report 152–3, 155, 260
Settle–Carlisle line 261–4
Stedeford committee 80–81
1960 White Paper 81
1974 White Paper 148
1977 White Paper 148, 149
coach services 190–91, 277, 299
coal wagons 92–3
Cockerell, Christopher 77
commercial railway 24, 135,
    152, 258
common carrier obligation
    24, 65
computerization 203–4
Concorde 175
Conran, Terence 109
consultants 239–40
container traffic 86, 92, 93, 131
continuous welded rail 201,
    253, 281
Coopers & Lybrand 247
Cornwall Skippers 271, 319
cost-benefit analysis 61, 156–7
Cotton, Ron 262
Coventry station 10, 118
Covid-19 pandemic xv, 342
Crosland, Tony 144–6, 148
Cross Country 185, 186, 298
Cuisine 2000 232, 233
Cyclists Special (British Transport
    Film) 49

Daily Mail 172
Dalgleish, Angus 244
Dartmoor 72

Davies, Hunter 94, 95, 96
Day, Robin 109
Deltic diesel locomotives 5, 15,
    84–5, 95, 185, 301
Deming, Edwards 313
Denning, Lord 78
Department of the Environment
    353
  closures 140
  rail to road conversion 245
  see also Ministry of Transport
Department of Transport 353
  Capitalcard 281
  Great British Railways xvii
  rail privatization 331, 334, 335
  see also Ministry of Transport
Derbyshire, Nick 238
Design Panel 107, 111
Design Research Unit 107
The Development of the Major
    Railway Trunk Routes
    (second Beeching report)
    95–8, 99, 101, 133, 240
diesel locomotives 5, 13, 84,
    120–21, 125, 252
  and APT 170
  Deltics 5, 15, 84–5, 95, 185, 301
  diesel-electrics 64, 125
  diesel-hydraulics 64, 125–6
  HST 162, 165, 176–86
  and loading gauge 27
  Modernisation Plan 63, 64–5,
    72–3, 233
  staffing 5–6, 123–4, 206–7
diesel multiple units 28–9, 121,
    159, 269

Blue Pullmans 159–62
  Pacers 269–71, 318–19
  Sprinters 272–3, 319, 323
disabled travellers 43, 114
Disconnected! (Austin and
    Faulkner) 156
Docherty, Marie 171
Doncaster 47
Doncaster workshop 233,
    235, 239
double arrow design 109–110,
    342, 343
Drive (AA) 131–2
driver only operation (DOO)
    216, 219, 221–2
Dudley 101
Durie, Alexander 131–2

East Coast Main Line 298
  Azuma 186
  Deltics 5, 84–5, 95
  electrification 15–16, 63,
    301–3
  High Speed Train
    183–5, 275
  InterCity 225 174
  OfQ 311
  sleeper cars 38
Economist 62
Edgar the Swan 289
Edmonds, John 313, 327
Edmondson, Thomas 128
electric locomotives 306
  APT 169–70
  InterCity 225 303–4
  staffing 206–7

electrification 9–10, 29–31, 57, 85
    Beeching 94–5
    East Coast Main Line 15–16,
        301–3
    Great Eastern Main Line 302
    Great Western 303
    Modernisation Plan 5, 6, 63
    West Coast Main Line 3–16,
        85, 106, 301–2
    Woodhead tunnel 30, 134
The Elizabethan 35
engineering workshops 138,
        206–7, 226
    OfQ 312–13
    privatization 233–6, 239
Epstein, Brian 100
Euston station 3, 4, 10–11, 14,
        106, 115, 116, 237
Evans, Harold 144
Evening Standard (locomotive) 286
Evening Standard (newspaper) x,
        286, 297
Evening Star 28, 63, 122
Executive Service 300
Exeter St David's 49
External Financing Limit
        (EFL) 193

Far North line 141
fares 30, 190
    advance tickets 120, 317
    choking off 307
    discounts 12, 190, 287–8
    increases 306–7, 328
    market pricing 120
    restrictions on rises 58–9

Faulkner, Richard
    Beeching report 86, 88–9, 98
    on bias towards affluent rail
        passengers 145
    on closures 156
    Settle–Carlisle line 264
    Stedeford report 79–80
Fenchurch Street station 237
Fenchurch Street to Southend
        line 297, 316
ferries 113, 228–9, 230
Fiat 175
Field organization 257, 258
Fiennes, Gerard 66–7, 68–9, 82,
        90, 92
Financial Times 190
FirstGroup 277
Flèche d'Or 229
flexible rostering 151, 216, 217,
        219–20, 224, 244
Flying Scotsman 33, 163
Folkestone Central station 118
fonts 110–111
football specials 47–8
Ford, Roger 177, 180–81, 183,
        327
Foster, Sir Christopher 157,
        336
Fowler, Norman 191
France
    electrification 13
    high-speed routes 165–6
    steam locomotives 123
franchising system xv–xvi, 337,
        340–42
Fraser, Tom 98, 99, 130

freight services 188, 191–2, 328
  Beeching report 86, 92–3
  computerization 204
  container traffic 92, 93, 131, 137
  and electrification 13–14
  marshalling yards 65–7
  merry-go-round coal wagons 92–3
  Modernisation Plan 59, 60
  National Freight Corporation 137
  at nationalization 19
  Red Star 192–3
  sectorization 258
  staff reductions 202
  steam locomotives 121
  Woodhead route 134
Freightliner 93, 137
Freud, Clement ix, 232

gas-turbine engines 166, 169
Gatwick airport 279, 280, 299
gay community 42–3
GEC (General Electric Company) 236
general managers 64–5, 126, 161, 250, 251, 254, 260, 268
Germany 123
Glasgow 63, 85
Gleneagles 227, 228
Gold Star Holidays 230
Golden Arrow 229
The Golden Hind 301
Goswick rail crash 33

Goundry, Bob 272
Gourvish, Terry
  Beeching 84
  Grosvenor Hotel 227
  managers 326–7
  Modernisation Plan 60, 62, 63
  nationalization 18, 21, 22, 23
  OfQ 313
  privatization 338
  sectorization 260–61
  workshop privatization 235
Grange, Kenneth 179
Great British Railways xvi–xvii, 342–3
Great British Railways (White Paper) xvi, 342–6
Great Central Main Line 91
Great Eastern Main Line 302
Great Western Main Line
  APT 169
  electrification 303
  HSTs 181–2, 186
Great Western Railway 18, 25, 28, 251
Greater London Council (GLC) 281, 282, 283
Greater Manchester 136
Greece 316
Green, Chris 273, 275, 327
  driver only operation 221
  and electrification 4, 14–15
  graduate training scheme 4, 240, 275
  at InterCity 275, 317–18
  and mystery trains 46–7

Green, Chris – *cont.*
  at Network SouthEast 273,
    275, 278, 280–81, 282,
    283–8, 312, 315–16
  North London line 280–81
  and privatization 331–2
  and regional structure 253
  at ScotRail 275–8
Gresley, Nigel 177
Grosvenor Hotel 227
Guardian 152, 219–20
Guillebaud, Claude 199

Habitat 109
Haig, Andrew 108
Hall, Peter 245, 247
Hampton Court flower show
  289
Hancock, Tony 289
Hanks, Reggie 65
Hardy, Richard 92, 93
Harlow station 118
Harrison, Karen 197
Harrow and Wealdstone rail
  crash 34
Hatfield rail crash 339
Heath, Ted 140
helicopters 57
Hemingway, Brian 293–4
Henshaw, David 53–4, 78
  Beeching report 85, 89, 101
  Branchline Committee 69–70
  steam locomotives 27, 29
  Transport Act 1953 58
Herald of Free Enterprise
  disaster 229

Hidden, Anthony 293, 295–6
High Speed Train (HST) 95,
  162, 165, 176–86, 275, 303,
  305, 328
Hitachi IEP 185–6
Hither Green rail crash 291
Holding the Line (Austin and
  Faulkner) 79–80, 86, 88–9,
  98, 145, 264
holiday specials 49–50, 87
homosexuality 42–3
hop pickers 48
Hope, Richard 153
Hope Valley line 134
Horwich Foundry workshop
  235, 239
hotels 19, 226, 227–8
hovercraft 77, 229–30
Howell, David 154
Hull 237
Hunslet-Barclay 271
Hurcomb, Sir Cyril 20, 21
hydrokinetic brakes 168

Independent 223
industrial relations 187, 194–200,
  210–24, 244, 248, 290,
  291, 328
  see also unions
integrated transport 56, 57, 130,
  136–7
InterCity (Inter-City) 4, 10,
  162–4, 185, 186, 193
  branding 164–5, 183, 317
  business-led project
    management 304

economic turnaround
  304–6
Executive Service 299–300
OfQ 310, 311, 317–18
on-board catering 231–3,
  300–301
and privatization 338
sectorization 258, 266, 267,
  273, 275, 280, 298–301, 309,
  320, 327
InterCity 225 174, 303–4
InterCity Express Project (IEP)
  185–6
Issigonis, Alec 109

J. Walter Thompson 282
Jackson, Tanya 32, 40, 300
Japan
  high-speed routes 165–6
  management techniques 313
Jenkins, Roy 139
Jenkins, Simon 118–19
Johnson, Boris xvi, 77, 78
Johnson, H. C. 13
Jones, Colin 13
Jones, Sydney 167
Joseph, Sir Keith 246

Kelly, Phil 34–5
Kensington Olympia 39
King, Paul 322–3
Kingmoor marshalling yard 67
Kinneir, Jock 110
Kirby, David 280
Knight, Ray 194–5, 196,
  208, 221

Ladbroke Grove rail crash 34,
  297, 339
Landmark Hotel 255
Lawrence, David 115,
  117–18
Lazard 239
Leith, Prue ix, 231
Lennon, John 100
Leppington, Leslie 196
level crossings 138
Lewisham rail crash 34
Leyland 270, 271, 272
Lindblom, Charles 260
line closures see closures
Liverpool Street station 238
Livingstone, Ken 281
Llangynog 70
Llanyblodwel 70
Lloyd, Thomas 244
loading gauge 27, 168
locomotives
  livery 31–2, 113–14
  naming 119–20
  regional fleets 252–3
  see also diesel locomotives;
    electric locomotives; steam
    locomotives
Loft, Charles 67–8, 78, 130, 140,
  143
London
  economy 291
  ringways 246–7
London & North Eastern
  Railway 25, 240
London & North Western
  Railway 113

London & South East 258, 266, 273, 278–80
see also Network SouthEast
London Midland Region
  livery 114
  Mod-X 116
  signalling 201–2
  speeds 35
  West Coast Main Line electrification 7, 65
London, Tilbury & Southend line 279
London Transport 18, 20, 107–8
London Underground
  Capitalcard 281–2
  driver only operation 221
  electrification 29
  map 285
  Victoria Line 157
Looe 134
Louth 90–91

MacGregor, John 335–6, 337, 341
Macmillan, Harold 40
Major, John xi–xiv, xv, 332, 334
Manchester 136
Manchester airport 323
Manchester Piccadilly station 10
Mansfield 101
Mark 1 coaches 41–6
Mark 2 coaches 11
Mark 3 coaches 301
Mark 4 coaches 304
marketing
  HST 182–3
  Inter-City 164–5

Network SouthEast 288–90
West Coast Main Line electrification 12–14
Marples, Ernest 76–9, 81, 100–101, 129, 130, 132, 148
  and Beeching 82, 84, 85–6, 93–4
Marples Ridgway 76
Marsh, Richard 136, 142, 143–4, 147, 156, 245
marshalling yards 65–7
The Master Cutler 301
May, Theresa xvi
Meara, David 38
Mechanical and Electrical Engineering Department 167, 177, 234
merry-go-round coal wagons 92–3
Merseyside 136
Metro-Cammell 272, 317
Mid-Wales line 139
Midland Main Line 185, 305
Miller, Terry 177, 178–9
Mini 109
Ministry of Overseas Development 129
Ministry of Transport 353
  APT 166
  electrification 7–8
  first woman minister 128, 129–30
  pro-road bias 156
  see also Department of the Environment; Department of Transport

Missenden, Sir Eustace 20
Mitchell, David 263, 290
Mitchell Cup 290
Mod-X 116
Modernisation Plan 6, 9, 17,
    59–63, 67–9, 84, 100,
    108, 128
  diesel locomotives 233
  electrification 5, 63
  engineering workshops 234
  marshalling yards 65–7
  steam locomotives 120
Monopolies and Mergers
    Commission 278–9
Morning Star 219
Motorail 38–40
motorways 55, 60, 78, 187,
    299, 319
Moule, Gerald 40
Muir, George 260
multiple units *see* diesel multiple
    units
Multiprinter Major 203–4
mystery tours 46–7

NASA 112
National Freight Corporation
    137
National Union of Railwaymen
    (NUR) 197, 200,
    213, 214
  and ASLEF 218–19
  Beeching report 92
  Blue Pullmans 160
  driver only operation 219
  flexible rostering 217
    strikes 60–61, 198, 212,
        217–18
    see also RMT
nationalization 17–25, 53–4
Naughtie, James ix–x
Nelson, John 254, 260, 329
  on Bob Reid 310–311
  OfQ 312, 314–15
  on Robert Reid 249,
      251, 302
Network Rail xvi, 329, 340,
    346
  see also Railtrack
Network SouthEast 266, 275,
    280–81, 282–4, 288, 291,
    297–8, 309, 320, 327
  accidents 291, 292–7
  branding 284–7
  Cannon Street station rail
      crash 297
  Capitalcard 281–2, 283
  Clapham Junction rail crash
      291, 292–6
  discounted fares 287–8
  and *Evening Standard* 286, 297
  marketing 288–90
  OfQ 310
  and privatization 338
  rolling stock 316–17
  total route modernization
      315–16
  see also London & South East
Networker 316–17
Ninian Park, Cardiff 47
Nock, O.S. 15
North London line 280–81

Northern Ireland 346–7
NUR *see* National Union of
    Railwaymen

Observer 307
Office of Road and Rail 329
    see also Rail Regulator
open stations 90, 188, 216
Operation Pride 286
organizing for quality (OfQ)
        309–310, 311–15, 326
    InterCity 311, 317–18
    Regional Railways 318, 319
Oxford Companion to British
    Railway History 332

Pacers 269–71, 318–19
Padmore, Sir Thomas 129
Panorama 218–19
Parker, Peter 84, 150–51, 243–4,
        248–9
    APT 172, 174, 175, 176
    Commuters' Charter 278
    industrial relations 217–19,
        220, 248
    London & South East 279
    public relations 154, 188–91,
        272
    rail to road conversion 244,
        246–7
    and Reid 248
    and Savile 165
    and Serpell report 151, 153–5,
        215
Parkfield Group 235
Parkinson, Cecil 316, 333, 334

Party Outings (British Rail
    brochure) 49
passenger services 188, 191
    APT 165–77
    classes 183, 300
    disabled travellers 43, 114
    Inter-City 162–5, 174
    Modernisation Plan 59–60
    Motorail 38–40
    Pullmans 35–6, 301
    sectorization 258, 266–7
    slip coaches 52–3
    specials 46–50
    through coaches 51–2
    see also catering; closures; fares;
        rolling stock
Passenger Transport Executives
    (PTEs) 136–7, 270–71,
        318, 324
Paxman Engineering 178
Pay Trains 90
Pendolino tilting trains 168, 172,
        175
Perth marshalling yard 67
Pettitt, Gordon 284
    Clapham Junction rail crash
        294
    industrial relations 211–12,
        221
    Regional Railways 318–24,
        325
    sectorization 259
Peyton, John 141–4
Poole, Stephen 232, 233, 252–3,
        255–6
Portillo, Michael 263

Portugal 316
Potter, Stephen 166–7, 172
Potters Bar rail crash 339
Powell, Enoch 80
Preston 238
Prideaux, John 153, 327
privatization 226–7, 230–31,
    238–40, 241, 309, 329,
    331–46
  catering 231–3
  and closure procedures 264
  engineering workshops
    233–6, 239
  franchises 323–4, 337, 340–41
  and Great British Railways
    xvii, 342–3, 346
  hotels 227–8
  Major xi–xiv
  property 237–8, 328
  ships and ports 228–30
  Thatcher xi, 225–6, 333
Provincial Railways 258, 266–73,
    320, 327
  and Intercity 267, 299, 306
  OfQ 310
  Pettitt 284, 318
  see also Regional Railways
Public Service Obligation (PSO)
    147, 193, 319
  after privatization 339–40
Pullmans 35–6, 41, 51, 163, 301
  Blue Pullmans 159–61
Purley station rail crash 297

Quant, Mary 109
Queen of Scots 35

Quicksnack 231
Quintinshill rail disaster 34

race discrimination 194–7
Race Relations Act 1965 195
Race Relations Act 1968 196
race specials 47
The Rag Trade (TV sitcom) 223
Rail Alphabet 110–111
rail closures see closures
Rail Express Systems 310
Rail Regulator 329, 341
  see also Office of Road and Rail
rail to road conversion 244–8
Railfuture 325
Railtrack xiii, 329, 337, 340, 346
  see also British Railways;
    Network Rail
Railway Conversion League 81,
    244, 247–8
Railway Development Society
    71, 325
Railway Executive 20–21, 24–5
  abolition 57
  investment plan 56–7, 59
  livery 31–2
  steam locomotive policy 26,
    27, 31
Railway Invigoration Society 71
Railway Rates Tribunal 24
Railway Staff Joint Committee
    (RSJC) 211, 213
Railway Staff National Council
    (RSNC) 211, 213
Railway Staff National Tribunal
    (RSNT) 211, 213

railway stations *see* stations
Railway Technical Centre 166
Railways Act 1993 xiv, 343
Randall, Chris 46, 209–210, 223
Raymond, Stanley 133
Rayner, David 295
Rayner, Peter 239–40
Red Star 192–3
Regional Railways 318–24
  see also Provincial Railways
Reid, Bob (chairman 1990-1995)
  224, 241, 243, 310–311, 327
Reid, Robert (chairman 1983-
  1990) 243, 248–51, 264–6
  Clapham Junction rail crash 294
  East Coast Main Line
    electrification 302
  Fenchurch St to Southend line
    297–8
  and Green 275, 277–8
  InterCity 298, 301
  organizing for quality 308,
    309–310
  and regional structure 253–4,
    257
  and Ridley 257, 264–5, 302
  sectorization 258, 260, 267,
    279
  Settle–Carlisle line 262, 264
Reshaping of British Railways (first
  Beeching report) 84, 85–95,
    100, 101, 162
restaurant cars 37
RFS Industries 235
Ribblehead viaduct 123, 261,
  263, 264

Richards, John 42–3
Ridley, Nicholas
  East Coast Main Line
    electrification 301, 302
  and rail privatization 226,
    333
  and Reid 257, 264–5
Rifkind, Malcolm 334
RMT (National Union of Rail,
  Maritime and Transport
  Workers) 197, 222
Road Haulage Association
  76–7
road safety 132
Roberts, Norwell 196
Robertson, Sir Brian 57–8, 82,
  83, 94
Robin Hood line 325
Rodgers, Bill 148–9
rolling stock 269
  APT 328
  camping coaches 50–51
  coach interiors 114
  coal wagons 92–3
  HST 328
  livery 113–14
  lounge first compartments
    163–4
  managers' private saloon cars
    256
  Mark 1 coaches 41–6
  Mark 2 coaches 11
  Mark 3 coaches 301
  Mark 4 coaches 304
  Network SouthEast
    316–17

Networker 316–17
restaurant cars 37
sleeper cars 37–8
see also diesel multiple units;
   locomotives

safety 33, 223, 291–6
  Automatic Warning System
   34, 252, 297
  Mark 1 coaches 45–6
  see also accidents
St Ives 134
St Pancras station 116
Sampson, Anthony 82
sandwiches ix, x, xvii, 231
Savile, Jimmy 164–5
Scotland
  closures 141
  HSTs 186
  reopenings 325
ScotRail 275–8, 327
Sea Containers 230
Sealink 113, 229, 230
Second World War 17, 18–19
sectorization 258–60, 266–7,
   307–8, 309
  see also InterCity; Network
   SouthEast; Provincial
   Railways
Serpell, Sir David 79, 150, 151
Serpell report 79, 151–5, 193,
   215, 248, 260, 299
Settle–Carlisle line 91, 155,
   261–4, 324, 326
Shapps, Grant x, xvi, xvii
Shaw, Jon 335–6, 341

Sherman, Sir Alfred 154–5,
   245–6, 247
ships 113, 226, 228–9
signalling 126–7, 201–2, 328
  Automatic Warning System
   34, 252, 297
  Clapham Junction rail crash
   293–4, 296
  Modernisation Plan 60
  staff culture 204–5
singling 137–8, 267
Skeggs, Tony 288–9
Skippers 271, 319
Slade Green depot 316
sleeper cars 37–8, 41
slip coaches 52–3
snow, wrong kind of ix–x
Snow Hill tunnel 282–3
social railway 70, 135, 139, 191,
   258, 266–7
solid state interlocking 328
Somerset & Dorset Joint
   Railway 91
South Croydon rail crash 33
Southall rail crash 34, 297, 339
Southern Railway 20, 29–30
Southern Region 284
  CLASP 116
  electrification 5, 6, 9–10, 63
  ferry connections 229
  singling 137–8
Spearman, Sir Alexander 99
Speller amendment 324
Sprinters 272–3, 319, 323
staff 19, 188, 207–9, 326–8
  alcohol abuse 209–210

staff – *cont.*
APT 169
assaults on 209
Blue Pullmans 160
diesel locomotives 123–4
driver only operation 216
engine maintenance 205–7
flexible rostering 151, 216,
217, 219–20, 224, 244
freight services 202
hierarchy 255–7
HST 179–80
killed on duty 292, 295
level crossings 138
management training scheme
4, 240–41, 326
managers 326–7
Network SouthEast 286, 287
OfQ 314
pay 215
reductions 138, 207
signallers 201, 204–5
at stations 202–3, 216
steam locomotives 123–4
track maintenance 201
uniforms 119
women 119, 197
Stagecoach 277
Stansted airport 323
stations x, 34–5, 188
de-staffing 90, 188, 202–3, 216
modernization 115–19
Network SouthEast 286–7,
290
redevelopments 10–11, 237–8
signs 110

steam locomotives 26–8, 29, 54
phasing out 3, 5, 56–7, 63,
120–24, 127, 138
staffing 206
Stedeford, Sir Ivan 79
Stedeford committee 79–81,
150, 151
Stephenson, George 26
stopping trains 89
Strauss, George 98
Sunday Times 144, 286
Swindon works 235
Switzerland 142

Tanat Valley Light Railway
70, 72
Thatcher, Denis 257
Thatcher, Margaret 150, 189,
193, 215, 223
and GLC 283
and rail privatization xi,
225–6, 333
Thomas, Cecil 32
through coaches 51–2
tilting trains 165–6, 168, 171–2,
175, 328
The Times 84
timetables xvii, 326, 332
clock-face 163
and diesel locomotives 125
May 2018 xvi, 345
West Coast Main Line
11–12
Today programme ix–x
TOPS (Total Operating
Processing System) 204

total route modernization
315–16
Towler, James 264
Townsend Thoresen 229
track
commuter lines 281
continuous welded rail 201,
253, 281
gauge 26–7
loading gauge 27, 168
rail to road conversion 244–8
singling 137–8, 267
tamping machines 126
track authority model 334, 335–6
traction *see* electrification;
locomotives
Trades Union Congress 220
Trafalgar House 236
Train Protection and Warning
System 297
trains *see* rolling stock
trainspotters 47, 122
Transport Act 1953 57, 58
Transport Act 1962 79, 81, 99, 324
Transport Act 1968 23–4, 135–6,
137, 156
Transport Act 1974 147
Transport Salaried Staffs'
Association (TSSA) 197
Transport Users' Consultative
Committees 71–2, 85–6, 263
Travelcard 281
Travellers Fare 231
Treasury 139, 184, 193
British Transport Hotels 227
discounted rail fares 288

HST 183
and London & South East 279
Modernisation Plan 61, 62,
68, 75
rail privatization 334, 335, 336
Trewin, Peter 249, 250, 257
Trusthouse Forte 231–2, 233
Tyneside 136

uniforms 119
unions 209
and privatization 331–2,
341–2, 346
racism and sexism 196–7
and Thatcher government 215
see also ASLEF; industrial
relations; National Union
of Railwaymen
Upper Crust 231

vacuum brakes 67
Vale of Rheidol steam railway
123, 230, 239
Varsity line 66, 139–40
Victor Britain Rent-A-Car 41
Victoria Line 157, 221
Victoria station 237
Virgin Trains 168, 175

Wales, proposed closures
141, 143
Walker, Herbert 30
Walker, Mark 192–3, 213–14
Walters, Sir Alan 246
Warburton, Ivor 10, 310
Waterloo station 255–6, 287, 289

Waverley route 91
Weighell, Sid 146, 218–19, 246
Welsby, John 266, 267, 268–9,
    272, 273, 318, 320–21
West Coast Main Line
    APT 171–2
    electrification 3, 4, 5, 6–10,
        12–16, 63, 85, 94, 95, 106,
        301–2
    InterCity 162, 163, 298
    Pendolino tilting trains 168,
        172, 175
West Germany 123
West Midlands 136
West Yorkshire 271
Western Region 65, 122, 251–2
    Automatic Warning System
        252

locomotives 28, 64, 125–6,
    251–2
seasonal trains 50
Williams, George 107, 108
Williams, Keith xvi, 342
Williams-Shapps review xvi
Wilson, Harold 97–8, 128, 129,
    130, 215
Woodham's scrapyard, Barry 122
Woodhead route 30, 134–5
workshops see engineering
    workshops
Worrall, Terry x

Xavier, Asquith 195–6

Your New Railway (British
    Railways) 12–14

These are permissible arrangements for the use of the Symbol and Logotype together. No other variations are permitted. Refer to Sheet 1/08 for proportions.

a. Symbol and logotype in positive

b. Symbol and logotype in positive within two ruled rectangles

c. Symbol and logotype reversed out of solid or